Vietnam's Rural Transformation

This volume is included in Westview's series

Transitions: Asia and Asian America

Series Editor, *Mark Selden*

Vietnam's Rural Transformation

EDITED BY

Benedict J. Tria Kerkvliet
and Doug J. Porter

WestviewPress

A Division of HarperCollins*Publishers*

ISEAS

INSTITUTE OF SOUTHEAST ASIAN STUDIES

for

Nguyễn Kim Thư

This volume is included in Westview's series
Transitions: Asia and Asian America

Published in 1995 in the United States of America by Westview Press, Inc., 5500 Central Avenue, Boulder, Colorado 80301-2877, and in the United Kingdom by Westview Press, 12 Hid's Copse Road, Cumnor Hill, Oxford OX2 9JJ

Library of Congress Cataloging-in-Publication Data
Vietnam's rural transformation / edited by Benedict J. Tria Kerkvliet
  and Doug J. Porter
     p. cm. — (Transitions—Asia and Asian America)
  Includes bibliographical references and index.
  ISBN 0-8133-8950-X (hc)
  1. Vietnam—Rural conditions. 2. Rural development—Vietnam.
I. Kerkvliet, Benedict J. II. Porter, Doug J. III. Series.
HN700.5.A8V55 1995
307.1'412'09597—dc20   95-15855
                                                                                        CIP

Published in 1995 in Southeast Asia, Japan, Australia, and New Zealand by the Institute of Southeast Asian Studies, Heng Mui Keng Terrace, Pasir Panjang, Singapore 0511, Republic of Singapore

ISBN 981-3055-01-4 (hc)
ISBN 981-3055-00-6 (pb)

The paper used in this publication meets the requirements of the American National Standard for Permanence of Paper for Printed Library Materials Z39.48-1984.

10   9   8   7   6   5   4   3   2   1

Contents

Tables, Figures, Maps, and Plates

Figures

Maps

Plates
Between Chapters 4 and 5, beginning after page 138

Acknowledgments

We are grateful to the sponsors and participants who contributed to the 1993 Vietnam Update conference held at the Australian National University during December 1993 at which earlier drafts of many of the chapters in this volume were presented. The Vietnam Update, an annual event at the ANU, was generously supported by the Research School of Pacific and Asian Studies (RSPAS), the Australian International Development Assistance Bureau (AIDAB), and the Australian Council for Overseas Aid. Within RSPAS, Pacific and Asian History, Political and Social Change, Human Geography, National Centre for Development Studies, and Anthropology deserve principal credit for getting this book underway. Bev Fraser of the Department of Political and Social Change, RSPAS, ably managed all aspects of the conference organization. Assisting her were Allison Ley, Claire Smith, and Lulu Turner. We also want to thank other members of the conference organizing committee: Adam Fforde, David Marr, Steve Sénèque, and Carlyle Thayer.

Many other individuals contributed particular skills and energy to the production of this volume. Several maps, figures, and illustrations were skillfully prepared by Kay Dancey and Nigel Duffey of the Cartographic Unit, RSPAS. Christine Tabart made an enormous contribution to the final drafts, helping us search data sources for Chapter One, and providing valuable editorial advice. Christine Attema gave vital assistance during the final stage of formatting the manuscript. The photographic skills of Jerry Galea are reflected in the plates at the centre of this volume and on the cover. We are grateful to Jerry for allowing us to include his work in this volume. In addition, we wish to record our appreciation for the assistance and counsel of Susan McEachern, Senior Editor at Westview Press; Roselie Ang, Acting Managing Editor at the Institute of Southeast Asian Studies; and Mark Selden, series editor for Westview.

Benedict J. Tria Kerkvliet
Doug J. Porter

About the Contributors

Dang Xuan Thu, who recently graduated from the University of Canberra, teaches English at the National Foreign Languages University, Hanoi.

Dang Phong is a researcher with the Price Committee of Vietnam, Hanoi, and is the editor of that committee's *Market and Price Review*.

Dao The Tuan is an agronomist whose research interest is agricultural and rural development. Since 1983 he has been the Director of the Vietnam Agricultural Science Institute in Hanoi. He is also the Head of the Institute's Department of Agrarian Systems and Coordinator of the National Research Program on Rural Development.

Adam Fforde has been working on various aspects of the Vietnamese economy since 1977. He lived in Vietnam in 1978-1979 and 1987-1992 and has been based in Canberra since 1992. He is a Visiting Fellow at the Department of Economics, Research School of Pacific and Asian Studies, Australian National University; Director and Economist, ADUKI Pty. Ltd., Consultants, Canberra; and Chairman of the Vietnam Educational Trust. He is currently focusing his academic work on a collaborative study of contemporary economic and institutional change in Vietnam funded by the Australian Research Council.

Benedict J. Tria Kerkvliet emphasizes agrarian studies in Vietnam and the Philippines and is in the Department of Political and Social Change, Research School of Pacific and Asian Studies, Australian National University.

Viviane Lowe is a graduate student in Anthropology at the Australian National University.

Nguyen Manh Huan (also known as Nguyen Dinh Huan) is an economist specializing in rural development in Vietnam, particularly with reference to environmental and social impacts of current reforms. He has extensive experience in project design, management, and evaluation as a result of working with government institutions, international organizations, and NGOs.

Doug J. Porter is a researcher in the Department of Human Geography, Research School of Pacific and Asian Studies, Australian

National University. He is an adviser to various non-governmental organizations and development agencies working with marginal rural peoples in Indo-China and the Philippines.

Steve Sénèque is currently completing his doctoral dissertation in the Department of Economics, Research School of Pacific and Asian Studies, Australian National University. He is studying the impact of recent economic reforms on agricultural and economic development and on farm household economic behavior. He did fieldwork in Vietnam during 1991 and 1992.

Carlyle A. Thayer has studied Vietnam politics for over twenty years. He is currently an Associate Professor at the University of New South Wales's Australian Defence Force Academy in Canberra. He recently completed a three year Visiting Fellowship at the Department of Political and Social Change, Research School of Pacific and Asian Studies, Australian National University.

Tran Thi Van Anh is a researcher with the Center for Women's Studies in Hanoi. Her work has focused on rural women and policies towards women during periods of transition.

Vo-Tong Xuan, an agronomist emphasizing farming systems, is the Director of the Mekong Delta Farming Systems Center and Vice Rector of the University of Can Tho, Vietnam. He also holds several other prominent positions, including Member of Vietnam's National Assembly, where he is Vice Chairman of the Committee on Science and Technology. His international affiliations include being a member of the Board of Trustees of the International Rice Research Institute, Los Baños, Philippines.

1

Rural Vietnam in Rural Asia

Benedict J. Tria Kerkvliet and Doug J. Porter

Introduction

Vietnam's economic liberalization since the early 1980s provokes praise and alarm. Though still a cub, this new "tiger" has quickly come to symbolize the "Confucian" passion, power, and daring for the many who herald Vietnam's bold transformation. But Vietnam's economic race to "catch up for lost time" as a result of wars, international ostracism, and failed national policies is now just as often counterposed with another "race against time." Environmental conditions and, by some claims, social conditions in the countryside look set to stymie Vietnam's bright economic future. These contradictory appraisals are reflected in the broad compass taken by contributors to this volume. Each chapter emphasizes the remarkable transformation that has been underway in recent years; each also points to problems and worrying features of the changes. It is premature, however, to attempt firm conclusions. The themes running through the volume regarding the role of the state, society-state relations, and social, economic, and environmental consequences of economic liberalization are matters requiring further research and debate. We hope this book makes a significant contribution to the discussion.

The purpose of this introductory chapter is to contextualize the book in two ways. First, the issues implied in the title of this collection, *Vietnam's Rural Transformation*, have international relevance. What does rural transformation mean, particularly when it is often expressed as "rural development," and how is it related to the rapid economic change taking place in Vietnam today? Barrington Moore has suggested that development in any nation can be conceptualized in terms of three "social co-ordination" questions: how should resources be distributed; how should production be done; and who shall make decisions and rule on these matters? (Moore 1978:9). More recent debate, under the rubric of "sustainable development," has added a fourth question: how can questions about production, consumption, and governance be answered in such a way that they do not compromise the ability of future generations who must also address them? Answers to these questions are not immutable nor fully agreed upon within societies. Different constellations of answers can be ascendant in different regions of a country and at different times. As we point out, contested answers have certainly characterized Vietnam in recent decades.

The second purpose of this introduction is to compare and contrast the situation in rural Vietnam with other nations in Asia, namely China and several Southeast Asian countries during the 1970s to early 1990s. Each nation has addressed these "social co-ordination" questions in unique ways, but striking similarities have emerged in recent years with respect to three basic features of agrarian arrangements. One is that the rural household is the principle unit of agricultural production. Secondly, in all the countries, the market has become the primary means for determining the allocation of resources available for production and consumption in rural society. Thirdly, in all cases, but in different ways, the state continues to be a major influence on relations between rural households and national and, increasingly, global markets.

We first review broad features of agrarian arrangements in Vietnam and neighboring countries, then examine the gains in rural productivity and the incomes that they have experienced. Equity and environmental considerations, which bear directly on the sustainability of the gains in productivity and incomes generally found across Southeast Asia, are examined. Next, as evident from international debates on sustainable development, we consider how states act with regard to the country-side. We end with a discussion of relations between the peasantry and the state and the locus of change in state policies, particularly in Vietnam and China, where the turn-about in answers to social co-ordination questions in the countryside has been most pronounced.

Recent economic changes in Vietnam began for a number of reasons, some of which have parallels in other countries previously governed by Communist parties (Kornai 1992:383-386). The accumula-tion of economic difficulties is often highlighted as a reason, but also important was the questioning of the party's competence and disaffection in the cities and countryside. While the specific policies and measures adopted by the Vietnamese government had a strong indigenous character (Turley 1993:6), they were fashioned with an awareness of serious problems in other socialist countries and of the rapid economic growth in several neighboring countries, such as Malaysia, Thailand, Indonesia, Taiwan, and South Korea. Moreover, economic reform, as a set of policies and procedures, has an international genealogy, albeit a fractured one. This is not to say that economic policy changes in Vietnam were carefully wrought from international reforms; indeed, as Jozef Van Brabant (1990:209) notes, the policies "emerged by default, the authorities apparently having abandoned any hope of ensuring adequate and equitable growth in an impoverished country by central means." Nevertheless, the strong international parallels are not coincidental. Economic liberalization is a key expression in what, during the 1980s, came to be called "the counter-revolution" in development thinking (Toye 1987). And in part, as Vietnam's national leaders revamped the country's economy, they aimed to restore the confidence of international financial agencies and other governments by demonstrating a commitment to what those audiences regarded as sound and efficient, i.e., "liberal," policies.

The ideas and opinions characteristic of the "counter-revolution" development strategy are diverse, but are united by the belief that the problems of development can only be solved by a free market economic system and a government that undertakes a minimum of functions.[1] In Vietnam, liberalization has included dismantling central state planning and moving toward a state-regulated market; eliminating subsidies and replacing socialist accounting with profit and loss accounting; de-collectivizing production and distribution; adopting market exchange rate policies; reforming banking, investment, and property laws in the direction of more market-driven transactions; and adopting austere monetary and fiscal policies. These specific policies entail three views that are consistently espoused by international proponents of economic liberalization. First, economic performance is damaged by an over-extended public sector, and the state should avoid intervention in the sphere of production. Secondly, at the heart of economic growth problems are domestic policies. The contention is that governments have been overly concerned with accumulating physical assets of production and have neglected improvements in "human capital." And thirdly — most marked in nations with a strong historical commitment to egalitarianism — government controls and policy measures get in the way of economic efficiency.[2] "Economic liberalization" is shorthand for reducing the role of the state in relation to the market and privileging economic production and efficiency considerations over others, such as the creation and maintenance of public and social goods. The strategy normally implies political/administrative de-centralization in some degree and a reduced role for the public service sector.

Vietnam's recent experience of "rural transformation" is broadly common to its neighboring countries. Transformation is not simply about changes in agricultural production or shifts in the distribution of resources and population, but includes issues of wealth distribution, social justice, the fiscal capacity of rural institutions for governance as well as health, education, agricultural extension, and rural credit. Economic liberalization has touched each of these aspects of rural life. Proponents presume that these changes are positive. Rural development, in this sense, is understood also in the language of "catching up," "efficiency," "integration," and a host of other terms common within the discourse of economic liberalization. Other analysts have pointed to mixed positive and adverse results of rural transformation in the context of economic liberalization.

The chapters in this volume analyze various aspects of economic liberalization and rural change. Two chapters emphasize political aspects. Carlyle Thayer's chapter outlines the broad political conditions in Vietnam in recent years, current policy emphases on the countryside, and changing relations between state and society that have become more apparent since the late 1980s. Chapter three by Ben Kerkvliet takes up the question of society-state relations at the local level by analyzing evidence from villages and districts; he concludes that a range of unauthorized political activities by villagers have influenced the state's shifts in policies. Next are three chapters on economic conditions and changes, again using different approaches. In chapter four, Adam Fforde and Steve Sénèque carefully examine national economic trends, particularly with regard to agriculture, while wrestling with questions concerning the extent to which state policy makes a difference in economic outcomes. Dao The Tuan's chapter five uses quantitative data from several surveys to analyze rural household income patterns in several regions of the country and some of the resulting social consequences, particularly social differentiation. Dang Phong in chapter six synthesizes qualitative material collected from many rural areas to describe the growing vitality of economic life in the countryside. The final three chapters take up different themes in rural transformation in the context of recent economic changes. Vo-Tong Xuan, in chapter seven, highlights ecological problems in Vietnam's countryside, especially regarding rice production in the Mekong delta. Tran Thi Van Anh and Nguyen Manh Huan, in chapter eight, point to several beneficial but also costly aspects of the alterations in cooperatives and other state-initiated institutions. In chapter nine, Doug Porter analyzes the impact of national macroeconomic and public sector administration policies on local governance and marginalization. In the process, he pulls together some of the main threads running through the volume regarding the role of the state, differentiation, and new economic conditions in rural Vietnam.

Agrarian Arrangements

Agrarian arrangements are central to the three social co-ordination questions that Barrington Moore argues all societies must address. We have noted that current arrangements are often debated or reconsidered and even resisted or subverted. At the extreme are rebellions, revolutions, wars, and other violent social upheavals, which are often fought precisely over how best to answer these fundamental questions. But a society cannot afford to be interminably in turmoil about how to answer such questions; some solutions, hopefully ones reasonably satisfactory to a wide range of interests and sectors in society, need to be institutionalized in order for people to get on with other aspects of life.

For the better part of thirty years, 1945-1975, Vietnam was at war with France and the United States, whose governments opposed the country's independence and unification. For part of that time, from the mid 1960s to 1975, the country was also being torn apart by civil war as two Vietnamese governments fought for territory, power, and people's allegiance and support. Millions of lives were thrown into disarray, hundreds of thousands of people were killed, and immeasurable damage was done to the nation's natural environment and human-made infrastructures. Central to this tumultuous era were disputed answers to production, distribution, and authority questions that profoundly involved rural society. Indeed, to a considerable degree the upheavals in Vietnam were agrarian upheavals. Society was often polarized over how land should be distributed; how production should be done and by whom; how the produce should be divided among those who had made an input into the farming process, those who had not, and the state; who had authority to decide on these vital questions; and what relations should be between authorities and villagers, especially those tilling the land? Answers to these and related questions compose what we call agrarian arrangements.

Two striking features of rural Vietnam are that agrarian arrangements have changed rather drastically in the last thirty years and those changes have been multi-directional. Their path has been akin to an elliptical but shifting orbit, moving rather far away from where they had been earlier in the century then recently bending back, not to where they had been before but nevertheless pulled in part by lingering influences from the past.

Similar is the situation in rural China, which, like Vietnam, earlier this century experienced a revolution in which agrarian arrangements were violently contested. Upon the establishment of Communist party-led political regimes, both Vietnam and China created agrarian arrangements with several similar hallmarks. The state socialized all land and outlawed private land ownership. The state in each country also has tried to distribute access to productive land rather equally. Each carried out radical land reforms, initially redistributing land more or less equally among farming households with no compensation paid to the previous owners, and then trying to consolidate most household lands (along with such other means of production as work animals and equipment) for collectivized farming. Generally speaking, households in each country were allowed to retain, though not own, a small amount of land for their private use. Collectives, organized and managed by local officials, were the principle linkage between a village (or cluster of villages) and the state. The state, through various mechanisms including quotas and fixed prices, took a portion of what collectivized villagers produced. The rest of production was distributed among all those living within a collective's jurisdiction according to guidelines combining the labor each person contributed with equity or need considerations. Only production from individual household plots was exempt from claims by the collective and state. Some of these features were not entirely new in Vietnam's history. That land belongs to everyone or the state, rather than being privately owned, is a theme in several parts of pre-French dominated Vietnam. Communally owned land within a village also has a heritage in numerous (though by no means all) parts of Vietnam and China. And the socialist state's intervention to redistribute land and thereby reduce inequalities parallels what the pre-modern Vietnamese state did from time to time.[3]

We hasten to add that within these similarities between China and Vietnam, there were also important differences, and within each country the pattern was not uniform. For example, the process of redistributing and then collectivizing land and other resources was done faster and more extensively in China than in Vietnam. Civil war and wars with France and the United States prevented Vietnam's Communist party leaders from quickly implementing these changes or doing them comprehensively throughout the country. Land redistribution followed by collectivization was carried out most extensively in the north and parts of the central region, from the early 1950s through the 1970s. Even within these areas, the coherence and strength of collective farming varied considerably. In the south, land redistribution, which began while the country was at war and continued after the fighting ended in 1975, was extensive. But collectivization, which commenced after 1975, rarely came close to the prescribed model. Most land there was never collectively cultivated.

Nevertheless, broadly speaking and reducing Vietnam and China's model of agrarian arrangements to their basic elements, the state and collectives were supposed to — and in many areas did — direct production, the distribution of produce, and the use of land and other vital means of production. Peasant households, though they had some input into decision making within their collectives, often had little control over their work and numerous other facets of their lives. Collectives and the state dominated the economy in much of both countries, leaving little room for autonomous markets for agricultural produce, labor, capital, and other resources.

Since the late 1970s and early 1980s in both Vietnam and China, a new arrangement of these main elements has emerged. Now in each country the state and collectivized production have receded into the background while households and the open market have moved to the foreground. Households, not leaders of collectives, are now the principal units for deciding what and how to farm; and markets, not states or their local agencies, are the main means by which produce and other resources are distributed. Those household plots that previously represented a tiny fraction of all land have enlarged in recent years to encompass, with the blessing of the state, nearly all the land in most areas. Though private ownership remains illegal, land is no longer (except in a few places) farmed collectively. Instead, each household has been leased land for twenty or more years in Vietnam, depending on the kind of crops. In China, the length of lease is shorter (Selden 1993:227). In Vietnam, but not yet in China, leased land can even be bought and sold (for the duration of the lease) at prices negotiated between buyer and seller, though laws attempt to put limits on land accumulation. Market forces are now at work and in contention with strong values still favoring an equitable distribution of land. Emerging now in both countries is a small but apparently growing proportion of village households that are, in effect, tenants and wage laborers. They work the land held by households controlling more than can practicably be farmed by one family.

An important difference between Vietnam and China as agrarian arrangements have changed since the late 1970s are the numerous flourishing village and township enterprises, which have played a key role in the rising diversification of China's rural economy (Selden 1993:232, 234). Many of these enterprises are not privately owned but instead are owned and run by collectives, often carrying over from the time when collectives focused on farming. They have been refitted for manufacturing a range of products. Other enterprises are owned and managed by townships and villages. Such businesses are relatively few in Vietnam, and it is not at all certain that they will flourish.

Relative to China and Vietnam, land distribution, production relations, and other agrarian institutions have been fairly constant in Laos, Thailand, Malaysia, Indonesia, and the Philippines. Though contentious agrarian arrangements have led to agrarian revolts in parts of the Philippines and occasional bloodshed in rural Indonesia and Thailand, disagreements have never been sufficiently widespread, vehement, nor organized in these and other Southeast Asian countries to produce radical rearrangements. Private property, the market, and households as the main unit of agricultural production have been the core of agrarian arrangements in these countries for decades. Except for Laos, land is not socialized. Though states in these countries do own land, much of it is forested "public land." Most farm land in Thailand, Malaysia, Indonesia, and the Philippines is privately owned and used. In Laos, though in theory all land is common property, the state recognizes villagers' proprietary rights to their land. Years of war and revolution in Laos have had relatively little to do with agrarian arrangements (Evans 1990).

Land distribution in Laos has been reasonably equitable, even prior to the establishment in 1975 of the Lao People's Democratic Republic. Land is much more unequally distributed in Thailand, Malaysia, and Indonesia, though a large portion of farmers in these countries own at least some of what they till. The proportion of tenant farmers has historically not been high in these countries, though the percentage has been increasing in recent decades. Tenancy in Indonesia rose from 7 per cent in 1963 to 15 per cent in 1980 (Booth 1988:53); in Thailand it increased from 4 per cent in 1963 to 13 per cent in 1988 (Medhi Krongkaew et al. 1992:210). Only the Philippines, where land concentration has for decades been significantly higher than elsewhere in Southeast Asia, has there been a long history of high tenancy, in the range, for instance, of 50-60 per cent of farming households during the 1930s. The percentage has gradually declined since the 1950s due to modest land reform efforts and other factors, although the lack of recent reliable data prevent one from saying by how much.[4] Agricultural wage labor has a long history in Southeast Asia, though most laborers previously were from households that also had land of their own to till. In recent decades, however, the proportion of rural households that neither own nor rent land and rely heavily on working for other farming households has become large in several Southeast Asian countries (Quibria 1993:14). By the mid 1980s in the Philippines, for instance, landless agricultural workers composed an estimated one-third of all rural households (Kerkvliet 1987:205).

From this comparison of agrarian arrangements emerge two features common now to all the countries. One is that the rural household is the principle unit of agricultural production. It persists along with the intensification of capitalism in Indonesia, Malaysia, Thailand, and the Philippines; it remains in Laos and Myanmar (Burma); and it has resurfaced in Vietnam and China after years of being submerged under a state-directed effort to collectivize agriculture and centrally plan the economy. Second, in all cases markets have become the primary means for determining prices for farming inputs, produce, labor, land, and so forth. In none now does the state attempt to control these transfers (though, as we will elaborate later, the state is a major player in and influence on markets).

A final observation is a new dynamic between cooperatives and private enterprise in several countries. Though collectivized production has proved to be inadequate, cooperatives for marketing produce and certain services appeal to many peasants. An underlying attraction for farming households in the Philippines, Thailand, Indonesia, and Malaysia is to eliminate the "middle man" thereby retaining more profit from what they produce and reducing prices on the inputs and credit that they consume. Such middle men are among the ubiquitous private entrepreneurs that have long flourished in these countries. Cooperatives are still few, but those that succeed do so because they provide a better deal for farming families than do private entrepreneurs. Meanwhile in the new market-oriented environment, those same kind of entrepreneurs are beginning to flourish again in China and in some parts of Vietnam. But the cooperatives in Vietnam that are surviving the transition from collectivization to household farming are those that can supply their members inputs, credit, irrigation, and other services or market their crops at better prices than private business people offer.

Rural Production and Economy

Farming and other agricultural activities are principal ways of making a living for large sections of the population in Vietnam and all the other Asian countries we have mentioned. But within that shared characteristic are two variations; in one group of nations the rural economy remains heavily agricultural while in another the rural economy has become much more diversified, especially since the 1960s.

The heavily agricultural rural economies are Vietnam, Laos, and Myanmar. Agriculture as a percentage of total production exceeded 38 per cent in all three during the late 1980s and during the early 1990s whereas in the other countries considered here the percentage ranged from 12 to 27 per cent (Table 1.1). Agricultural products as a percentage of exports has also been relatively high in these three countries and has not changed dramatically since the mid 1970s (Table

1.2). In the other countries, meanwhile, the changes have been rather remarkable. In China, Thailand, and the Philippines, exports have risen noticeably but the percentage that is agricultural has dropped nearly threefold. This is particularly striking in Thailand, where agricultural products in the mid 1970s accounted for three-fourths of all exports but by 1992 were less than one-third. In Malaysia and Indonesia, the importance of agriculture for foreign exchange earnings has also declined significantly.

Over three-quarters of the population in Vietnam, Myanmar, and Laos live in the countryside and most of these people depend heavily on farming and fishing for their livelihood. This is not to say people only farm and fish. Trade, crafts, carpentry, weaving, and other non-agricultural activities are among the other ways rural people in these countries provide for their own needs and supplement their incomes. Nevertheless, the best available figures show that over 80 per cent of Vietnam's labor force is agricultural (including forestry and probably fishing); the comparable figure is 76 per cent in Laos and 64 per cent in Myanmar.[5] Agricultural work is by far the most important source of income for most rural families in these three countries and has been for decades. Moreover, the predominate crop grown is rice, much of it for local consumption. In Vietnam, for example, rice accounts for nearly 55 per cent of agricultural production and 64 per cent of cultivated land in the late 1980s was used primarily for growing rice (McCarty et al. 1993:72-73); in Laos over 80 per cent of cultivated land is devoted to rice (UNDP 1991a:70).

Elsewhere in Asia what is farmed and how rural people earn a living is considerably more diverse. In Malaysia, peasant households producing mainly rice have been in the minority for decades; they constituted only 16 per cent in 1980 (Lim and Said 1989:183). In fact in many parts of Malaysia, farming families get half of their income from work other than farming (Lim and Said 1989:187). Nationally, Malaysia now relies on eight large-scale irrigation schemes for the majority of its rice production (Taylor 1994). In the Philippines, rice growing accounted for only about 38 per cent of cropped land in the early 1960s and 24 per cent by the mid 1980s, even though the area of rice land had slightly increased. A major reason was the much larger areas for, and therefore share of, other crops, especially corn and coconut (Boyce 1993:64). The Philippines' Department of Agriculture has adopted crop diversification as a strategy to increase agricultural production and farm incomes. In Thailand, the particulars are different but the pattern is similar, with agricultural policy and practice decreasingly oriented to rice farming (Taylor 1994; Turton 1989:55). The proportion of non-farm income for farming households has been rising in many parts of each

TABLE 1.1: Agriculture as a Percentage of GDP in Southeast Asia and China

	1960	*1970*	*1980*	*1984*	*1988*	*1992*
China	na	na	31	36	32	27
Indonesia	54	45	26	26	24	19
Laos	na	na	60	81	59	na
Malaysia	37	29	24	21	21	na
Myanmar	33	38	46	48	46	59
Philippines	26	30	23	25	23	22
Thailand	40	26	25	20	17	12
Vietnam	na	na	40	38[b]	38	39[a]

a 1990 figure.
b 1986 figure.

Sources: Brookfield 1993:8; McCarty et al. 1993:42; World Bank 1982:114-115; World Bank 1986:184-185; World Bank 1990b:182-183; and World Bank 1994:166-167.

TABLE 1.2: Agricultural Products as a Percentage of Total Exports in Southeast Asia and China

	Total Value of Exports (US$million)			*Agricultural Products as Percentage of Total Exports[a]*		
	1976	1984	1992	1976	1984	1992
China	6,558.1	24,848.4	127,694.9	36.8	22.0	9.6
Indonesia	8,556.3	21,887.8	33,815.5	24.9	14.0	14.9
Laos	11.6	7.2	97.5	59.8	57.9	53.8
Malaysia	5,294.8	16,483.6	42,288.1	57.6	39.3	21.3
Myanmar	192.6	447.2	638.6	92.9	74.0	84.6
Philippines	2,484.7	5,265.9	9,789.6	59.3	35.6	18.8
Thailand	2,950.2	7,279.1	28,733.0	74.1	61.1	30.6
Vietnam	na	698.5[b]	2,475.0	na	56.9[b]	37.6

a Includes food, animals, fish, tree products such as rubber and copra, and forest products.
b Figures relate to 1985.

Sources: IEDB, UN Comtrade Data, November 1993; SRVN 1993b:193; Fforde 1993a:40.

country. As cities have sprawled, towns have grown, and modes of transportation have become easier and faster, the proportion of peasant households with members earning money as vendors, mechanics, drivers, factory workers, construction workers, domestic helpers, and the like has steadily grown. In Indonesia and China, the shift has been more abrupt and hence more noticeable within the last ten to twenty years.

Economic growth and rural diversification appear to be intertwined. China's GDP grew by an extraordinary 9.5 per cent during the 1980s; agriculture (including forestry and fishing) grew at over 6 per cent. This represents considerable employment generation and expanded opportunities for rural people, particularly in the context of the rapid change in agrarian arrangements giving more freedom of choice and movement for rural households. Economic growth averaging in the 5.0-7.5 per cent range (with agriculture in the 3-4 per cent range) from 1965 to 1990 in Indonesia, Malaysia, and Thailand represents similar conditions for rural people there. And growth averaged 5.7 per cent in the Philippines during the period 1965 to 1980 (before dropping to an average of 1 per cent in the 1980s).[6]

Laos, Vietnam, and Myanmar, on the other hand, have not had sustained and relatively high economic growth. In such economic environments, rural people have had little opportunity or incentive to diversify production or sources of income. Although national policy urges agricultural diversification (SRVN 1993a:56), the situation in Vietnam is unclear. National surveys suggest some shrinking of the population engaged in non-agricultural occupations. (Nguyen Sinh Cuc 1992:13). But other evidence presented by Dang Phong and Fforde and Sénèque in this volume points to the diversifying effects of several factors, including the new agrarian arrangements. Encouraging signs for Vietnam are GDP growth rates above 5 per cent since 1988, reaching over 8 and 7 per cent in 1992 and 1993, respectively. Agricultural growth, meanwhile, was 6.3 per cent and 3 per cent (Fforde 1993a:10, and 1993b:7, 51).

Economic Liberalization, Equity, and Environment

Internationally, there are conflicting views on how changes in agriculture and the liberalization of a developing economy affect the poor or the degree to which economic liberalization has environmentally friendly or detrimental outcomes. The presumption is usually that liberalization will enhance rural productivity, improve incomes, and thereby food consumption of the poor. A second view is pessimistic, often adduced from instances where the poor are unable to participate in green revolution technologies, or where they are displaced by rising indebtedness and resultant land concentration. A third view, more optimistic, is that economic liberalization can and should be "engineered" in such a way that the poor can participate in economic growth — via technologies targeting poor people's crops, or special rural development projects and financing schemes and government interventions, such as preferential access to agricultural credit and extension services (Binswanger and von Braun 1991). In large part, these differing views provide the framework for the chapter by Fforde and Sénèque. The same debate is also evident in contributions from Vo-Tong Xuan and Porter, and evidence from other chapters suggests that the situation in Vietnam is complex and mixed.

Despite the voluble international debate about the equity consequences of economic liberalization, international policy discussions about Vietnam initially said little regarding social justice or equity considerations. Where these were broached, they tended to be eclipsed by the focus on macroeconomic efficiency and national growth. Vietnamese academics and leaders and their foreign advisers, often approvingly refer to the "trickle-down" theory of development. It is often argued that economic stagnation most severely affects the poorest, and therefore anything that ends the economic crisis serves them. Further, it is believed that freeing rural society of the fetters of an expensive, unresponsive, and corrupt officialdom will create opportunities for the emergence of a dynamic civil society, both political and economic, which should benefit small traders, the informal sector, and small farmers alike. Liberalization of agriculture, so the argument goes, should therefore undeniably benefit the rural poor.

But one of the main lessons of thirty years of experience in developing countries is that economic growth, while a necessary condition, is not a sufficient one for the eradication of poverty. Meanwhile, there is no agreement about the long term effects on the rural poor of liberalized economic policies and the near wholesale withdrawal of the state. Links are said to exist among export-oriented, labor intensive industry (a common aspect of liberalization policies), economic growth, and the alleviation of poverty, including rural poverty (Quibria 1993:92-93). Further, rapid economic growth appears to be a precondition for sustaining high levels of expenditure on poverty-oriented "safety net" programs and social investment in health, education, and nutrition, all of which can make a significant contribution to poverty reduction. But there can be no presumption that those who previously benefited from the pre-liberalized economy will be those first to lose, nor that those who previously were marginal will not continue to be so under the new system.

The potentially deleterious effects of liberalization in Vietnam are now cautioned in policy documents. For instance, the World Bank in 1990 noted that, "while in the medium and long term, these measures should result in increased economic growth and family incomes, the path of adjustment is likely to create increased stresses in the short term for some groups adversely affected by these reforms ... fiscal constraints may already be weakening education and health indicators and increasing the risk of lower quality and coverage of basic services" (1990a:87-88). Such conditions are also now being documented by research findings; some of them are referred to later in this section and in other chapters of this book.

For now, at least since 1970, living conditions on average seem to be improving in several Asian countries including Vietnam. One can get a sense of this from available statistical data on several indicators. Limitations in how such data are gathered and measures are compiled mean that one cannot take the numbers themselves too literally. But they do point to trends that are generally supported by other evidence. While life remains very hard for the majority of rural people in these Asian countries, trends suggest that people on average ate better, were more healthy, lived longer, and were more literate in 1990 than in 1970 (Table 1.3). According to certain indicators, Vietnam's living conditions have improved more than in some neighboring countries. Life expectancy in 1970 was lower in Vietnam than in the Philippines or Thailand but by 1990 it was higher. Other indicators suggest, though, that conditions have not improved as rapidly in Vietnam as they have in several other Asian countries, and earlier advantages that Vietnam had over some countries have diminished or disappeared. For example, whereas per capita calorie figures in 1970 were higher in Vietnam than in China, Indonesia, Myanmar, and the Philippines, they had become lower by 1989. Similarly, while the proportion of the Vietnam government's budget allocated to health has increased to about 3.1 per cent (up from 2.1 per cent five years ago), this is less than comparable to figures in the Philippines, Thailand, and Myanmar, though more than in Indonesia (World Bank 1991:224-225).

In Vietnam's countryside, living conditions have improved, however this is more evident in some areas than others. Food availability (calories per capita) declined between 1970 and 1980 as a consequence of numerous factors, including war, recovering from war, and inappropriate economic policies. But as the country overcame the legacies of war and discarded collectivized production and central planning, agricultural production increased. Levels of food availability were higher in 1989 than they had been since the early 1960s, at the

TABLE 1.3 Quality of Life Indicators

(i) Food

	Calories per Capita/Daily			Ratio 1989 1970	Food Production per Capita Index 1979-81=100 1988-1990
	1970	1980	1989		
China	1,982	2,331	2,639	1.33	132
Indonesia	2,061	2,397	2,730	1.32	128
Laos	2,256	2,418	2,630	1.17	121
Malaysia	2,518	2,716	2,774	1.10	155
Myanmar	2,070	2,343	2,440	1.18	101
Philippines	1,839	2,421	2,375	1.29	86
Thailand	2,213	2,300	2,316	1.05	105
Vietnam	2,167	2,045	2,233	1.03	119

(ii) Social Indicators

	Life Expectancy (years)				Infant Mortality (per 1,000)				Adult Literacy (%)		
	1970	1980	1990	Ratio 1990 1970	1970	1980	1990	Ratio 1990 1970	1980	1990	Ratio 1990 1980
China	62	67	70	1.13	69	41	29	0.42	69	73	1.06
Indonesia	47	55	62	1.32	118	99	61	0.52	67	77	1.15
Laos	40	45	50	1.25	146	127	103	0.70	44	na	na
Malaysia	62	67	70	1.13	45	30	16	0.36	60	78	1.30
Myanmar	51	57	62	1.22	104	84	64	0.62	66	81	1.23
Philippines	57	61	64	1.12	66	52	41	0.62	83	90	1.08
Thailand	58	62	66	1.14	73	44	27	0.37	88	93	1.06
Vietnam	55	63	67	1.22	104	57	42	0.40	87	88	1.01

Source: Based on data in Johansen 1993:49, 51-52.

outset of the second Indochina war and the big push to collectivization in northern Vietnam. Meanwhile, since 1970 life expectancy has been increasing and infant mortality has been declining. Literacy, which was one of the lowest in Southeast Asia in the 1950s, jumped considerably of the highest in the region. Especially significant is that literacy among women, which previously was much lower than among men, was by 1990 nearly the same as literacy among men; and among people below 45 years of age, literacy levels for men and women were nearly equal

(Vietnam, Ban Chi Dao 1990:44-46). Such improvements made while the country fought and recovered from wars are in considerable measure the result of policies by the government in Hanoi to improve the country's health and education standards. Several authors in this volume present material that reinforces the impression that living standards have become less severe in the last decade or two. A 1990 national survey into rural living conditions prompted by the Council of Ministers noted an average rise in incomes of 4.59 per cent over 1988, and a rise of 9.35 per cent over the 1981-87 period (Nguyen Sinh Cuc 1992:14). Figures in Tuan's chapter show a decline in poverty in each of the five major regions. On average the drop was from 25 per cent of rural households with incomes below the poverty line to 12 per cent between 1989 and 1992.

While the downward direction in poverty is encouraging, the minimal definition used (the equivalent of twenty kilograms of rice per person each month or about 847 calories per day) greatly under-represents the proportion of poor people. Vietnam remains in the World Bank's list of the world's poorest nations. The official per capita figure of $220 (US) is well below the poorest ASEAN country (Indonesia, with a per capita $570 in 1990). Even if Vietnam were to maintain a growth rate of 10 per cent a year over ten years, per capita income would likely rise to only $500.

Agricultural prices across all regions have increased, but it is not certain this has been a uniformly good thing for the poor. Market-relevant infrastructure (commune level markets, farm to market roads, etc.) continue to be poorly developed as the chapter by Porter indicates for Quang Nam Da Nang and its importance is stressed in the chapter by Fforde and Sénèque. With poorly developed market competition, increased prices tend to be more theoretically beneficial than real for the remote and poorest sections of the population. Increased prices tend to concentrate around localities with better infrastructure. In areas with poor infrastructure, the translation of improved prices into better rural wages tends not to occur. Within particular regions, differentiation is becoming particularly marked in areas close to urban centers or in areas where the market economy has been more developed. As Ngo Vinh Long (1993:189) remarks of these areas "the income spread between well-off and poor rural households had (in 1990) reached forty to one." And official concern is evident. In a January 1992 interview with the Communist party daily, Prime Minister Vo Van Kiet warned of "the confrontation between luxury and misery, between cities and countryside" (*Nhan Dan* 31 January 1992).

In the early 1990s, trends in health care and education may reflect some adversities of new economic and social policies in Vietnam. Most observers laud Vietnam's past achievements. In 1986, Vietnam had estimated gross enrollment ratios of 100 per cent for primary education and 43 per cent in secondary education, second only to China among low income countries (World Bank 1990a:84). And Vietnam's adult literacy rate compares favorably with more economically advanced neighboring countries. But there is evidence of "slippage" in recent years, largely as a result of the austerity measures taken during economic liberalization. The proportion of children aged 6-12 in school has consistently declined in the past few years, as has the percentage of children in nursery schools and in secondary schools (Nguyen Sinh Cuc 1992:16-19). These trends are reported to be more marked in remote and upland rural areas, especially where there is a high proportion of ethnic nationalities. Although education spending increased from 6.7 per cent of the national budget in 1986 to 12 per cent in 1991, actual per capita spending has not kept pace with population growth because in the meantime local levels (especially communes) have withdrawn from education spending (Hiebert 1993:68; World Bank 1990a:93).

Various contributors to this volume address the recent changes occurring in rural health and query the extent to which trends may be attributed to measures associated with economic liberalization. The privatization of health care in 1989 has pushed health care beyond the reach of many rural households and, as Porter argues, the costs of health care are often the single most important cause of chronic indebtedness for the bottom 15 per cent of the population. But the evidence is mixed on whether the decline in access to affordable health care can be attributed purely to economic liberalization. Anecdotal reports indicate that health workers believe conditions are better than before; others have argued that the quality of health workers and facilities have probably been falling since 1975 due to factors which pre-date economic liberalization (Allen 1993). The government notes that "support for the health system has been less than desired" during the transition to the market economy (SRVN 1993a:25). Some programs have been scaled back, and malaria is resurgent in the mountainous border regions. More serious, and also officially acknowledged, widening income disparities and downgrading of facilities formerly provided by cooperatives, particularly child care, "have contributed to increasing malnutrition" since the later 1980s (SRVN 1993a:25) which stands, according to national surveys, at 36 per cent of children (Nguyen Sinh Cuc 1992:16-19).

Among the other Asian countries considered here, improvements in quality of life indicators and the reduction of poverty has been most remarkable in China and Indonesia. Two decades ago the calories per capita measure in those two countries was considerably lower than

Malaysia's (which was the best among those countries we are considering). Now the indicator for China and Indonesia is close to Malaysia's (Table 1.3). Food production per capita, life expectancy, and other measures have also advanced noticeably. Meanwhile, poverty levels have dropped significantly. A measure of poverty that has been standardized so as to make reasonable comparisons among countries over time shows China's very poor rural population declining from nearly 40 per cent in 1970 to 11 per cent in 1990 while the percentage in Indonesia went from 58 to 14 (Table 1.4). Both countries were previously worse than the Philippines and Thailand; now they are in better shape. Meanwhile, on the same measure, poverty in Malaysia, which in 1970 was not comparatively pronounced, has declined considerably more to about 4 per cent. We stress that because the definition used is minimal (though not as minimal as the Vietnam one referred to earlier), the figures in Table 1.4 do not represent the extent of poverty.[7] Serious poverty remains and is especially pronounced in more remote parts of each country. It is also likely that the recent remarkable growth will plateau or has done so already and that the trickle-down effect may be reduced to a dribble. Nevertheless, the drop that has occurred in this one measure of poverty within twenty years is significant, indicating that the rapid economic growth in China, Indonesia, and Malaysia has been beneficial to large sectors of rural people.

China, Indonesia, and Malaysia's experiences in recent decades suggest that sustained high economic growth is associated with improved economic conditions in the countryside, including a significant reduction in rural poverty. But the cases of Thailand and the Philippines show that the relationship is not automatic. Thailand's growth rates were comparatively high throughout the 1970s and 1980s, yet quality of life indicators suggest modest improvements. Income distribution, on the other hand, became more unequal and there are indications that rural incomes have declined in recent years (Hirsch 1994:324). Indeed, absolute poverty levels, after declining in the 1970s, actually went up a little in rural areas between 1980 and 1990. Studies argue that the benefits of overall economic growth accrued disproportionately to Bangkok and other urban areas at the expense of many rural regions (Ikemoto 1991; Medhi Krongkaew et al. 1992; Hirsch 1994).

In rural areas, the gradient of differentiation, becoming more pronounced closer to urban centers, observed for Vietnam is typical across Southeast Asia. Technically, the green revolution strategy was one of "betting on the strong" (Oasa 1981), developing rice varieties for areas where the social and physical infrastructure would most favor a significant increase in yields. Throughout most of Asia, these are the

TABLE 1.4: Estimated Absolute Poverty (per cent of population)

		1970	1980	1990
China	Rural	39	na	11
	Entire	33	28	9
Indonesia	Rural	58	28	14
	Entire	60	29	15
Malaysia	Rural	21	na	4
	Entire	na	na	na
Philippines	Rural	42	35	27
	Entire	35	30	21
Thailand	Rural	30	19	20
	Entire	26	17	16

Note: Absolute poverty means 2,150 calories per person per day, 90 per cent from grains, and non-food basic needs or equivalent. No comparable data are available for Laos, Myanmar, and Vietnam.

Source: Johansen 1993:4.

lowland areas, where irrigation is possible and proximity to urban centers ensures relatively good extension supports and transportation networks. That the political and economic advantages of economic liberalization and the accompanying green revolution-type intensification of agriculture tend to accrue to local elites has been well documented, although considerable controversy persists (Buttel et al. 1985). However, the positions taken by advocates and critics have become less conflicting in recent years. Advocates recognize the problems that arise from rapid market penetration and when development efforts become biased around high-yielding varieties and petrochemical inputs. Critics are more prepared to agree with advocates that it has stimulated productivity, though they question whether this translates into income increases. There is growing evidence from Vietnam and throughout the region, however, that the massive increases in agricultural productivity have slowed or plateaued (Brookfield 1993; Buttel et al. 1985; and Rambo 1994) prompting another look at the argument that long term generalized economic growth in rural areas will inevitably trickle-down to the poorer majority.

In the Philippines, meanwhile, where economic growth was respectable in the 1970s but extremely low during the 1980s, various measures indicate that absolute poverty, nevertheless, declined and income distribution became somewhat less unequal (Balisacan 1992:131, 134). The explanation could be that the data on poverty are seriously flawed and that more reliable indicators are, as Boyce (1993:47-49; 146) argues, real wages, which in the Philippines have been declining since the 1960s, especially in rural areas. Similarly, real income was also declining in Thailand's rural areas in the 1980s (Medhi Krongkaew 1993:7, table 7). In contrast, real wages and real income, consistent with trends in poverty reduction, have been generally increasing in rural Indonesia, Malaysia, and China (Booth 1988:186; Rogers 1992:96; Kueh 1993:235-236). For the Philippines, the evidence from measures just cited and numerous other studies is mixed. If there has been a reduction in poverty during a time of little or no economic growth, declining real wages, and (as the next section suggests) few or no redistribution policies by the state, perhaps one reason is the growing significance of remittances and other assistance from relatives and friends working abroad (Balisacan 1992:146).

Regarding environmental conditions, activists claim "Vietnam is in an ecological race against time" (Kemf 1991:32), and it is equally clear from recent legislation and pronouncements that official concern is deep-seated and rising. The Vietnam government recognizes two kinds of environmental problems: "brown" environmental issues, concerning water, air, and industrial waste management in urban areas; and "green" issues in the countryside. The latter are listed to include "problems caused by fertilizers and pesticides used in intensive agriculture, deforestation, destruction of wetland ecosystems, the careless exploitation of aquatic resources, the misuse of water resources, and the reduction of biological diversity" (SRVN 1993a:27). For a new generation of policy makers, the environment appears to have a high status. The Vice Minister of Transport was reported to remark recently "If we shoot a pistol at the environment, it will fire a cannon back at us" (England and Kammen 1993:161).

The shift from the undeniably wasteful command system of resource allocation brought to an end the practice of enterprises off-loading their inefficiencies to the state budget. And the lack of a "hard budget constraint" was a major impediment to the discipline of economizing on resource use (Spoor 1988:103). But free market conditions, such as prevailing in neighboring countries, could also accelerate environmental degradation. In Thailand, the well known deterioration of the country's natural ecology is said to "reflect a classic case of myopic attention to economic growth leading to widespread exploitation and destruction of natural resources, together with poisoning of land and water" (Hirsch 1994:325). Indeed, the literature on Southeast Asia is replete with general statements on soil erosion, nutrient cycling disruption, degradation of vegetation cover, disturbance to hydrologic cycles, and the resurgence of pests and diseases in agriculture, all as a result of increasingly intensive agricultural activities.

One major environmental problem concerns forests. Wood remains the primary fuel source for 80 per cent of 65-70 million Vietnamese, contributing to the plunder of natural forest cover. In 1943 about 41 per cent of the forest cover remained, but by 1975 this had fallen to only 29 per cent. Besides logging and using forest for fuel wood, additional causes for forest depletion were the US military's deliberate defoliation and other adverse consequences of wars in Vietnam. Since 1975, forests have continued to decline by 200,000-300,000 hectares per year.[8] The sustainable level of biomass consumption is estimated at 80 million tonnes per year, well above current levels of demand. But already only about 18 per cent of natural forest cover remains, soil erosion is reported to threaten 40 per cent of the country's land area, and some areas of northern Vietnam have been losing 100-200 tonnes of soil annually (Hiebert 1990:46; England and Kammen 1993:139). Table 1.5 indicates that the forest situation in Vietnam is among the most perilous in Southeast Asia.

Vietnam's 2.8 million shifting cultivators have been resettled, but with limited success; more than half continue traditional agricultural practices while settled in permanent villages. Serious land degradation problems are now reported in every ecological zone. Vast area of the uplands, and the midlands of northern Vietnam require massive rehabilitation efforts (Rambo 1994; Le Trong Cuc 1991). That Vietnam is among the most densely populated countries in Asia, especially in the major agricultural areas of the Red River and Mekong River deltas, also poses environmental challenges. High rural density does not necessarily mean economic stagnation and ever greater pressures on land and other resources. But it may mean precisely that if greater economic diversification is not occurring — which is presently the situation in Vietnam.

It is too early to judge whether the potentially deleterious effects of economic intensification will be countered by Vietnam's recent environmental protection law, passed by the National Assembly in December 1993. But the "economic race" mentality is a worrying sign. This is reflected in the widely held view among officials that "environmental protection is a luxury that Vietnam cannot afford" (England and Kammen 1993:140). Economic growth and poverty reduction must come first, environmental improvement will follow. As one official source says, "Vietnam must aim to eliminate poverty in

TABLE 1.5: Estimated Land Area Under Forest in Southeast Asia and China

	Year	Percentage
Indonesia	1990	56
Malaysia	1989	56
Laos	1990	47
Myanmar	1989	47
Cambodia	1989	41
Philippines	1988	22
Vietnam	1991	18
Thailand	1991	15
China	1990	12

Sources: Potter 1993:105; Asia 1990 Yearbook 1990:6.

order to remove this fundamental cause of environmental degradation" (SRVN 1993a:28). Official attitudes are echoed at the farming household level throughout Vietnam.

Whether this "economic synthesis" that casts environmental sustainability as an outcome of maximizing economic growth (Schnaiberg 1980) can itself be sustained in practice is chastened by the conclusions of recent agro-ecological research. A study of areas in the Red River delta concludes that simply maintaining current agricultural production levels in the future is problematic, given the farmers' dependence on imported technology in the form of seed, fertilizer, pesticide, and fuel for irrigation pumps. Further, because these areas are so intensively managed, the agro-ecosystem is highly vulnerable to even minor perturbations. Gradual degradation is more likely, consistent with experience from elsewhere in Southeast Asia where yields have often declined, and certainly plateaued (Rambo and Le Trong Cuc 1993). A recent summary of issues relating to population pressures and economic intensification provides a sobering reminder of the very different circumstances in Vietnam compared to its more successful ASEAN neighbors two or three decades ago. "At that time, Malaysia, Thailand, or even Indonesia, had relatively favorable ratios of people to land, seemingly limitless frontier areas for resettlement and agricultural expansion, abundant forest resources, and seemingly damage proof environments.... [Vietnam] must start off already carrying a heavy burden of excess population, depleted resources, and a seriously degraded environment. It has no margin of error, no unexploited cushion of resources on which to fall back" (Rambo 1994:10). The problems are daunting. Some cause for hope comes from studies of government policy interventions showing that credit, tenurial rights, and area specific technologies can improve the lives of rural poor and even reverse environmental degradation (Brookfield and Blaikie 1986).

The State and the Countryside

In Vietnam, as in other Asian countries, the state has been, and remains a major force in determining how "social co-ordination" questions about economy, equity, and environment are resolved. State institutions — including the bureaucracy, military, government, and dominant political parties — in all these countries extended to more corners and recesses of society by the end of the twentieth century than they did at the beginning. The reach of the state, however, is firmer in some than in others. And the extent to which the state tries to control rural society and the use of natural and other resources or makes an effort to favor the peasantry over other sectors of rural society varies from one to the other and has fluctuated over time.

Until recent years the states in Vietnam and China, each dominated by its own Communist party, were trying to control, plan, and direct most aspects of society and resource use, including economic and political ones. No other states among the countries we have been considering were as assertive and insistent. To a considerable degree these states in China and Vietnam have reached deep into the social, economic, and political life of rural people, though inevitably their grips varied over time and from region to region.[9] At the same time, each state leadership in Vietnam and China claimed to be ruling on behalf of the working class and the peasantry, and staked much of its credibility and legitimacy on satisfying the needs of these classes at the expense, if necessary, of propertied, capitalist, and other previously more privileged classes' interests.

Laos and Myanmar are similar to Vietnam and China in claiming to favor peasantry and attempting to direct rural production and distribution, including the socialization of land in both and the imposition of collective farming in Laos (Evans 1990:chs.6, 8; Taylor 1987:300, 323-324, 347-352). But neither state has yet been able to dictate changes in production to the extent that China and Vietnam did. Both states are also far less able than those in China and Vietnam to monitor and govern other aspects of rural life and the distribution of resources. This is especially the situation in Myanmar in which the state, dominated by elite Burmans, continues to have inordinate difficulties projecting its authority over many areas of the country. This is despite recent truce accords with significant sections, though by no means all, of rebel groups that have been fighting against the state's political and economic claims since the 1950s (Brown 1994:ch.2).

In China and Vietnam, each state since the early 1980s has been relaxing or lifting completely its hold on numerous economic activities regarding production, marketing, and price setting in an effort to bring the economy out of doldrums and despair. This has not so far resulted in major shifts toward greater popular participation in rural life, since the state continues its attempts to control or at least steer most "non-economic" activities, ranging from religion to political associations. Pressures are building in each country, fuelled in part by changes set in motion by the economic liberalization, for the state to relax its hold on these activities as well. State leaderships calculate that economic improvement and eventually prosperity for most rural and urban people will replenish the reservoir of legitimacy they want peasants and workers to accord them. Economic success, leaders hope, will reverse the trend, corroborated in national surveys of declining confidence among the peasantry in village officials and a decrease in participation in mass organizations (Nguyen Sinh Cuc 1992). Vietnam and China's leaders also continue to give some attention to equity issues and to soften the harshness of emerging capitalism with policies and programs such as fertilizer subsidies, crop insurance, agricultural credit, agricultural price supports, rural infrastructure developments, social security programs, and the like, many of which are not yet in place but are being considered. Revenues are a major constraint, though sustained economic growth is bringing larger tax revenues in both countries.[10] Vietnam's leaders are looking especially to foreign assistance and loans to help, a task made easier by the lifting of the US trade embargo. But the nature of government priorities is problematic. While policy indicates a commitment to basic education and primary health care, government requests for assistance often focus on high cost university facilities and curative medical technologies. These high quality services inevitably benefit only a few.

Often threatening or undermining efforts to assist the peasantry are powerful interests in some localities which use their positions in the bureaucracy, government, military, and police to: monopolize agricultural credit and fertilizer trade, take a cut for themselves of rural development funds, and extract payments from residents for their own, not public, good (for Vietnam, see Fforde and Sénèque's chapter, this volume). As Kerkvliet's chapter indicates, corruption rates high among the concerns of rural Vietnamese.

The role of Vietnam's state and its stance toward the countryside seems to be evolving toward something like what now exists in Malaysia and Indonesia. The Malaysian and Indonesian states, as major suppliers and consumers of labor, capital, and land, influence the market but do not seek to control it. They encourage capitalistic relations of production and distribution while at the same time emphasizing rural development and giving some attention to assisting the peasantry. The state in both Malaysia and Indonesia has devoted significant proportions of tax revenues and other income (especially from oil in Indonesia) to assist rural producers. Hallmark programs, particularly in the 1970s and early 1980s, included fertilizer subsidies, low interest and interest-free production loans, protection for farmers' rice prices, rural education and health care, and irrigation expansion.[11] While certainly other factors have contributed to the reduction of rural poverty, government programs in these countries have been important (Quibria 1993). By no means have all rural Malaysians and Indonesians benefited equally from such programs; villagers who were better off or more powerful to begin with benefited disproportionately and local officials often abused their positions to take a cut at the expense of average residents.[12] But without these state efforts, the new wealth from economic growth during the last two decades probably would not have trickled down nearly as much as it did.[13]

The states in Thailand and the Philippines are different. An important (though not only) reason why rapid economic growth in Thailand during the last decade has not reduced rural poverty levels or improved average real incomes in the countryside is the state's relative indifference to or inability to alter rural conditions. While the Thai state has funded considerable public works projects, it has devoted little resources to other rural development efforts or to resource redistribution programs (Medhi Krongkaew 1992:215-224; Ikemoto 1991:150). The same has been true of the Philippine state. Particularly telling for the Philippines, where land inequalities and tenancy rates are highest, has been the extreme reluctance of the state to redistribute land or, until recent years, improve tenancy conditions. States in the Philippines and Thailand have generally pursued policies that are biased against agriculture or, if not, then primarily for agribusiness and large-scale farming. Other than irrigation and additional infrastructure efforts, these states have not been particularly concerned with the majority of small farmers and landless agricultural workers (Turton 1989:64-67; Boyce 1993:chs.4, 5, 7, 8). Also important is that the central leadership of each state often has to strike bargains with, even give way to, those who monopolize or significantly control local political and economic power and who frequently have their own armed forces beyond the control of the state. Often the result is that the state cannot or does not protect villagers against extortion, expropriation, violence, and other illegal behavior.

Peasant-State Relations

Earlier we argued that among the Asian countries considered in this chapter, changes in agrarian arrangements have been most marked during recent decades in Vietnam and China. We have not yet said much about how and why these sharp changes came about. We did highlight in the introduction some reasons in Vietnam for economic liberalization generally, including international influences and serious domestic economic and political problems — factors that were to some extent at work in China, too, though economic conditions there were much better than in Vietnam. To explain the turn-about in agrarian arrangements specifically, one also has to take into account what peasants did and how their actions affected both countries' national economies, state plans, and ultimately state policies.

We would not contend that peasants' actions are by themselves sufficient to explain the shift, but we are persuaded that villages in both countries were the source of significant pressures to dump collectivized agriculture, state-run distribution of produce, state pricing, and so forth, in favor of more household-based and market-oriented production and distribution. Moreover, a striking feature of such pressures is that by and large they were conveyed not through large organizations and overt political protest but through cumulative effect of unobtrusive foot dragging and other forms of everyday resistance that characterize what James Scott (1985) has called the "weapons of the weak."

In both Vietnam and China the Communist party-dominated state has prevented the growth of large political or advocacy organizations other than those it approves, indeed instigates. An organization that is "non-government" is practically unheard of in Vietnam or China, unless it is a foreign one involved in health, education, or other such development assistance work. This situation holds true for organizations that are supposed to represent interests of key sectors of society, like peasants and workers. The state-formed organizations for these sectors have a history of being primarily top-down — characterized more by conveying information and imperatives from the central leadership of the state to the rural people below than by transmitting concerns and criticism from below to the higher levels. An example is the official organization for peasants, which both Vietnam and China have; another relevant one to the peasantry is each country's association for women. Despite some signs that such organizations may be straining to become somewhat independent, they remain part of the state. Organizations independent of the state are generally small, localized, and involved in activities that have little or no direct political significance. Examples in recent years, with the changed agrarian arrangements in which household farming is of central importance, are the numerous informal credit associations and labor exchange networks that have been springing up across the countryside in Vietnam and China.

In Laos and Myanmar, officials have also sought to restrict peasant organizations to those established by the state. But compared to Vietnam and China, the state in each country is far less able to penetrate all rural localities and thereby direct rural organizations in all regions. In Laos the state has not been able to institutionalize the official mass organizations (Evans 1990:188), while in Myanmar, villagers are involved in significant organizations, even armed resistance, well outside the state's sanctioned ones.

Despite the absence of peasant-initiated, rural-based organizations to bring clearly into public view their grievances and demands, villagers' discontent with and opposition to the state's insistence on collectivized production and state-controlled markets and their preference instead for family-based production and more open markets contributed directly to the state's turn-about. Collectivized agriculture and central planning of the economy was a major priority project of the Communist party leaderships in both China and Vietnam. But over the years, the whole approach encountered considerable hesitation, resistance, and opposition by peasants whose lives were being reorganized and whose village societies were being reshaped to conform to the state's blueprint. In both China and Vietnam, how collectives really worked deviated noticeably, in some places significantly, from the prescribed model. Local leaders charged with implementing policies found they needed to bargain with villagers and accommodate at least some of their concerns in order to get a modicum of compliance. In southern Vietnam after 1975, villagers' opposition to collectivized farming was so persistent and extensive, though still low keyed and not highly organized, that the national leadership silently backed away to reconsider whether to try again. Gradually and increasingly during the 1970s, the whole collectivized agricultural structure became extremely shaky in much of both countries. Moreover, due to locally initiated experiments based on household production, often with no official blessing, more productive and viable agrarian arrangements were emerging. These provided those national leaders who themselves had become more critical of official policies with additional evidence to argue in the party's Central Committee and Politburo that a major shift was necessary.[14]

A small-scaled and much shorter version of China and Vietnam's experience occurred in Laos. The Communist party there, too, envisaged socialized production in the countryside. In the second half of the 1970s, after winning control of the state, the party leadership tried to impose on villages a system of cooperatives and other radical changes in land use and production arrangements. But, so uniform and durable was the Laotian peasantry's day-to-day, month-to-month foot-dragging and other such forms of opposition that the national leadership was soon forced to abandon the idea, leaving agrarian arrangements much as they had been before 1975 (Evans 1990).

Before considering why peasants in Vietnam and China have considerable influence on the state while having relatively little political room to maneuver openly and confrontationally, let us look at peasant-state relations in some of the other countries in the region. In Malaysia and Indonesia, peasants have somewhat more latitude than their counterparts in Vietnam and China to mobilize independently. State leaders strive to channel political activism among villagers into state-sponsored organizations — such as the Farmers Association in Malaysia (FAM) and the Indonesian Farmers' Association (HKTI) and Village Unit Cooperatives (KUDs) in Indonesia — and the dominant political party (Barisan Nasional in Malaysia, GOLKAR in Indonesia), from which loyal members can derive material and other benefits. Yet Indonesian and Malaysian villagers may join organizations that press what concerns them even though at odds with the dominant party and government. At the same time, there are many disincentives to such confrontation that peasants have to weigh, including possible violation of anti-subversion laws. An easier route is to support minority political parties, that sometimes attempt to press matters important to rural people and, in Malaysia, occasionally actually win enough votes to form local governments (Kessler 1978).

In Thailand and the Philippines peasants are even freer than in Malaysia and Indonesia to organize themselves and join other groups as they please. And they do, especially in the Philippines, which has had numerous peasant organizations during this century. In both countries, frequent visible forms of rural discontent include strikes, barricades, and demonstrations. In addition peasant politics ranges from considerable everyday, non-confrontational resistance against state agencies, local officials, landlords, logging companies, and others to outright armed rebellion. While state leaders in Thailand and the Philippines frequently resort to repression and other forms of intimidation to counter such rural organizations, they rarely attempt to organize or mobilize the peasantry in ways more to the state's liking. Occasionally some such effort is made, such as the government-initiated village associations (*Samahang Nayon*) in the Philippines in the 1970s, but they are not sustained. Nor does either state have a dominant political party into which rural people are recruited as a way to channel their political energies.

Interestingly enough, there is no direct relationship between the degree of autonomy that peasant organizations have and the extent to which peasants influence state policies toward the countryside or rural people's access to the state's resources. The countries with the most independent organizations — the Philippines and Thailand — are also the countries in which policies have been least favorable to villagers. To get the state's attention in these countries, peasants practically, if not actually, must resort to armed rebellion. Malaysia, Indonesia, Vietnam, and China have had no significant rural uprisings in recent decades and states there allow much less scope for independent peasant organizing, yet they tend to be more peasant-oriented. What might explain this?

For Vietnam and China, part of the answer goes back to the peasant-based revolutionary origins of present regimes. Despite major departures from earlier ideals and despite programs and practices that have been at the expense of the peasantry, these states still subscribe to an ideology which extols tillers of the soil and working class people generally. As peasant-based revolutionary states, they repressed or eliminated landlord, agribusiness, and other such interests that, were they still to exist, might well oppose peasant-oriented policies and even control the state. Another factor is fear and self-interest on the part of ruling elites who realize the power peasants have to affect what can happen locally and even nationally. An angry countryside can mean not only lots of trouble for them but possibly their downfall, just as they themselves came to power during a torrent of rural unrest. While state leaders might well employ surveillance, intimidation, and repression to inhibit and counter rural discontent, their own experience and understanding tell them such methods alone will not work. They must also pay attention to rural concerns.

Some of this last element may help to explain the Indonesian case as well. The present regime headed by President Suharto came to power in the mid 1960s when Indonesia was in the throes of considerable rural and urban unrest and, from the point of view of many military leaders who took power, was on the verge of becoming ruled by a Communist party (PKI). Besides smashing the PKI and its affiliated organizations, including a large one for peasants, the New Order's leadership pursued agrarian policies to reduce the bases of that earlier agrarian conflict, recognizing the power of rural producers to upset the country's economy and political stability. Perhaps entwined with this is what William Liddle (1987:144) refers to as a "populist" orientation of many state leaders to give high priority to the needs of "the people." Though a major purpose may have been, as some analysts have said, to "incorporate the rural elite into the state apparatus" (Hart 1986:42),

Indonesian policies also have had the effect of improving economic conditions for a significant proportion of villagers.

Malaysia has not had a history of rural revolt, and certainly the regime is not the result of rural revolution. The state's leadership wants to keep rural people reasonably happy for reasons having to do with the combination of ethnic and electoral politics in the country (De Koninck 1992:191; Crouch 1993). Briefly, a very important constituency for the major partner, United Malays National Organization (UMNO), in the ruling political coalition party are the Malays. And a large proportion of these voters are rice growers, rubber producers, and other rural people. Other political parties also compete for Malay votes, particularly Islamic ones which have proven to be serious contenders in several elections, especially in certain parts of the country. Consequently, UMNO and the ruling party coalition have been rather attentive to the countryside.

In so far as states in the Philippines and Thailand try to improve peasants' conditions, they have focused mainly on those parts of each county with agrarian unrest, usually after concluding that repression alone cannot stop peasant revolts (Brown 1994:ch.5; Kerkvliet 1990:29-31). Other pressures on the state to devote considerable resources to benefit a majority of rural people are typically overwhelmed by stronger business and other elite interests that greatly influence policy making and implementation. While elections can be occasions in which such power holders can be challenged, for various reasons the outcomes usually bring minimal change in the status quo.

Conclusion

Whereas ten or fifteen years ago Vietnam would have been widely understood as significantly different from many other Asian countries, now the similarities are more striking. With regard to the countryside, both Vietnam and China experimented with agrarian arrangements that were unusual in the region. But now in both countries, rural households are the main units of agricultural production, just as they are in most other Asian countries. Cooperatives and collectivized farming have, if not entirely disappeared then certainly receded into the background, no longer being the primary institutions that distinguished Vietnam and China's rural political economy from their Asian neighbors. This reflects another feature that Vietnam now shares with most Asian countries that a short time ago it did not — a market economy. Central to the economic liberalization that Vietnam has been undergoing in recent years is the rise and expansion of markets, reducing if not replacing the scope for state involvement in the use, production, and distribution of resources. Now the market is the primary means for allocating resources for production and consumption. The domineering role in these matters once played by Vietnam's state has diminished considerably, just as it has in China, making the role of the state generally, and its involvement in rural affairs particularly, more like many of its other Asian neighbors. That is, the state in Vietnam remains a major actor in economic, political, and social matters and is prominent in setting and implementing development agendas. But it is not as intrusive as it was earlier.

Now in an economic situation rather comparable to other Asian countries, Vietnam has dilemmas that are also common to neighboring countries. Growth, expansion, entrepreneurship, and personal financial success are encouraged and celebrated, but concerns about equity, distribution, quality and extent of public services, and environmental costs and sustainability are also evident. How to combine these components is a basic question reflected in many debates in numerous quarters of the country, government and non-government alike. No doubt economic growth is necessary, but if that alone is the primary goal, then environmental and social costs can be immense. Countries in Asia that seem to be doing best in terms of steering growth in directions that distribute the benefits of growth somewhat judiciously to poorer sectors of society are ones in which the state is proactive. But that requires the state to have the inclination and ability to remain rather autonomous from powerful economic interests who are primarily concerned with advancing their own narrow interests rather than public good. Hopefully, the Vietnam polity's legacy of concern for equity and for the welfare of rural people will remain vital and be a modulating influence on forces that otherwise, if left unchecked, could wipe away achievements Vietnam has made regarding land distribution, public health, education, among others, and direct some gains of growth to those areas of society and the environment most vulnerable to crass market-driven forces.

Notes

1. Key figures internationally include the late Harry Johnson, Ian Little, Bela Balassa, and Peter Bauer. Toye (1987) provides an analysis of this new political economy of development.

2. Toye (1987:47-70).

3. For recent discussions of Vietnam's land use history, see Phan Dai Doan 1992:32-40; Minh Quang Dao 1993.

4. About the most one can say is that roughly 56 per cent of rural households in the mid 1980s had little or no land (Putzel 1992:25). This includes tenants as well as non-tenants, who relied on wage labor, fishing, and other ways to live.

5. For Vietnam, see McCarty et al. 1993:101; for Laos and Myanmar, see UNDP 1991b:151.

6. All growth figures are from World Bank 1992:220-221.

7. If poverty is defined somewhat more loosely, then about 36 per cent of China's and 23 per cent of Indonesia's rural populations were poor in 1990. The comparable percentage for the Philippines was 54 and for Thailand it was 29 (Johansen 1993:29).

8. The figures for depletion range from 100,000 to 380,000 hectares per year (Collins, Sayer and Whitmore 1991; Fearnside 1990; and Rao 1990).

9. Specialists disagree about how pervasive and invasive the Communist Party-led state actually was in China before the 1980s. See, for instance, Shue 1988 and Unger 1989. For Vietnam, debates on this matter have been less pointed but interpretations do vary (see Kerkvliet's chapter in this volume).

10. For Vietnam, see Porter's chapter in this volume.

11. For example, see Rogers 1992:82, 86, 94, 129-130; Lim and Said 1989:183-186; Booth 1988:150-158; Tjondronegoro et al. 1992:79, 83-84.

12. This is a central argument in Gillian Hart's book on Indonesia (1986) and her comparative analysis of Indonesia, Thailand, Malaysia, and the Philippines (1989). James Scott (1985) has evidence along this line for Malaysia. Anne Booth, though, doubts whether the biases for local political and economic elites in Indonesia were as pronounced as Hart claims (Booth 1988:253-255).

13. For Malaysia, see De Koninck 1992:189-191; Lim 1989:209. For Indonesia, see M. Ravallion and M. Huppi, Poverty and Undernutrition in Indonesia during the 1980s, World Bank, Washington, D.C., mimeo., 1989. (discussed in Coxhead 1990:67-68).

14. For China, see Kelliher 1992. For Vietnam, see Kerkvliet and Xuan chapters, this volume.

References

Allen, S. 1993. "Health and the Current Situation and Recent Changes," in Carlyle A. Thayer and David G. Marr eds., *Vietnam and the Rule of Law*. Pp 38-49. Canberra: Department of Political and Social Change, Australian National University.

Asia 1990 Yearbook. 1990. Hong Kong: Far Eastern Economic Review.

Balisacan, Aresenio. 1992. "Rural Poverty in the Philippines: Incidence, Determinants and Policies." *Asian Development Review* 10(1): 125-163.

Bautista, Romeo. 1990. *Poverty Alleviation, Economic Growth and Development in East Asia*. Working paper no. 90/5. Canberra: National Centre for Development Studies, Australian National University.

Binswanger, Hans, and Joachim von Braun. 1991. "Technological Change and Commercialization in Agriculture." *World Bank Research Observer* 6(1):57-80.

Booth, Anne. 1988. *Agricultural Development in Indonesia.* Sydney: Allen and Unwin.

Boyce, James. 1993. *The Philippines: The Political Economy of Growth and Impoverishment in the Marcos Era.* Honolulu: University of Hawaii Press.

Brookfield, Harold. 1993. "The Dimensions of Environmental Change and Management in the South-East Asian Region," in Brookfield and Byron, eds. Pp. 5-32.

Brookfield, Harold and Yvonne Byron, eds. 1993. *South-East Asia's Environmental Future: The Search for Sustainability.* Tokyo: United Nations University Press.

Brookfield, Harold and P. Blaikie. 1986. *Land Degradation and Society.* London: Basil Blackwell.

Brown, David. 1994. *The State and Ethnic Politics in Southeast Asia.* London: Routledge.

Buttel, F., M. Kenney, and J. Kloppenburg. 1985. "From Green Revolution to Biorevolution: Some Observations on the Changing Technological Base of Economic Transformation in the Third World." *Economic Development and Cultural Change* 34(1):31-55.

Collins, M., J. Sayer, and T. Whitmore, eds. 1991. *The Conservation Atlas of Tropical Forests, Asia and the Pacific.* London: Macmillan for International Union for the Conservation of Nature.

Coxhead, Ian. 1990. "The Identification and Measurement of Poverty," appendix in Romeo Bautista. Pp. 53-69.

Crouch, Harold. 1993. "Malaysia: Do Elections Make a Difference?," unpublished paper, 24pp.

De Koninck, Rodolphe. 1992. *Malay Peasants Coping with the World.* Singapore: Institute of Southeast Asian Studies.

England, S., and D. Kammen. 1993. "Energy Resources and Development in Vietnam." *Annual Review of Energy and Environment* 18:137-167.

Evans, Grant. 1990. *Lao Peasants under Socialism.* New Haven: Yale University Press.

Fearnside, T. 1990. "Figures for Vietnam." Fax to S. Midgley, Seed Centre, CSIRO, From Institute of Foresters of Australia, quoted in Potter (1993:107).

Fforde, Adam. 1993a. *Vietnam: Economic Commentary and Analysis.* No. 3, May.
_____. 1993b. *Vietnam: Economic Commentary and Analysis.* No. 4, December.

Hart, Gillian. 1986. *Power, Labor, and Livelihood: Processes of Change in Rural Java.* Berkeley: University of California Press.
_____. 1989. "Agrarian Change in the Context of State Patronage," in Hart et al., eds. Pp. 31-49.

Hart, Gillian, Andrew Turton, and Benjamin White, eds. 1989. *Agrarian Transformations: Local Processes and the State in Southeast Asia.* Berkeley: University of California Press.

Hiebert, Murray. 1990. "Taking Cover." *Far Eastern Economic Review* 148(23):46.

_____. 1993. "Vietnam Notebook." *Far Eastern Economic Review*. Bangkok.

Hirsch, Philip. 1994. "The Thai Countryside in the 1990s." *Southeast Asian Affairs 1994*. Pp.320-336. Singapore: Institute of Southeast Asian Studies.

Ikemoto, Yukio. 1991. *Income Distribution in Thailand*. Tokyo: Institute of Developing Economies.

International Economic Data Bank (IEDB). 1993. UN Comtrade Data, November.

Johansen, Frida. 1993. "Poverty Reduction in East Asia: The Silent Revolution." *World Bank Discussion Paper 203*. Washington: The World Bank.

Kelliher, Daniel. 1992. *Peasant Power in China: The Era of Rural Reform, 1979-1988*. New Haven: Yale University Press.

Kemf, Elizabeth. 1991. "Casualties of Vietnam's Recovery." *New Scientist* 14 September:32-35.

Kerkvliet, Benedict. 1987. "Peasants and Agricultural Workers: Implications for United States Policy," in Carl Lande, ed., *Rebuilding a Nation: Philippine Challenges and American Policy*. Pp. 205-218. Washington, D.C.: Washington Institute Press.

_____. 1990. *Everyday Politics in the Philippines: Class and Status Relations in a Central Luzon Village*. Berkeley: University of California Press.

Kessler, Clive. 1978. *Islam and Politics in a Malay State: Kelantan 1838-1969*. Ithaca: Cornell University Press.

Kornai, Janos. 1992. *The Socialist System: The Political Economy of Communism*. Princeton, N.J.: University Press.

Kueh, Y.Y. 1993. "Food Consumption and Peasant Incomes," in Y. Y. Kueh and Robert F. Ash, eds., *Economic Trends in Chinese Agriculture: The Impact of Post Mao Reforms*. Pp. 229-271. Oxford: Clarendon.

Le Trong Cuc. 1991. "Rehabilitation of the Ecologically Degraded Midlands in Northern Vietnam," in Nguyen Manh Hung, Neil Jamieson, and Terry Rambo, eds., *Environment, Natural Resources and the Future Development of Laos and Vietnam*. Pp. 45-56. Papers from a Seminar, Indochina Institute Papers. Fairfax: George Mason University.

Le Trong Cuc and Terry Rambo, eds. 1993. *Too Many People, Too Little Land: The Human Ecology of a Wet-Rice Growing Village in the Red River Delta of Vietnam*. Honolulu: East West Center.

Leslie, Joan, and Michael Paolisso. 1989. *Women's Work and Child Welfare*. Boulder: Westview Press.

Liddle, R. William. 1987. "The Politics of Shared Growth: Some Indonesian Cases." *Comparative Politics* 19 (January):127-146.

Lim Teck Ghee. 1989. "Reconstituting the Peasantry: Changes in Landholding Structure in the Muda Irrigation Scheme," in Hart et al., eds. Pp.193-212.

Lim Teck Ghee and Muhammad Ikmal Said. 1989. "Malaysia: Rice Peasants and Political Priorities in an Economy Undergoing Restructuring," in Hart et al., eds. Pp.181-192.

McCarty, Adam, Merlyene Paunlagui, and Vu Quoc Huy. 1993. *Vietnam Data Bank: 1976-1991*. Canberra: National Centre for Development Studies, Australian National University.

Medhi Krongkaew. 1993. "Thailand's Internationalisation and its Rural Sector," unpublished paper.

Medhi Krongkaew, Pranee Tinakorn and Suphat Suphachalasai. 1992. "Rural Poverty in Thailand: Policy Issues and Responses." *Asian Development Review* 10(1):199-225.

Minh Quang Dao. 1993. "History of Land Tenure in Pre-1954 Vietnam." *Journal of Contemporary Asia* 23(1):84-91.

Moore, Barrington Jr. 1978. *Injustice: The Social Bases of Obedience and Revolt.* White Plains, N.Y.: M. E. Sharpe.

Ngo Vinh Long. 1993. "Reform and Rural Development: Impact on Class, Sectoral, and Regional Inequalities," in William Turley and Mark Selden, eds, *Reinventing Vietnamese Socialism: Doi Moi and Comparative Perspective.* Pp.165-209. Boulder: Westview Press.

Nguyen Sinh Cuc. 1992. "The Actual Economic and Social Situation in Rural Areas of Vietnam following the 10th Resolution." *Economic Problems* January-March:9-16.

Oasa, Edmund. 1981. "The International Rice Research Institute and the Green Revolution: A Case Study on the Politics of Agricultural Research." Unpublished PhD Thesis. University of Hawaii, Honolulu.

Phan Dai Doan. 1992. *Lang Viet Nam: Mot So Van De Kinh Te Xa Hoi [Vietnam Village: Some Social Economic Problems].* Hanoi: NXB Khoa Hoc. Xa Hoi.

Potter, Lesley. 1993. "The Onslaught on the Forests in South-East Asia", in Brookfield and Byron, eds. Pp. 103-122.

Putzel, James. 1992. *A Captive Land: The Politics of Agrarian Reform in the Philippines.* New York: Monthly Review Press.

Quibria. M. G. 1993. "Introduction." in Quibria, ed., *Rural Poverty in Asia: Priority Issues and Policy Options.* Pp.1-100. Hong Kong: Oxford University Press.

Rambo, Terry. 1994. "Poverty, Population, Resources, and Environment as Constraints on Vietnam's development." Paper to Eleventh Annual Berkeley Conference on Southeast Asian Studies, University of California at Berkeley, Feb 26-27.

Rambo, T. and Le Trong Cuc. 1993. "Prospects for Sustainable Development in the Villages of the Red River Delta," in Le Trong Cuc and Terry Rambo, eds. Pp. 165-186.

Rao, Y. 1990. *Forestry in Vietnam: An Overview.* Bangkok: Food and Agriculture Organization. Referenced in Potter (1993:127).

Rogers, Marvin. 1992. *Local Politics in Rural Malaysia.* Boulder: Westview Press.

Schnaiberg, A. 1980. *The Environment: From Surplus to Scarcity.* New York: Oxford University Press.

Scott, James. 1985. *Weapons of the Weak: Everyday Forms of Resistance.* New Haven: Yale University Press.

Selden, Mark. 1993. "Agrarian Development Strategies in China and Vietnam," in Turley and Selden, eds. Pp. 209-253.

Shue, Vivienne. 1988. *The Reach of the State: Sketches of the Chinese Body Politic.* Stanford: Stanford University Press.

Spoor, Max. 1988. "Reforming State Finance in Post-1975 Vietnam." *The Journal of Development Studies* 24(4):102-114.

SRVN (Socialist Republic of Vietnam). 1993a. *Vietnam: A Development Perspective.* Prepared for the Donor Conference (September) Hanoi.

SRVN (Socialist Republic of Vietnam). 1993b. General Statistics Office. *Nien Gian Thong Ke — 1992 [Statistical Yearbook — 1992].* Hanoi: NXB Thong Ke.

State Committee for Sciences, with UNDP, UNEP, SIDA, and IUCN 1991. *Vietnam National Plan for Environment and Sustainable Development 1991-2000 Framework for Action 1991.*

State Planning Committee and UNDP. 1990. *Report on the Economy of Vietnam.* Hanoi: UNDP and SPC.

Taylor, Donald. 1994. "Agricultural Diversification: An Overview and Challenges in ASEAN in the 1990s." *ASEAN Economic Bulletin* 10(3):264-279.

Taylor, Robert. 1987. *The State in Burma.* Honolulu: University of Hawaii Press.

Tjondronegoro, Sediono M.P., Irland Soejono, and Joan Hardjono. 1992. "Rural Poverty in Indonesia: Trends, Issues and Policies." *Asian Development Review* 10(1):67-90.

Toye, John. 1987. *Dilemmas in Development: Reflections on the Counter Revolution in Development Theory and Policy.* Oxford: Basil Blackwell.

Turley, William S. 1993. "Introduction," in Turley and Selden, eds. Pp. 1-15.

Turley, William S. and Mark Selden, eds. 1993. *Reinventing Vietnamese Socialism: Doi Moi in Comparative Perspective.* Boulder: Westview Press.

Turton, Andrew. 1989. "Thailand: Agrarian Bases of State Power," in Hart et al., eds. Pp. 53-69.

UNDP (United Nations Development Program). 1991a. "The Economy of Laos: An Overview," in Joseph Zasloff and Leonard Unger, eds., *Laos: Beyond the Revolution.* Pp. 67-83 . London: Macmillan.

_____. 1991b. *World Development Report.* New York: UNDP, Oxford University Press.

Unger, Jonathan. 1989. "State and Peasant in Post-revolution China." *Journal of Peasant Studies* 17 (October):114-136.

Van Brabant, Jozef. 1990. "Reforming a Socialist Developing Economy: The Case of Vietnam." *Economics of Planning* 23(3):209-229.

Vietnam, Ban Chi Dao Tong Dieu Tra Dan So Trung Uong (Central Census Steering Committee). 1990. *Ket Qua Dieu Tra Mau (Sample Results).* Hanoi.

World Bank. 1982. *World Development Report 1982.* Oxford: Oxford University Press.

_____. 1986. *World Development Report 1986.* Oxford: Oxford University Press.

_____. 1990a. *Vietnam: Stabilization and Structural Reforms.* Economic Report. Washington DC.: World Bank.

_____. 1990b. *World Development Report 1990.* Oxford: Oxford University Press.

_____. 1991. *World Development Report 1991: The Challenge of Development.* Oxford: Oxford University Press.

_____. 1992. *World Development Report 1992: Development and the Environment.* Oxford: Oxford University Press.

_____. 1994. *World Development Report 1994.* Oxford: Oxford University Press.

2

Mono-Organizational Socialism and the State

Carlyle A. Thayer

Introduction

Political, economic, and social change has accelerated dramatically in Vietnam since the mid 1980s. One consequence has been an explosion in the amount and quality of information about Vietnamese society generated from within Vietnam. This in turn has led to a re-evaluation of long-held assumptions about state-society relations, such as the applicability of the Leninist model. Some observers claim that socio-economic change has resulted in "creeping pluralism" in Vietnamese society (Porter 1990, 80-81; Kerkvliet chapter, this volume) or perhaps the development of "nascent civil society" (Thayer 1992a and 1992b). Others have called for a re-conceptualization of the nature of state-society relations in Vietnam (Fforde and Porter 1994). This chapter presents a critical evaluation of the Leninist model (or mono-organizational socialism) in the post-unification period.

Vietnam's reform program pre-dates the landmark Sixth National Party Congress which popularized the term *doi moi* or renovation. As economist Adam Fforde (1993) has pointed out, "bottom up" economic reforms began in the late 1970s and accelerated in the 1980s prior to the sixth congress. Calls for political reform were first heard in 1981 prior to the Fifth Party Congress. However it was not until the Sixth Congress that an explicit officially endorsed program of political reforms was adopted. This involved mainly a shake-up of the Vietnam Communist Party's (VCP) bureaucratic structures, the retirement of unsuitable cadre, and the rejuvenation of mass organizations and the

Vietnam Fatherland Front. The press and other media were called upon to lend extra-bureaucratic support to the reform campaign (Thayer 1992b). These efforts led to a two-year period of political liberalization (1987-89).

In 1989, events in China, Eastern Europe, the Soviet Union and in Vietnam itself, prompted party officials to apply the brakes and slow — but not halt — the momentum of reform. In 1991 the Seventh National Party Congress agreed to proceed with political reform, but only gradually. According to then party Secretary General Nguyen Van Linh (1991:20):

> We do understand the importance of renovation of the political system. However, the issue here is to find the appropriate context, forms, and steps. At this early stage, the Party takes economic renovation as the central focus.
>
> Simultaneously with economic renovation, we have step by step renewed the political system. Politics is an extremely complicated area. A hasty acceleration of political renewal without the necessary foundations, and incorrect renovation will result in political instability which subsequently will cause numerous difficulties and hindrances in the whole course of renovation. This is a major lesson drawn from reality in our country as well as from the experience of restructuring and reform in some fraternal countries.

Post-congress political reforms focused on the state apparatus, government structures, and the National Assembly. Much energy and publicity was accorded to the amendment of the 1980 state constitution and the conduct of national elections under a new electoral law (Thayer 1993). It was only after these foundations had been laid that Vietnam's leaders turned their attention to the rural areas where the vast majority — 80 per cent — of Vietnamese live and where economic reforms were having a major impact on state-society relations.

For example, in 1988 the VCP Politburo issued Resolution 10 which switched rural production from agricultural cooperatives to the peasant household. The results in terms of production output were quite spectacular. Vietnam, once a rice deficit country, became self-sufficient and then the world's third largest exporter of rice. Rice also became the third largest earner of foreign exchange after oil and gas and sea food products. Increased agricultural production led to the emergence of the "new rich" in the countryside and the revival of lively market activity due to the availability of a wide variety of consumer goods.

But there was a "down side" to this development. The gap between rich and poor has increased and disparities in the level of socio-economic development between regions, such as Vietnam's northern mountain provinces and the Red River delta, has widened.[1] The rural cooperative system has been dismembered. Subsidies are no longer available for health, education, and welfare services as they once were (a matter discussed further in chapters by Anh and Huan and by Porter in this volume). User fees are now being applied, though there are exceptions. The quality of health, education, and welfare services has deteriorated; and access is now more limited.

Other factors led to adverse rural conditions and the spread of poverty. Vietnam's all time high rice production in 1993 produced a glut and a fall in price. The terms of trade for the ordinary peasant farmer have been adverse, making it difficult for peasant farmers to purchase necessities such as fertilizer, pesticides, petrol, oil, and electricity.[2] Local light industries were devastated by rampant smuggling. The situation of the unemployed and underemployed was only made more difficult by these developments.

In 1993 the VCP's Central Committee held three plenary sessions, one more than required by party statutes.[3] This was the first time since 1987 that three such meetings had been held. One entire plenary session was devoted to rural conditions. The fourth plenum (4-14 January), focused on the "human factor" in development. This was placed within the context of the well-known slogan "to make the people prosperous, the country strong and society civilized." In his opening speech to the plenum, Do Muoi noted that education and health services had deteriorated (*xuong cap*) and culture, literature and art had become commercialized (*thuong mai hoa*).[4] By way of response, the plenum adopted five major resolutions on culture and arts; family planning; health; education and training; and youth affairs.

The fourth plenum decided that the time had come to reverse these negative trends. But it did not fully address the vital question of where funds would be found to meet the costs of these new priority programs. For example, Deputy Prime Minister Phan Van Khai noted in his 1993 mid term review of the economy that government spending was expected to rise 67 per cent while revenue would only increase by 32 per cent. The huge jump in expenditures was due to infrastructure construction, salary reform, and national security needs. Khai noted that the government had decided not to finance the deficit by printing money (as in the past) but through borrowing.[5] Funds would be mobilized from ordinary people's domestic savings which had not been deposited in the banking system. Funds would be obtained by overseas loans.

Vietnam's stress on the rural areas was accompanied by a shift in how it set out its priorities. No doubt under the influence of UN agencies and foreign non-governmental organizations (as well as pressures from below), the new party Secretary General Do Muoi stated in his opening address to the fourth plenum that the first priority of economic development must be accorded to human beings and not just an increase in GNP figures as in the past. Progress in economic development, he said, should be measured by three indicators: income, educational level, and life expectancy.[6]

Do Muoi returned to this theme in his closing speech to the plenum where he highlighted three points: the importance of the "human factor" in development, the necessity to construct appropriate social infrastructure, and the need to formulate the correct policy line.[7] In these respects Do Muoi noted that although Vietnam was a poor country and budget constraints were tight, it was necessary not only to "practice thrift and fight corruption" but to mobilize the resources of "individuals, the people, and society." Later in the year the Politburo issued resolutions on mobilizing women (June) and national unity (November).

It was at the fifth plenum (3-11 June) that for the first time the VCP Central Committee adopted a policy towards peasants, agriculture, and rural areas with the aim of concretizing the resolutions of the Seventh Party Congress.[8] The plenum drew up a balance sheet of the pluses and minuses in agriculture and rural development before adopting a resolution entitled, "On Continued Socio-Economic Renovation and Development in the Countryside."[9] On the plus side, the plenum noted that because Politburo Resolution 10 had been successfully implemented Vietnam had been able to increase food production. According to the final resolution of the plenum, "Victory on the agricultural front has contributed decisively to the gradual extrication of our country from socio-economic crisis and the maintenance of political stability."

On the negative side, the plenum detailed the effects of Vietnam's low level of development on agricultural production, light industry, trading, and services. It also noted the environmental effects of unregulated exploitation of Vietnam's natural resources, such as forest timber. The plenum considered the politically sensitive issue of rural conflicts which had arisen over the implementation of the party's policy on the long term allocation of land and forests to peasant households. Finally, the plenum noted that "democracy and social justice in the rural areas have been ignored," "bureaucratism, authoritarianism, and corruption in state apparatuses are still prevalent" and that party organizations, local administration, and mass associations had been slow in renovating their activities.

The plenum set three broad objectives to be reached by the year 2000: to end unemployment in the countryside by promoting "agro-forestry-fishery, industrial, small industrial, handicraft, and service development in the countryside"; to end rural poverty and malnutrition, especially in remote ethnic minority areas; and to guarantee "democracy and social justice" by maintaining political stability and social order.

The third objective was related, in part, to the changed role of the agricultural producers' cooperative. Previously the agricultural cooperative exercised the functions of "state management over all areas of social life in the localities." These were now transferred to the village administration. In the past, as Do Muoi noted in his report to the party meeting, agricultural cooperatives "used to directly manage the land, direct production, and distribute products" but now they are concerned with "guiding and serving production activities of peasant households, promoting the development of small industries, handicrafts, and rural industries." At the same time, the autonomy of peasant households was to be respected. In areas where the cooperative had not been completely disbanded, their management committees were to be directly elected by members. In areas where the cooperatives no longer existed, peasants were urged to set up cooperative organizations to assist in labor exchange, irrigation and other tasks such as marketing. As Do Muoi noted, "we cannot apply a rigid or coercive method to carry out this task, rather we must satisfactorily ensure effective leadership for these forms of cooperation."

The impact of socio-economic change on the countryside not only affected the role and functions of the agricultural producers' cooperative, but had led to the emergence of a number of new organizations and activities. As noted by Do Muoi, "the general trend shows that more and more branches of trade and professions are emerging in the countryside, ranging from those involved in agriculture, artisan industry, and handicrafts to those dealing with trade and support services." These developments only served to reinforce the need to "renovate the substance and work methods of the current political system" including the party and its mass organizations. Party organs were assigned the role of guiding the transformation of existing agricultural cooperatives and other forms of cooperative activities (e.g., labor exchange, marketing, etc.). Finally, the secretary general called for a "drastic change in the substance and work methods of the Fatherland

Front and other mass organizations (Peasants' Association, Women's Union, Communist Youth Union, War Veterans' Association and other professional societies)."

The fifth plenum was followed by the convening of the third session (ninth legislature) of the National Assembly. The National Assembly passed eight major pieces of legislation including the law on land use and the law on agricultural tax which are discussed elsewhere in this volume.

These developments have implications for political scientists and their approach to the study of state-society relations in contemporary Vietnam. Historian David Marr has argued, for example, that people in Vietnam are increasingly able to organize their lives without reference to the party (1988:26). This is not to say that the Vietnamese state is no longer authoritarian or incapable of repression. However, socio-economic changes underway in Vietnam have led to a revival of traditional activity and an explosion of private associational activity which cannot be accounted for by the mono-organizational model of state-society relations. This poses methodological problems for political scientists. If Vietnam is no longer a typical communist or Leninist political system, what is it? Should political scientists develop a "transitional model" based on other East Asian states to explain the transformation currently underway (see the discussion in Kerkvliet, this volume; Ljunggren 1994a; and Turley 1993). If so, "from what, to what"? Or is Vietnam developing its own unique political model?

Mono-Organizational Socialism

Up until the mid 1980s, it was common to analyze Vietnam's political system in the context of comparative communism. Vietnam was compared with the Soviet Union and China because it had modelled its constitution and political institutions on those states. In communist states, the constitution enshrined the Communist party's monopoly leadership role over the state bureaucracy and societal activity. The party was supposed to control and lead all legal organizations and associations. The party set the goals and objectives for these groups, and it determined their structures and approved their leading personnel. These associations were in turn welded into a single organizational matrix which the party directed. In the economic sphere, land, the means of production and economic units were state owned. Economic activity took place under central direction according to long term plans. In brief, these political systems were examples of "mono-organizational socialism" (Rigby 1991:111-112).

Under the system of mono-organizational socialism, the Communist party controlled and directed the operations of the state bureaucracy, armed forces, and mass organizations by appointing party members to overlapping leadership positions in these bodies. In this respect, party members were "dual role elites." For example, in Vietnam central level party officials were also ministers in the government, generals in the armed forces, or chairmen of mass organizations. The same pattern was also replicated at province and village levels. Party officials assigned to such bodies were organized into branches at each administrative echelon and linked in a separate vertical chain of command within their host organization. In other words, the party maintained a parallel hierarchy inside the government, military, and mass organizations. Throughout the rest of the system non-party members were grouped into functional mass organizations (for workers, peasants, youth, women) or special interest groups (for lawyers, writers, artists, journalists, scientists, etc.). These groups were placed under the direction of an umbrella organization, the Vietnam Fatherland Front (VFF). By mid 1990, the Vietnamese government had authorized 124 national mass societies, including 41 friendship associations, and over 300 provincial or municipal level associations which operated under central control (Voice of Vietnam, Hanoi, 7 June 1990).

In a mono-organizational socialist system the economy was organized as a centrally planned economy. Banking and industry were nationalized. Land and the means of production were owned collectively. Agricultural production was also collectivized through the institution of rural cooperatives. A State Planning Committee set material targets to be achieved over a set time period, the hallmark of which was the five-year plan with priority on industrialization. The goal of each economic component was to meet these targets. The state budget was financed by remittances from state-run enterprises and collectives. The state then allocated central funds according to plan. It set wages and prices, and provided housing, education, and welfare services. Employment was guaranteed. Inefficient state owned enterprises were propped up by state subsidies and favorable bank loans. Foreign trade was mainly confined to other socialist states in barter-type arrangements. As the experience of Eastern Europe and the Soviet Union has made clear, mono-organizational socialism resulted in an economy of aggravated shortages due to its inefficiencies. Attempts to reform these economies led to further economic crises, political instability, and eventually the overthrow of the authoritarian one-party state. Vietnam has avoided a similar fate. Why?

There are several very important differences between Vietnam and its European counterparts. Vietnam is overwhelmingly an agrarian society. The market has never been completely eradicated. Vietnam is also "deeply underdeveloped" (Ljunggren 1993:39). Thirdly, Vietnam has been the recipient of large amounts of external assistance. Finally, Vietnam's ruling political party gained power primarily through its own efforts in a popular revolutionary struggle. The Vietnam Communist Party based its legitimacy to rule on the charisma of Ho Chi Minh and moral authority gained in the protracted 30 year struggle against French colonialism and American intervention. It was not installed in power by the Soviet Red Army.

The political system which emerged in North Vietnam after 1954 mirrored the essential features of mono-organizational socialism discussed above. Vietnam specialists have labelled this system the "DRV model" (de Vylder and Fforde 1988; Ljunggren 1993:41, 77-78) or "neo-Stalinist model" (Fforde 1993:295). In 1960, a state constitution was formally adopted which enshrined the ideology of Marxism-Leninism and the party's leading role in society in line with other communist systems. Communist organizational forms and methods, which had been successfully employed against the French, and which formed the basis of the Democratic Republic of Vietnam after 1954, were replicated in the south during the struggle for national reunification. After 1975, Vietnam's communist leaders moved quickly to impose the "DRV model" on the south even when the model was inappropriate to local conditions. For example, a Second Five-Year Plan (1976–80) was adopted which placed southern Vietnam under central planning for the first time. Southern government structures, political parties, and administrative units were disbanded and/or declared illegal. Southern provinces were merged into larger units.

Post-Unification: The Regularization of Politics

Since unification the nature of Vietnam's political system has been changed in significant ways. For example, the political process has become "regularized" (Thayer 1988) and Vietnam has attempted to "liberalize" its political institutions. There are three main elements of the regularization process. The first is the regular convocation of national party congresses in accordance with party statutes. Vietnam's political calendar is now set on a five-year cycle. In the past there were gaps of nine (1951-60) and sixteen years (1960-76) between national party congresses. Since unification national party congresses have been held regularly in accord with party statutes. The Fourth National

Congress, held in December 1976, was followed by the Fifth (March 1982), Sixth (December 1986), and Seventh (June 1991).

Congresses at grass-roots and provincial level held in advance of the congress, as well as the national congress itself, provide a regular venue where policy can be reviewed critically and where party leaders can be held accountable for their actions. Vietnam's party leadership now comes under much closer scrutiny and criticism for its actions than before. The party statutes also make provision for the convocation of a party conference in mid term to review policy implementation and leadership performance. Vietnam's first mid term national conference was held in January 1994.

Secondly, the sectoral composition of the party Central Committee has changed. In the past, the party Central Committee was dominated by senior officials who served in the central party apparatus, central government or in the highest command positions in the military. Since unification, provincial party leaders and other secondary level officials have been brought into an expanded Central Committee. There is now a balance between officials with responsibility at the central level and those operating at provincial level. As Vietnam has moved from war to peace, the military's representation has been reduced accordingly but regional commanders have been given more prominence than before.

Finally, since unification leadership change has been institution-alized in a carefully managed process of generational transition. This process has been most dramatic on the Politburo but has occurred on the Central Committee and other national party organs as well. The pattern of change involving members of the Central Committee is equally significant. There is now a regular turn over of membership. Figures gathered by the author for the period 1960–91 indicate that approximately one-third of the membership is routinely replaced at each national congress.

The Seventh Congress (June 1991) marked a maturation of the regularization process. Both the Politburo and Central Committee experienced leadership turnover comparable with previous congresses. The Politburo continued to reflect a careful mix of ideological, regional, and institutional interests. Four of its seven new members were southerners. In sectoral terms, the military's representation on the Central Committee increased slightly, while the balance between the center and the provinces was maintained The pattern of leadership renewal was taken a step further by the voluntary retirement of Nguyen Van Linh as Secretary General of the VCP after only one term in office.

The regularization of the political process in Vietnam — leadership accountability, expanded sectoral representation and the institution-alization of leadership change — has contributed to a more open political system. The Central Committee is now more representative of society than before and its plenary sessions have become a forum for lively debate. The Politburo is no longer dominated by a stable group of leaders all drawn from the same generation. The position of party secretary general has changed. Since 1986 each new incumbent has had to rely less on the automatic acceptance of his personal authority and more on consensus building within the party to secure support for policy (Stern 1993).

Political Liberalization Vietnamese Style

The need for political reform of Vietnamese political institutions was identified as long ago as 1981 in the lead up to the Fifth National Party Congress. At that time Dr Nguyen Khac Vien, a leading intellectual, addressed an open letter to the National Assembly pointing out deficiencies in the political system and calling for democratic reforms. The issue of institutional reform, as distinct from political liberalization, was addressed in key documents delivered to the Fifth Congress but little was achieved over the next five years.

In 1986, the impact of Gorbachev's reform program in the Soviet Union combined with pressures which had been building up internally to produce a consensus in favor of political reform. This was especially noticeable in the lead-up to the Sixth National Party Congress where widespread criticism of the party and its policies emerged in the local congresses of party organizations. Vietnam's Sixth Party Congress, which saw the elevation of Nguyen Van Linh to the party's secretary generalship, marks the start of Vietnam's attempt to liberalize its political institutions. The Central Committee's Political Report declared, for example, that "the errors and shortcomings in economic and social leadership originated from shortcomings in the party's ideological and organizational activity and cadre work. This lies at the root of all other causes." The reform program was a limited one and basically confined to rejuvenating the party, mass organizations, and state institutions to make them more efficient if not more popular.

During the years 1987-89 Vietnam entered a period of genuine political liberalization. Elements of the press and mass media took up the call by Nguyen Van Linh to assist the renovation process by reporting cases of corruption and abuse of power. In one celebrated case, a corrupt provincial chief was exposed and forced from office. There was also a flowering of literary activity by writers, poets, dramatists, and publishing houses as previously rigid ideological controls were loosened. Students, the intelligentsia, war veterans, and peasants became politically active. Some deputies in the normally quiescent National Assembly were emboldened to speak their minds and to criticize government ministers. In 1988 they even challenged the party *nomenklatura's* right to nominate a single candidate for the post of chairman of the Council of Ministers (Thayer 1992a and 1992b). Gareth Porter concluded a review of developments during this period by arguing that Vietnamese society was beset by "creeping pluralism" (1990:80-81).

If we enlarge our view of Vietnamese society in the 1980s, it is evident that much more was going on than the emergence of activity that could be considered overtly political. Vietnam's shift to a market economy, which was all but complete by 1989-90, led to the emergence of spontaneous activity at all levels of society. In the countryside, for example, agricultural producers' cooperatives were disbanded in favor of the household or family production. This abrupt shift led to serious disruptions in the provision of health, education, and social welfare services. It also led to the emergence of numerous new institutions to replace the cooperative in providing loans and social services. Anthropologists have noted the re-emergence of village traditions and traditional village organizations (Hy Van Luong 1992; Kleinen 1993).

In urban areas, there has been an explosion of private entrepreneurial activity. Petty traders have made their appearance everywhere.[10] Established mass organizations have taken on new roles, while new groups and associations have been formed. Journalist and old Vietnam-hand Barry Wain (1990) has captured the spirit of these developments:

[The party's] hard-line stance belies what is actually happening in Vietnam. Three years of *doi moi* or "renovation" have transformed the political as well as the economic landscape. Many Vietnamese now feel free to say and do almost anything — so long as they don't question the supremacy of the Communist Party.

Newspapers expose current corruption while writers uncover the abuses of the past. Politicians openly debate controversial policies. Interest groups, some potentially powerful, are forming or being reactivated.

The government is walking a tightrope as it attempts to respond to popular demands, influenced by events in Eastern Europe, while keeping its grip on power. That grip is slipping, some Vietnamese say, not because the party is being directly challenged but because the whole system is being loosened by a multitude of developments.

In this heady atmosphere, officially sponsored mass organizations, such as those grouping peasants, youth or women, are beginning to question the policies of the party they have always passively obeyed. Other bodies are being registered or revived, outside party controls. Although their objectives are largely innocuous — helping the disabled, restoring temples, assisting the poor — they are nascent pressure groups that didn't exist before.

In mid 1990, at the same time Wain was writing, the Council of Ministers was forced to issue a directive demanding compliance with government regulations concerning the establishment, organization, and operation of mass societies. The existing regulations, dating to 1957 and 1959, were unsuited to current realities and were therefore flouted. According to one report,

> .... some of the societies have recently operated at variance with the state stipulations.... Mass societies and clubs with characteristics similar to mass societies must complete adequate procedures for requesting authorization for their establishment and only after receiving such authorization can they operate. They must comply with the state law and their own regulations and correctly report on their activities to authorized agencies. Any change in their regulations must be reported to the agencies that have authorized their establishment (Voice of Vietnam, Hanoi, 7 June 1990).

Events in 1989 — the massacre of pro-democracy demonstrators in China, the armed resistance activities of overseas Vietnamese,[11] and the collapse of communism in Eastern Europe later in the year, brought the period of political liberalization to a close. Eight magazines and newspapers were closed down while the editor-in-chief of *Saigon Giai Phong* was dismissed. In December 1989, the National Assembly passed a new press law which reasserted party control over the media. In July the following year, the VCP issued a directive on management of literature and arts which tightened party controls in this area.

Tran Xuan Bach, a proponent of political liberalization, was expelled from the Politburo, while journalist and retired army Colonel Bui Tin, and dissident writer Duong Thu Huong were expelled from the party for their outspoken views. Several well-known Vietnamese intellectuals who advocated political reform, such as Doan Viet Hoat, Nguyen Dan Que, Huynh Tan Mam, Le Quang Vinh, Doan Thanh Liem, and Pham Quoc Toan (editor of *Vung Tau Con Dao* newspaper) were arrested. Amnesty International (1992) reported that at least 60 political prisoners, including eight writers and journalists, were arrested during 1990-91 alone. The party banned public discussion of pluralism (Bui Tin forthcoming), while key officials and the party press repeatedly intoned against the threat of "peaceful evolution" (*dien bien hoa binh*).[12]

The crackdown on advocates of political reform curtailed public discussion but did not stop party members and other intellectuals from outspoken criticism of party policy in the lead up to the Seventh National Party Congress and at the congress itself. Indeed, the party encouraged frank discussion as long as it was kept in-house. Retired party veteran Dr. Nguyen Khac Vien, in a repeat of his actions prior to the Fifth Party Congress, once again put pen to paper to make his views known. Well-known mathematician Dr. Phan Dinh Dieu and Hoang Minh Chinh, the former head of the Institute of Philosophy, who had been twice jailed for opposing the party's ideological line (1967-72 and 1981-87), separately issued trenchant critiques of key documents to be put before the party congress.

The Seventh Congress firmly rejected calls for any form of political pluralism or a loosening of the party's monopoly role. It did endorse gradual and limited efforts at political reform — the details of which were left to the Central Committee to work out. On the economic front, the congress endorsed continued economic renovation and further steps towards the creation of a free-market economy. In June 1992, the Central Committee's third plenum adopted various policies aimed at reforming the party apparatus, arresting the decline in party membership and rejuvenating the matrix of mass organizations.

The state apparatus was also subject to reform efforts and these were accorded greater publicity. The center-piece of post-congress reform was the amendment of the 1980 state constitution and electoral law. The party's leading role was acknowledged but made subject to the law (article 4). Three new state leadership positions were created: president, prime minister, and chairman of the National Assembly's Standing Committee. Collective leadership, the hallmark of the former Council of Ministers, was replaced by a cabinet government headed by a prime minister. Each minister was to take responsibility for the conduct of his/her portfolio.

In July 1992 elections were held for the National Assembly (ninth legislature) under Vietnam's most liberal electoral law. Each seat had to be contested. The procedures governing candidate selection were liberalized and independent candidates were permitted to nominate themselves. Although the results of Vietnam's elections were pre-determined and the party's grip on power remained as tight as it had been, the electoral process produced some surprises. One prominent non-party candidate, who had received central endorsement, and four representatives of mass organizations in Ho Chi Minh City lost. The pattern of voting suggested that independent public opinion was beginning to assert itself in urban areas, especially in the south (Thayer 1993). The 1992 elections changed the composition of the National Assembly, replacing peasant representatives with younger, better educated, and more professionally qualified deputies.

The Vietnamese State and Associational Activity

Vietnam's market reforms have not only given birth to a legalized private sector, but have led to the revitalization of group and organizational activity at the local level and the emergence of groups and associations formed as a result of local initiative. With the exception of groups which have attempted to engage in overtly political activity, state authorities have generally tolerated — if not encouraged — the activities of revitalized organizations and newly formed associations.

The emergence and continued existence of non-political associations and groups, formed in response to economic change and as a result of local initiative, cannot easily be reconciled with the mono-organizational model discussed above. Some newly active organizations are pre-existing ones which have evolved in the context of a market economy to take on new roles and functions (e.g., trade unions). Others are newly formed which have emerged to meet needs peculiar to a market economy (e.g., Vietnamese NGOs, consultancy groups, etc.). The legal status of these groups and associations is unclear (Beaulieu 1994). Some were previously registered but now engage in activities beyond the scope of their original charters. Others have petitioned for legal registration only after their formation. Still others remain unregistered but are tolerated because they perform what authorities perceive to be a useful function. In contrast, the state has moved to repress any group which has taken an overt political stance (see Table 2.1).

Vietnamese party and state authorities have attempted to control the activities of these groups by bringing them under existing regulations. In many cases, existing regulations do not cover the activities of groups formed to cater to the needs of a market economy, such as the Vietnam Bankers' Association.[13] Vietnam has responded in an ad hoc fashion by issuing new directives or by drawing up legislation to legalize the activities of these groups. For example, when foreign owners of joint enterprises reportedly defaulted on contract conditions and provoked a spate of walk-outs by local trade unions,[14] Vietnamese authorities responded by passing a new Labor Law which legalized the right to strike, but only as a last resort. The legalization of the activities of private groups and organizations, whether by decree or by law, is an illustration that the Vietnamese state is capable of responding to political pressures from below (as it did to economic pressures from below in the late 1970s).

Given the limited data available, Table 2.1 is schematic and is presented for illustrative purposes only. There are definitional difficulties in classifying various organizations by function as some may be multi-functional. The point here is to illustrate that the scope of group and associational activity in Vietnam has expanded greatly after the adoption of *doi moi*. There were fewer associations and societies in the pre-1986 period and these were grouped under the umbrella of the Vietnam Fatherland Front. Many organizations, like the Vietnam Union of Science and Technology Association, grew out of existing bodies and now include a plethora of affiliated groups and societies. It would appear that many of the new groups and associations, while not wholly autonomous from the state and therefore not purely popular, are in fact "semi-governmental" if not "quasi-governmental." According to Ljunggren (1994a:33):

> While hardly any of the organizations can be described as truly autonomous, it seems clear that a new realm of free social and cultural space for social organizations, discourse and advocacy is emerging, and that this development is affecting the Vietnamese model and, gradually, the inner dynamics of political life in Vietnam.

The impact of the *doi moi*, particularly the shift towards a market economy, has revealed facets of state-society relations in Vietnam that cannot be easily accounted for by the model of mono-organizational socialism. Traditional village associational activity, centered in the family and clan structure, is now being revived. State-society relations at grass-roots level are now conducted through the structure of the agricultural producers' cooperative. Both the Vietnamese party-state and new associations (as well as revived ones) have reached new forms of accommodation. The exceptions to this pattern are those groups, such as the Unified Buddhist Church, which resisted the imposition of mono-organizational socialism in the post-unification period, or new

TABLE 2.1:   Typology of Groups and Associations with New Roles or Newly
Formed

1. Political	Club of Former Resistance Veterans
	Freedom Forum; editor: Doan Viet Hoat
	High Tide of Humanism Movement;
	leader: Nguyen Dan Que
Mass Organization	Vietnam Peasants' Association
	Vietnam Women's Union
	Vietnam Confederation of Trade Unions
	Vietnam Federation of Youth
	Vietnam War Veterans' Association
2. Business, Commercial, and Professional	Vietnam Bankers' Association
	Vietnam Lawyers' Association
3. Science and Technology	Vietnam Union of Science and Technology Associations
4. Arts and Culture	Han Literary Society
5. Social Welfare/NGO	Club of Former Political Prisoners
	Towards Ethnic Women
	credit societies; *hui* (informal credit circles)
6. Religious	An Quang Buddhists
	Protestant Evangelical
	Unified Buddhist Church
7. Friendly Associations	clan and ethnic community groups
	groups to help the disabled and assist the poor
8. Public Affairs	consultancy and policy research institutes

Sources: Based on Thayer 1992a; Ljunggren 1994b; and Mark Sidel, personal
communication, 29 April 1994.

groups which have mounted an overt challenge to the party's political supremacy, particularly by appealing for overseas support.

Political and economic power is now no longer exclusively located in Hanoi as it was in the decade following reunification. Ho Chi Minh City has emerged as a countervailing economic center in its own right. Other centers, less powerful, are also emerging such as Da Nang in central Vietnam, the port city of Hai Phong, and regions, such as the Mekong delta, northern highland provinces and central Vietnam. For example, a caucus of southern deputies emerged during the National Assembly's eighth legislature (1987-92). Also, military regions have been recognized by the inclusion of their commanders on the party Central Committee (Thayer 1994:60-63).

The power of the Vietnamese state has always been constrained by provincial and village government. Prior to unification there were no provincial representatives on the party Central Committee. In the post-unification period, provinces were merged into larger units to ease central control and local officials were appointed to the Central Committee for the first time. The new enlarged provinces proved difficult to control and were likened to "independent kingdoms" by some Vietnamese critics. Eventually in 1991-92 the enlarged provinces became so powerful that they were broken up into their original units. Despite these efforts, the central state has still not succeeded in imposing its writ on local authorities. They still retain the negative power to thwart or undermine national policy with which they are in disagreement. When circumstances dictate, they have the capacity to act independently in pursuit of particularistic interests. For example, despite a central government decree banning the export of timber, it was discovered in 1993 that timber continued to be exported through the port of Qui Nhon. Government decrees requiring the payment of import taxes are regularly flouted by smugglers along the Sino-Vietnamese border.

In order to overcome the entrenched power of provincial people's committees, the executive organs of elected people's councils, an attempt was made in 1992 to amend the 1980 state constitution to give the prime minister the power to appoint the chairman of provincial people's committees. This was successfully resisted. Under the terms of the 1992 state constitution, the prime minister can only make such an appointment on the recommendation of local people's councils. The prime minister, however, may dismiss provincial leaders. Vo Van Kiet exercised this power in 1994 when he sacked local officials in Da Nang and Ba Ria-Vung Tau.[15]

As with state-society relations at the village level, Vietnam has witnessed an accommodation between central and provincial authorities too. For example, after the administrative break-up of the large provinces mentioned above, many of the new provincial party secretaries were appointed to the Central Committee following the January 1994 mid term party conference. There is a rough balance between representatives of the central party and state apparatus and provincial representatives on the Central Committee.

The proposition that socio-economic change has led to new forms of accommodation between the state and society may be illustrated with reference to two major issues which have confronted national party leaders in recent years: corruption and Buddhist dissidence. The problem of corruption in Vietnam's socialist system is not a new phenomena (Turner 1975:217-220). However, as a result of the transformation of Vietnam's economy in the 1980s, so-called "negative phenomena," emerged as a major political issue, resulting, for instance, in considerable animosity between local authorities and villagers (see Kerkvliet's chapter, this volume). The heart of the matter is the abuse of power by party and state officials who engage in corrupt acts. Corruption and abuse of power provoked popular outcry, and severely undermined the party's image of incorruptibility and self-sacrifice which it had cultivated during its struggles against the French and the United States. Party officials have publicly stated that corruption is the one issue which has the capacity to undermine the party's legitimacy to govern.

Nguyen Van Linh, the reformist party secretary general, made the eradication of corruption and abuse of power by party and state officials his personal crusade when he came to office in late 1986. Linh began his campaign in a newspaper column launched in May 1987 under the heading "things which must be done immediately". A party rectification campaign was launched during 1987-90. Eventually Linh's reformist push, including his campaign against corruption, stalled. Linh stood down as party leader at the Seventh Congress in June 1991 and was replaced by Do Muoi. The third plenum of the VCP's Central Committee (June 1992), considered the issue of eradicating corruption from within party ranks as an integral part of the party-building process. Later that year, after the amendment of the state constitution, national elections, and the formation of a new government, Vo Van Kiet, the new prime minister launched a national campaign against corruption and smuggling. The following year he appointed a high-level steering committee to direct this campaign. One of its priorities was to bring to trial ten cases said to involve corrupt high-level officials.

To date the major victim of the anti-corruption campaign has been Vu Ngoc Hai, the former Energy Minister and former member of the party's Central Committee. Hai was charged with arranging financial kickbacks during the construction of the north-south powerline. He was tried and found guilty in 1994. However, the overall results of the anti-corruption campaign have been limited. For example, a mid 1993 report to the National Assembly noted that only 2,900 cases of corruption had been uncovered and 1,000 brought to trial. In late 1993, Do Muoi himself proclaimed that the campaign had been ineffective and unless corruption was ended, the party's prestige would suffer.

A recent editorial in the party's daily newspaper *Nhan Dan* (1 July 1994, 1,4) concluded:

Steady progress has not been achieved. Noteworthy is the fact that many party organizations have not closely linked efforts to reorganize the party with efforts to fight corruption. In a number of sectors, primarily economic units, capital construction companies, budget allocation agencies, and key establishments in charge of handling money, goods, and rare and precious materials, there are indications of misappropriation, waste and loss of state property. As far as leading agencies are concerned, there are also indications that a number of cadres have been involved in embezzlement of public funds, bribe-taking and abuse of power to enrich themselves illegally. Meanwhile, the party organizations concerned have slackened inspection and failed to take timely action to clarify the responsibilities of collectives and individuals, particularly party members in charge of leadership. Some local party committee echelons and a significant number of party installations at central level do not make due efforts to direct the anti-corruption campaign. Many local anti-corruption and smuggling mechanisms perform poorly. In many provinces and cities, party organizations do not attach due importance to efforts to bring into play the strength of the mass movement against corruption. Almost all major corruption cases brought to trial were not the results of evaluation and criticism in the party but the outcome of denunciations by the people and mass media as well as of investigations conducted by the agencies in charge. The action against a number of corruption cases was not stringent enough. In certain cases, only light action was taken against wrongdoers. Worse still, a number of influential cadres also tried to protect

corrupt elements and bribe takers. That situation has lessened
the people's confidence in the party.

Problems in state relations with Buddhist dissidents in southern
Vietnam emerged in the post-liberation period (Nguyen Van Canh
1983). After unification, property belonging to all religious groups,
including the Unified Buddhist Church (UBC), was confiscated.
Religious social welfare, educational, and training institutions were
closed down. UBC leaders, and monks and nuns in local pagodas,
were subject to heavy-handed treatment at the hands of local security
authorities. Buddhist leaders charged the state with discrimination,
persecution, and interference in religious affairs. Religious leaders, such
as Thich Quang Do and Thich Huyen Quang, who engaged in non-
violent public protests were arrested and later given suspended
sentences. However, when they resisted government-initiatied moves
to merge all Buddhist groups into one officially-approved and state-
controlled organization, the Vietnam Buddhist Church, they were re-
arrested and placed under house detention. Further arrests of key UBC
leaders followed in 1984.

After the adoption of *doi moi*, the state relaxed its restrictions on
religion in general. This resulted in a revival of Buddhist activities,
temple restoration, and larger attendances at Buddhist-sponsored
events. Problems in UBC-state relations surfaced again in April 1992
when the patriarch of the UBC died and left a will reportedly
designating Thich Huyen Quang as his successor. State authorities
claimed the will had been forged and on this basis have refused to
recognize the new patriarch.

UBC-state relations worsened in May 1993 when a man reportedly
committed suicide on the grounds of the Buddhist Linh Mu temple in
Hue. UBC sources claim that the immolation was a protest against
state persecution of the Buddhist Church. Local authorities deny this.
In the event, a street confrontation developed between local security
authorities and a crowd of "several thousand" Buddhists led by monks
from the Linh Mu pagoda. A security vehicle was overturned and set
on fire. Four monks and five laymen were later brought to trial and
sentenced to prison for their alleged actions. A separate confrontation
between local security authorities and church officials took place at an
UBC pagoda in Vung Tau city later that year.

While estimates vary, it is generally assumed that the vast majority
of Vietnam's population is nominally Buddhist. The Unified Buddhist
Church is regionally based and represents at most several hundred
thousand Buddhists primarily in central Vietnam and Ho Chi Minh

City. What seems clear is that the local state authorities appreciate the popularity and influence of the UBC within these areas. Despite the occasional arrest and detention of outspoken UBC leaders, the state has backed away from wholesale repression of the UBC's mass following. A curious coexistence apparently prevails. The state, which does not recognize the legal existence of the UBC, nevertheless tolerates church activity which is not overtly political. Pagodas and temples which are associated with the UBC continue to function.

Conclusion

Political scientists have tended to view Vietnam as a typical Leninist political system where change is initiated from "the top down" and state-society relations are seen as antagonistic. Current social science research on Vietnam indicates that a multiplicity of changes is currently underway in that country. The scope and nature of these changes have begun to challenge long-held assumptions and concepts about the nature of the Vietnamese communist political system. Quite clearly Vietnam is in a transitional period. But "from what, to what"? Did the transition period begin in the mid 1980s? Or, were initial assumptions about the nature of the state-society relations and the Vietnamese political system mistaken? Was there much more local activity and scope for "everyday politics" in Vietnam in the 1960s and 1970s than previously imagined? Perhaps future detailed research on conditions in Vietnam in the 1950s, 60s, and 70s will cause us to modify our views of state-society relations and give more prominence to the influence of grass-roots organizations and initiatives in the period prior to the adoption of *doi moi*.

Vietnam has often been perceived as being a "strong state" because of the ability of its leaders to mobilize the peasant masses to resist foreign invasion and to conduct land reform and agricultural collectivization (Migdal 1988). This perception was reinforced by Vietnam's adherence to Marxism-Leninism as the model for its political system. Vietnam's political system probably best approximated the mono-organizational socialist model during the 1950s and early 1960s. It remains for future scholarship to analyze the impact of the Vietnam war (including the air war over north Vietnam from 1965-72) on state-society relations in the Democratic Republic of Vietnam, and to determine the extent to which village associational activity reasserted itself at this time. It is now clear that reunification in 1975 had a profound effect not just on the south but on the north as well. One Vietnamese scholar has recently argued that the seeds of economic reform were planted in the north at this time (Dang Phong 1994). It is now quite clear that mono-organizational socialism was never successfully imposed on the south. The peasantry in the Mekong delta resisted collectivization.

The Vietnamese political system, as indeed state-society relations, can no longer be viewed through the lenses of the Leninist model. For example, the Vietnamese state is unable to end endemic corruption within the party apparatus, nor is it able to incorporate the Unified Buddhist Church within the matrix of organizations forming the Fatherland Front. This suggests that the state is far from the monolith it has been portrayed. Nonetheless, the Vietnamese state retains the capability to repress those groups and individuals which seek to challenge one-party rule.

However, in other areas of socio-economic endeavor, the Vietnamese state has adopted a softer approach to the emergence of new groups and associations. Socio-economic development policies which encounter resistance from below are modified. Although party leaders still give lip service to "Marxism-Leninism and the thoughts of Ho Chi Minh" ideology is rapidly losing its salience as an organizational principle (Marr 1994:6). Even the basis of regime legitimacy is shifting, from charismatic authority under Ho Chi Minh and moral authority in the decades of struggle against foreign intervention, to economic legitimation at present.

Since reunification, the functioning of the political system has become regularized and open to influences from below and from the outside. The boundary between Vietnamese one-party state and society must be seen as a constantly shifting internal one as new groups and associations work out new forms of accommodation with the state (Mitchell 1991). At a national level, the Politburo no longer faces a common identifiable external threat, as it did during wartime, but a myriad of complex issues and contending priorities. The cohesion of the Politburo and its operational code has been replaced by a more fractious decision-making structure. The role of party secretary general has shifted from strongman to consensus builder. While the "chaotic and overlapping" nature of this decision-making structure has not been completely reformed, the Politburo has begun to turn over decision-making in these complex areas to state ministers and the state apparatus.

Political power at the national level is no longer exclusively held by the small party elite who make up the Politburo. Political power has devolved in part to the Central Committee, the Cabinet government, the National Assembly, mass organizations, provincial administrations, and local People's Committees. The partial devolution of political power is illustrated with reference to the party Central Committee where the number of provincial representatives has increased dramatically over recent years. Further, a much wider range of sectoral interests are represented on the Central Committee (and in the National Assembly) than in the past.

Change from within will also be promoted by pressures from without. Foreign investors and their governments will continue to pressure Vietnam to adopt legal-rational norms and become a "law governed state." While Vietnamese party conservatives can be expected to reject calls for political pluralism and multi-party democracy, their ability to repress domestic dissidents will be constrained to the extent that foreign countries which provide development assistance and trade privileges also insist on the adoption of internationally recognized standards of human rights.

According to Ljunggren (1994b) the most likely scenario for Vietnam's future is the evolution of the present system into a less authoritarian one. During this period of transition, the central party and state bureaucracies will be reformed to carry out their managerial tasks more efficiently. Societies, associations and other organized groups which are currently emerging will work out new forms of accommodation with the state at grass-roots, provincial, and central levels. The patterns of accommodation will vary and depend on their legal status as well as customary practice.

Notes

1. Ha Huy Thanh, "Socio-Economic Conditions Amongst Minorities in the Mountainous Region of North Vietnam," seminar presentation to Vietnam Studies Group, The Australian National University, 29 November 1993.

2. An encouraging sign, though, is that the terms of trade for agricultural producers have improved since the early 1990s (see the chapter by Fforde and Sénèque in this volume).

3. The sixth plenum (24 November-1 December 1993) was concerned mainly with preparations for the first mid term party conference, and unspecified national defence issues. The sixth plenum, the mid term conference (January 1994) and the seventh plenum (July 1994) stressed the importance of industrialization and modernization. The seventh plenum noted that agriculture remained the "foremost task."

4. *Nhan Dan* 16 February 1993, 3.

5. *Nhan Dan* 17 June 1993, 1, 3.

6. *Nhan Dan* 16 January 1993, 1, 3.

7. *Nhan Dan* 18 January 1993, 1, 3.

8. *Nhan Dan* 14 June 1993, 1, 3.

9. "Thong Bao Hoi Nghi Lan Thu Nam BCHTU Dang (Khoa 7)" [Communique from the fifth party plenum (7th Congress)]. *Tap Chi Cong San*, 2 (1993):3.

10. John Whitesides writes of the existence of "frog markets," so-called because of their ability to hop around and avoid control by local authorities; see Reuter, Hanoi, *The Jakarta Post*, 30 April 1994.

11. In August-September 1989, a group of 68 overseas Vietnamese resistance fighters led by Tran Quang Do was intercepted crossing Laos in an attempt to enter Vietnam. They were identified as members of the United National Front for the Liberation of Vietnam, whose leader, Hoang Co Minh, had been ambushed in 1987 attempting to infiltrate Vietnam. Each year the Vietnamese press reports on the arrest and trial of armed subversive groups composed mainly of overseas Vietnamese.

12. For a representative selection see: Bui Thien Ngo (1992), Pham Van Thach (1992), Tran Ba Khoa (1993) and Le Xuan Luu (1993).

13. The Vietnam Bankers' Association, a non-governmental organization grouping state-owned commercial banks, joint stock banks, and financial companies, was legalized by prime ministerial decree; Voice of Vietnam external service, Hanoi, 22 May 1994.

14. For reports on strike activity at South Korean and Taiwanese joint venture factories see: AFP, Hanoi, *The Nation* (Bangkok), 17 December 1992; Harish Mehta, Hanoi, *Business Times* (Singapore), 25 December 1992; Reuter, Hanoi, 15 February 1993; "Factory Staff Strike," *Far Eastern Economic Review*, 25 February 1993, p. 59; Reuter, Hanoi, 2 November 1993; Kyodo, Hanoi, *The Nation*, 20 November 1993; Voice of Vietnam, Hanoi, 24 December 1993; AFP, Hanoi, *Straits Times*, 30 December 1993; Reuter, Hanoi, 10 January 1994; AFP, Hanoi, *Straits Times*, 23 May 1994; *Vietnam Investment Review*, 23-29 May 1994; Radio Australia external service, Melbourne, 5 July 1994.

15. See: AFP. Hanoi, *Straits Times*, 24 May 1994 and Voice of Vietnam, 20 October 1994. The officials in Da Nang included the chairman and deputy chairman of the municipal People's Committee, the director of municipal housing, and director of a municipal marine products company. They were reported guilty of ignoring directives from the prime minister's office requiring that administrative practices and payments be made public. The accused officials reportedly collected unauthorized payments which they deposited in special funds. The chairman and deputy chairman of the Ba Ria-Vung Tau province people's committee were dismissed for irregularities in carrying out housing and land policy.

References

Amnesty International. 1992. *Viet Nam: Arrests of Political Prisoners, 1990-1991.* London: Amnesty International Secretariat (June).

Beaulieu, Carole. 1994. "Is it an NGO? Is it a Civil Society? Is it Pluralism Wriggling Along?" *Institute of Current World Affairs Newsletter* CB-26 (6 October).

Bui Thien Ngo. 1992. "Bao Ve An Ninh Quoc Gia trong Tinh Hinh Moi" [Protecting National Security in the New Situation]. *Tap Chi Cong San* 9 (September):3-7.

Bui Tin. forthcoming. *Following Ho Chi Minh: Memories of a North Vietnamese Colonel.* London: Hurst.

Dang Phong. 1994. "Viewing the Decade 1976-1986 in Vietnam Vertically and Horizontally". Paper presented to a seminar on Vietnamese Economic History, Macquarie University, Sydney (July).

de Vylder, Stefan and Adam Fforde. 1988. *Vietnam: An Economy in Transition.* Stockholm: Swedish International Development Authority.

Fforde, Adam. 1993. "The Political Economy of 'Reform' in Vietnam — Some Reflections," in Börje Ljunggren, ed. Pp. 293-325.

Fforde, Adam and Doug Porter. 1994. "Public Goods, the State, Civil Society and Development Assistance in Vietnam: Opportunities and Prospects." Paper presented to Vietnam Update 1994, Canberra: The Australian National University (10-11 November).

Hy Van Luong. 1992. *Revolution in the Village: Tradition and Transformation in North Vietnam, 1925-1988.* Honolulu: University of Hawaii Press.

Kleinen, John. 1993. "Responses to Economic Change in a North Vietnamese Village." Paper presented to Conference on Vietnam, Nordic Institute of Asian Studies, Copenhagen, Denmark (19-21 August).

Ljunggren, Börje, ed. 1993. *The Challenge of Reform in Indochina.* Cambridge: Harvard Institute for International Development.

_____. 1994a. "Challenge of Development and Democracy: The Case of Vietnam." Draft paper prepared for the Conference on "Democracy and Democratization in Asia," Center for Asian Studies, University of Louvain (30 May-2 June).

_____. 1994b. "Beyond Reform: On the Dynamics between Economic and Political Change in Vietnam." Unpublished paper.

Marr, David G. 1988. "Vietnamese Perestroika Slowly Realises Change." *Far Eastern Economic Review* (3 November):26.

_____. 1994. "Walking on One or Two Legs in Contemporary Vietnam." Paper presented to the Asian Studies Association of Australia Biennial Conference, Perth (13-16 July).

Migdal, Joel S. 1988. *Strong Societies and Weak States: State-Society Relations and State Capabilities in the Third World.* Princeton: Princeton University Press.

Mitchell, Timothy. 1991. "The Limits of the State: Beyond Statist Approaches and Their Critics." *American Political Science Review* (March) 85:1, 77-96.

Nguyen Van Canh. 1983. *Vietnam Under Communism 1975-1982.* Stanford: Hoover Institution.

Nguyen Van Linh. 1991. "To Continue Taking the Cause of Renovation Forward Along the Socialist Path," in *Communist Party of Vietnam 7th National Congress Documents*. Hanoi: Vietnam Foreign Languages Publishing House.

Pham Van Thach. 1992. "Dau Tranh Cong 'Dien Bien Hoa Binh' Gan Lien Voi Viec Tiep Tuc Su Nghiep Doi Moi" [The Struggle Against 'Peaceful Evolution' is Combined with the Work of Continuous Renovation]. *Nhan Dan* (30 December), 3.

Porter, Gareth. 1990. "The Politics of 'Renovation' in Vietnam." *Problems of Communism* 34 (May-June):80-91.

Rigby, T. H. 1991. "Mono-organisational Socialism and the Civil Society," in Chandran Kukathas, David W. Lovell, and William Maley, eds., *The Transition from Socialism: State and Civil Society in the USSR*. Melbourne: Longman Cheshire.

Stern, Lewis M. 1993. *Renovating the Vietnamese Communist Party*. Singapore: Institute of Southeast Asian Studies.

Thayer, Carlyle A. 1988. "The Regularization of Politics: Continuity and Change in the Party's Central Committee, 1951-1986", in David G. Marr and Christine White, eds., *Postwar Vietnam: Dilemmas in Socialist Development*. Pp.177-193. Southeast Asia Program. Ithaca: Cornell University.

_____. 1992a. "Political Developments in Vietnam: From the Sixth to Seventh National Party Congress." Regime Change and Regime Maintenance in Asia and the Pacific Discussion Paper Series No. 5. Canberra: Department of Political and Social Change, Australian National University.

_____. 1992b. "Political Reform in Vietnam: Doi Moi and the Emergence of Civil Society," in Robert F. Miller, ed., *The Developments of Civil Society in Communist Systems*. Pp. 110-129. Sydney: Allen and Unwin. .

_____. 1993. "Recent Political Developments: Constitutional Change and the 1992 Elections," in C. Thayer and D. Marr, eds., *Vietnam and the Rule of Law*. Pp. 50-80. Canberra: Political and Social Change, Australian National University.

_____. 1994. "The Vietnam People's Army Under Doi Moi." Pacific Strategic Paper No. 7. Singapore: Institute of Southeast Asian Studies.

Tran Ba Khoa. 1993. "Canh Giac voi Am Muu Dien Bien Hoa Binh cua cac The Luc Thu Dich" [Heighten Vigilance Against Hostile Forces' Schemes of Peaceful Evolution]. *Tap Chi Cong San* 1 (January):18-20.

Turley, William S. 1993. "Political Renovation in Vietnam: Renewal and Adaptation," in Börje Ljunggren, ed. Pp. 327-347.

Turner. Robert F. 1975. *Vietnamese Communism: Its Origins and Development*. Stanford: Hoover Institution Press.

Wain, Barry. 1990. "Vietnamese Find Political Taboos Fading." *Asian Wall Street Journal* (13 June):1, 20.

3

Rural Society and State Relations

Benedict J. Tria Kerkvliet *

Conceptualizing Society and State Relations

In recent years, collectivized farming and cooperatives, land arrangements, and the behavior of authorities have been among the paramount issues in rural Vietnam. In most parts of the country, land that was previously collectivized has been redistributed to farming households, and agricultural cooperatives are being transformed; the National Assembly in July 1993 passed legislation that substantially changed the previous 1988 Land Law; and a major concern among villagers is the abusive and corrupt local authorities they encounter.

These three issues are also avenues by which to analyze relations between the state and citizens in the countryside. What we can see is considerable political activity, often outside Communist party and other state sanctioned circles. Some actions are surprisingly bold and confrontational. Some of this behavior seems to have caused agencies of the state to take notice, even to have influenced the making and implementation of laws and policies.[1]

Western social scientists have been working with four broad representations or conceptualizations of society-state relations in Vietnam. One sees the governing and rule-making circles of the state as virtually self-contained; hence, social forces do not make a significant impact. As one scholar argues, "The model of the *bureaucratic polity*, in which major decisions are made entirely *within* the bureaucracy and are influenced by it rather than by extra-bureaucratic forces in society — whether parliamentary parties, interest groups, or mass movements — aptly describes how the Vietnamese political system works. Not only the determination of major policies but the power over the selection of political and governmental leadership is confined to a small group of party officials" (Porter 1993:101, italics in the original). This corresponds with the view that Vietnam is a "vast and coordinated party-state which pre-empts alternative and autonomous societal organizations from the national center down to the grass-roots of the village and the workplace" (Womack 1992:180). A similar way of conceptualizing this is "mono-organizational socialism" (see Thayer's chapter, this volume).

A second interpretation is that the state, particularly the Communist party, allows for societal influences but only in a corporatist fashion. That is, the state creates social institutions and organizations and uses them to advance its own agendas. William Turley argues that Vietnam is a "mobilizational authoritarian" state that, while having a reservoir of legitimacy acquired during the revolution and wars for unification, exercises a monopoly of power while allowing citizen participation through formal institutions dominated by the single Leninist party; "civil society is still weakly developed...." Stimuli for policy changes may come from below, particularly from among the peasantry, but only through organizations that the state initiates and controls (Turley 1993a:269-270; 1993b:330-331).

According to a third interpretation, the above conceptualizations attribute far too much power to the state and too little to society. In the first place, due to insufficient resources and other inadequacies, the actual administrative capacity of the state to co-ordinate programs and implement policies is considerably less than what a dominating state would require (Woodside 1979:318-401; Thrift and Forbes 1986:81-83, 101-104). A weak administrative structure combined with what Nigel Thrift and Dean Forbes (1986:82-83) call a "penetrating civil society" helps to explain the contrast between what the state claims and what actually occurs. At a time when the state was supposedly planning and running the economy, for instance, black markets were common. "Thus it would be wrong to depict the Vietnamese ... state as a monolithic force able to have its way on every issue..." (Thrift and Forbes 1986:165).

This analysis moves in a direction compatible with my understanding of society-state relations in recent decades. People individually and collectively do things that do not jibe with official plans and prescriptions and throw monkey wrenches into the state's ability to implement programs. But can society in Vietnam also influence what the state does? This third view implies that it cannot — that the situation is largely a matter of the state trying to impose policy on society rather than there being interaction such that what people do affects state decisions.

A fourth conceptualization makes room for social pressures and demands on the state, particularly from among peasants and workers, two classes the Communist party has persistently claimed to be serving. Though this process is dimly perceived and details are sparse, a number of studies indicate that Vietnamese authorities do accommodate pressures coming from outside the state apparatus and its own organizations (White 1985:111-112; Beresford 1988:116-118; Fforde 1989:ch. 12; Kerkvliet forthcoming).[2] Pushes and pulls, influences and counter-influences may indeed be channeled through official organizations, but they are also expressed through petitions and other methods on the margins of what is officially sanctioned and even through public protests and uprisings that directly confront agents of the state, as this chapter will illustrate. Perhaps by far the most important actions, cumulatively anyway, occur in the vast in-between terrain of "everyday politics," where people work out, come to terms with, and contest norms and rules regarding authority over, production of, and allocation of goods, services, and other important resources (Kerkvliet 1990:8-11). Sometimes such politics shade into the formal, state sanctioned forms of participation, and sometimes they tilt the other way into unauthorized, illegal activities. Everyday politics includes trying to live within, bend, or modify the prevailing contours as well as engaging in subtle, non-confrontational everyday resistance to slip under or to undermine them. In such everyday politics in Vietnam, villagers may have no expectations, perhaps even no intentions of affecting national policies, though they might well be trying to modify, even subvert policy implementation in their locality. But cumulatively such actions, even though not organized and co-ordinated, can have an impact on state agencies when done in large enough numbers, in generally the same direction, and "read" or understood by higher officials to mean that it is in their interest or the interest of the state to change. [3]

The next section contends that villagers' initiatives contributed to policies to replace collective production with household farming and related changes. The chapter then highlights a range of rural activities concerning (1) land use and land issues since the 1988 official endorsement of household-based farming and (2) local authorities' improper behavior and suggests that official deliberations and activities seem to be "hearing" what rural people have been "saying." The chapter concludes by suggesting the emergence of organizations that convey the concerns and interests of rural people.

De-collectivization and Rethinking the Cooperatives

The resolution from the Central Committee of the Communist party's June 1993 national conference on the countryside underscored the importance of "granting the right to long term use of land by peasant families" (Vietnam, Communist Party 1993:pt.3, item 4). Such a pronouncement, made so matter-of-factly then, would have been sensational ten years before. It symbolizes a seismic shift in policy and official ideology. National authorities have rejected what previously they insisted was mandatory, and they have adopted what they once said must be rejected.

In the late 1950s, at the top of the Communist leaders' agenda were cooperatives and collectivized agriculture, which were pursued in the north and later, after reunification, in the south. But following the "golden stage" in the north during the early 1960s, when cooperatives were small and organized mainly among extended families and close neighbors ("Sau 30 Nam" 1990:31-32), these national policies encountered considerable indifference and opposition from villagers. Resistance in the north was largely muted and unobtrusive, particularly during Vietnam's war against the United States and for national reunification from the mid 1960s to 1975. For those causes, villagers made huge sacrifices and suffered great losses. Perhaps because of those larger national needs and goals, they were more willing than they otherwise might have been to make do as best as possible in that situation, heeding the exhortations of national leaders that collectivized production was vital to the war effort.

Evidence of villagers' objections, primarily from northern Vietnam, can be summarized as follows: there was little or no personal incentive to work diligently nor disincentive to farm poorly.[4] Many villagers felt that no matter how hard they worked, they still would not have enough to eat. Consequently, often collective property — land, work animals, tools — were not well cared for, and yields, most importantly in rice, rose less than what the country needed in the face of rising population pressures, war requirements, and other demands. Living conditions in many areas stagnated or deteriorated from the mid 1960s to the late 1970s, even after the Third Indochina War had ended. Villagers often resented having to support numerous officials who did little or no agricultural work, were frequently seen as inept, and yet often seemed to live better than most other cooperative members. Moreover, some officials became tyrannical and abusive.[5] Also objectionable was that collective farming undermined the household and extended family as production and social units. In collectivized farming, people from different families and neighborhoods were expected to work together, cutting across kinship networks with which people were more comfortable. The sentiment favoring production by households surged in the north when families were reunited after the war, by which time the continuation of collective work made even less sense to many villagers. Yet precisely then, central authorities accelerated the push to consolidate cooperatives into even larger ones.

After 1975, resistance in the Mekong delta and several other areas of southern Vietnam against collective farming and even against small cooperatives was so intense that state authorities had to abandon the idea of achieving "higher level" cooperatives. And many of the initial small-scale cooperatives appeared only in official reports, not in reality.[6] In several areas, villagers in effect farmed their own fields, going contrary to the official model, often with the encouragement of agricultural specialists who saw the production team approach as an impediment to greater productivity.[7] In the north, too, during the late 1960s and through the 1970s villagers' behavior indicated they were "not deeply attached to cooperatives" ("Sau 30 Nam" 1990:48). They devoted prodigious amounts of time and energy to the small private plots that they had been allowed to keep, achieving yields more than twice as high as yields on collectivized land. By the 1970s many villagers derived 60-75 per cent of their actual income from these privately tended lands.[8] Peasants also surreptitiously encroached on collective land to expand their privately farmed patches. Five per cent of a cooperative's land was the legal limit for private use, but by the 1970s, the actual proportion in several areas was 7 to 13 per cent (Quang Truong 1987:91).

Meanwhile, when doing collective work, many northern villagers were "foot dragging," as one former production team leader told me, trying to gain as many work points as possible with the minimum amount of labor.[9] Disinterest and disgust was so serious in some areas that tens of thousands of hectares went unplanted. By the mid to late 1960s and through the 1970s, numerous northern villages were quietly tinkering with production arrangements, seeing how far they could deviate from the authorized model without attracting unwanted attention from officials, especially beyond the commune.

These local initiatives, often referred to as "sneaky contracts" (*khoan chui*), took various forms. In some villages, pig raising, which was supposed to be done by cooperative teams, was contracted to households (Luong 1993:202-203). In others, land used in the winter months for growing vegetables or land that could not be irrigated during the dry season was divided among interested households which paid a certain amount to the cooperative and did as they pleased with the rest of what they grew.[10] Some areas, encouraged by the results of these modifications, took the next step and contracted rice production to individual households.[11] Production team leaders in a commune of Ha Tay province told me that they unilaterally allocated under-farmed land to interested families.

Some local authorities turned a blind eye or even encouraged these modifications so long as production improved. In the late 1960s Kim Ngoc, the highest ranking Communist party official in Vinh Phuc (now part of Vinh Phu province), allowed limited family-based production until he was reprimanded and demoted by the national authorities.[12] The most widely known experiment, mainly because it later did receive official endorsement from Hanoi, occurred in Hai Phong, a city with over 90,000 hectares of agricultural land. Beginning with one cooperative in 1977-78, several stages of rice production were turned over to individual families who, upon fulfilling quotas, were permitted to keep the remainder. The results were impressive and in 1980, Hai Phong officials authorized all agricultural cooperatives to do this.[13]

In attempts to overcome opposition to collectivized farming and larger cooperatives, state officials tried exhortations, administrative reforms, and punishments. But because success was limited, authorities had to make concessions. At the commune and sub-commune level, local authorities modified what central directives stipulated in order to meet some of their villagers' needs and demands. By the late 1970s the country's exigent situation compelled the state's leaders to consider fundamental changes. The economy was grave, authorities were encountering great difficulties extracting produce from the countryside, and food shortages in the cities were mounting. These problems were, to a significant degree, a consequence of villagers turning their backs on the cooperatives and collective farming, determined to provide first for their own families' basic needs. "It is clear," summarized Adam Fforde, "that confronted with a severe economic crisis, the Vietnamese authorities" had to make "concessions to grass-roots pressures" (1989:205).

This provoked a series of decisions by the Central Committee and the Council of Ministers between 1979 and 1981 that gave individual households some leeway to farm on their own and keep for themselves what they produced after paying a contracted amount to their cooperatives. Though a significant improvement, it did not satisfy most villagers, for reasons outlined in Vo-Tong Xuan's chapter in this volume. Meanwhile, debate across the country was growing not only about how to organize agricultural production but the very idea of a state controlled and centrally planned economy. Out of that came "renovation" (*doi moi*). Then in 1988 the Central Committee's Political

Committee authorized cooperatives to make contracts with households who would farm land assigned to each one for about fifteen years. In effect, the party had come around to what numerous peasants had been saying, even surreptitiously practicing: replace collectivized agriculture with family-based farming and allot land to each household. In a sense, villagers had been leading the way; to keep up, national leaders had to change accordingly.[14]

The results of this major reform together with "renovation" have been beneficial for most villagers, though the results are certainly uneven (see other chapters in this volume). The general picture is that most rural people have enough rice and a diversity of other foods; many have sufficient money to repair and rebuild their houses and buy radios, televisions, bicycles, and other consumer items; and some can accumulate a surplus with which to start businesses. Production has been increasing, cereal grains per capita figures have been rising, and land previously idle is being farmed again. Vegetables, meats, and other produce are more plentiful than people can remember. Peasants have incentives to grow more and work more energetically because the energy and money they invest will directly benefit them. This is not to say that everyone is happy or even satisfied. Life for most rural people remains harsh, inequalities are more obvious and worrisome, and, as the resolution of Central Committee's June 1993 national meeting said, "poverty still prevails in the daily life of peasants..." and "democracy and social justice in the rural areas are still being violated" (Vietnam, Communist Party 1993:pt. 1). But most, I think, would agree that conditions would have been far worse without the changes.

While the idea of collective farming has been pushed aside, the concept of cooperatives remains, though their function, purpose, and future are much debated among villagers and in official circles. In practice, how "real" are cooperatives varies within regions and from one region to another (see Tran Thi Van Anh and Nguyen Manh Huan's chapter in this volume). A survey (apparently in 1990) of villagers in 26 districts across the country found that the majority of cooperatives has no funds to work with and does little more than provide farming advice and administer certain policies passed down from higher up (Tran An Phong and Cao Duc Phat 1991:12-13). Another study classified cooperatives and production groups (the "low level" forms of cooperation more common in southern and central Vietnam) as of 1989 into three categories: existing only in form with little or no substance; being somewhat active; and being active and innovative. The approximate percentages, respectively, were 40, 50, and 10 in the south; 30, 45, and 25 in the central region; and 23, 51, and 26 in the north (Hien Trang 1990:17-18). The activities of vibrant cooperatives include giving low interest production loans, buying farm machinery for cooperative members to use, expanding and improving irrigation facilities, organizing the building of local infrastructures, and establishing food processing and other small enterprises.[15] How many of the 50 per cent that are still marginally active will evolve into something meaningful rather than deteriorate into irrelevance is a question of some import-ance to many villagers and policy makers. Available information suggests that villagers generally see a role for cooperatives — though not necessarily configured as they now are — to help provide irrigation, develop markets for products, loan money, stockpile fertilizer and other inputs to sell at prices favorable to members, and develop new money-making activities.[16] Villagers in Thai Binh and Dong Thap provinces reportedly said, for instance, that cooperatives are needed to accomplish things that peasants cannot do individually (*Nhan Dan* 23 Sept. 1992:3, 5 July 1993:3), a sentiment that many villagers in Vietnam and elsewhere in Asia might well share.[17]

The state meanwhile, most importantly the Communist party's national leadership, now accepts the idea that cooperatives can have various forms and purposes. No longer do they insist on one model for the entire country. The party has also said recently that: hollow, inactive cooperatives should be disbanded, that peasants be allowed the latitude to create new cooperative organizations to meet their needs, and that they be permitted to join them voluntarily.[18] These significant alterations in the state's orientation are the product, in part at least, of a protracted struggle, spanning two or three decades, by villagers in many parts of the country. Along the way national state officials were forced to make some concessions and ultimately to realize that they had to abandon the entire idea of collective farming throughout Vietnam.

Controversies over Land and Authority

Activities in recent years point to villagers' concerns, frustrations, and anger on numerous issues. The two I want to highlight here concern land use and the behavior of local officials.

The decision in 1988 to permit land to be distributed to individual households released pent-up industriousness and stimulated agricul-tural production, but it also — unintentionally — contributed to numerous problems and questions that were difficult to resolve, in part because they were inherently so contentious but also because guidelines and laws were vague or inappropriate for the new situation. In particular, the 1988 Land Law, which had been passed in late 1987, was quickly overtaken by events on the ground.

Most obvious was that in the environment of a widening market economy, land use rights became a kind of property. And from that emerged an informal, technically illegal market in which use rights were bought, sold, mortgaged, and rented. Many villagers in the outskirts of Hanoi, Ho Chi Minh City, and other urban centers realized they could get high prices by selling their farm land use rights to urbanites who wanted lots for houses and businesses. In some semi-rural/semi-urban parts of Ho Chi Minh City, prices for such agricultural land reportedly rose more than tenfold in 1992, from 20-30 dong per square meter at the beginning of the year to 250-500 dong by the end (*Nhan Dan* 16 May 1993:4). In a commune outside of Hue, 70 per cent of the 465 houses built between 1988 and early 1993 were on farm land that had been illegally sold (*Nhan Dan* 17 April 1993:1). Meanwhile households with money are accumulating farm land that is sold or pawned by peasants who are strapped for cash or want to quit farming in order to try other livelihoods. By 1993 in several southern and some central provinces, numerous communes had households holding more than ten hectares of rice land each — which is large by Vietnamese standards. At least one family had 100 hectares (see Dang Phong's chapter, this volume). Individual holdings of upland and mountainous lands have reached 640 hectares (*FEER* 30 Sept. 1993:64-65). With land concentration has also come landlord-tenant arrangements and the hiring of agricultural laborers.

For some analysts, land concentration is a good sign for improved agricultural production and economic diversification, particularly if those who sell their land rights have alternative employment or can establish businesses (Dang Phong, this volume). Other observers, however, think that widening inequalities and economic classes will undermine previous gains. A survey revealed these matters greatly concern voters ("Report on Voters" 1993). Indicatively, a wounded former soldier in Bac Thai province also worries because, "In order to take the land from the hands of landlords, we lost half a century and paid with our sweat, blood, and bones. Now landlords are taking back the land..." (*Nong Dan* end of Aug. 1993:5).

Since the allocation of land to households, numerous disputes over fields and boundaries have emerged. Often such disagreements have been resolved through deliberations, frequently stretching over several months and facilitated by patient and dedicated local officials. But occasionally the conflicts burst into bitter confrontations. A Communist party document cites instances of villagers beating and killing each other, engaging in arson, and arousing the police to use force (Vietnam, Communist Party 1990).

The same source said that nation-wide there were 200,000 written complaints filed between 1988 and mid 1990 by villagers disputing how land use rights had been distributed in their localities (Vietnam, Communist Party 1990:1 appendix).   Some of the conflicts involve Buddhist temples, Catholic churches, and other religious groups that reclaim land they once used.   More often, however, former landowners, especially in the south, whose lands were redistributed to tenants in the 1970s prior to and after 1975, seek to retrieve some or all of their former holdings (Vietnam, Communist Party 1990:1, and 1 appendix).   Members of former landlord families might unilaterally try to retake fields that they once owned, or they might petition authorities to return those fields to them.   Such actions were numerous, for example, among the 976 reported cases of land being encroached and reclaimed during the first half of 1993 in Ben Tre province.[19]   Occasionally conflicts have become so heated that rival claimants kill each other and burn down houses.   In one tragic case, after local authorities had taken a field that a villager apparently had claimed he owned and had began to use, the man was so enraged that he murdered the four-year old son of the chairman of the local cooperative. He was subsequently sentenced to death.   His wife, embarrassed, distraught, and apparently harassed by other villagers, ended up committing suicide (*Nong Dan* end of August 1993:11).

In upland areas, minority groups have quarreled and clashed with lowlanders who have settled in these areas, with state enterprises and projects, and with foresters and other businesses seeking to exploit forest lands. Such tensions have existed for years, but the redistribution of land to individual households since the late 1980s has given more scope and reason for disputes to arise in many areas.[20] Many minority group people in the mountainous regions of northern and central Vietnam now reclaim some of the land which lowlanders have moved on to under the protection of the government.   Such land, minority groups have argued, rightly belongs to them because it had belonged to their forebears.[21]

Another locus of controversy concerns land (and sometimes ponds) set aside for distribution and use in a manner different from the rest. Frequently this is called the "second land fund" and apparently is more common in the Red River delta and some other northern provinces than elsewhere. Most arable land is in the "first land fund," which is distributed equally to each farming household on the basis of number of persons or numbers of working-age people or combinations of these and other entitlement considerations.[22]   Households have contracts (like leases) to farm fields in this first fund for a specified number of years (ranging from four to fifteen years before the new land law and up to twenty years since the 1993 Land Law), paying specified amounts per area to the cooperative for land taxes (which are passed on to the government), irrigation charges, and other fees. The second land fund, occasionally as large as 35 per cent but usually 10-15 per cent, is distributed differently.[23] Often all or a large portion of it is divided into parcels that are auctioned. The highest bidder for each parcel farms that field for a year or two, at which point the field should be auctioned again. Proceeds are typically supposed to be used for community purposes such as welfare funds, child care support, and senior citizen programs. In some places a portion of the second fund area is specifically reserved for such community needs rather than auctioned. While many villagers seem to like this system, peasants have complained that already second land fund areas have, in effect, been taken over permanently by individual households. Auctions are not held and old contracts are simply renegotiated out of public view, thereby denying others the opportunity to bid for the fields. Villagers in several areas also say that people are building houses on the land rather than farming it and some people even sell those fields to others who build houses on it, thereby diminishing the amount of arable land and violating the terms of the contracts. Others have complained that cooperative leaders have taken advantage of their office to award second fund land to relatives or to usurp it for themselves (*Nong Dan* 20 April 1993:3).

Boundaries and hence rights to fields and water have become controversial in several areas, causing friction between communes and between villages within the same commune. Previously, at least in many areas of northern Vietnam, the commune (*xa*) — the smallest administrative unit of the state governing apparatus — and the cooperative (which typically encompassed the whole commune or several villages within it) had managed to blur or make rather irrelevant the boundaries between villages (*thon, lang*). But villagers apparently have not forgotten where those boundaries "should be." Now, with the distribution of land use rights to households and the weakening of cooperatives and communal authority, many villages are reasserting their own identity, reviving old boundaries, and demanding that only people within the village should farm the land.

One study reported 6,000 conflicts nation-wide by 1990 involving disputed boundaries between villages, communes, and other administrative units (Vietnam, Communist Party 1990:1 appendix). From 1988 to late 1992, Thai Binh province had 50 serious clashes over land, many involving villagers wanting to secede from their present cooperative and commune (*Nhan Dan* 6 November 1992:3). A 1993 account about the Red River delta said that, although the number of land disputes had diminished, many "hot points" remained, often involving people apparently claiming autonomy for their own villages. A typical pattern, according to this unsympathetic account, is that a group of "instigators" (sometimes including a few party members and local cadre) mobilize fellow villagers to contribute money, rice, and energy to request district, provincial, and central government officials to look favorably on their land claims. And if they do not get their way, they "break the law, like refusing to pay land taxes and other fees, cry for cooperatives to be split, and organize fights for land between villages and communes" (*Nhan Dan* 16 May 1993:5). A more specific example, this time from the point of view of one side in a dispute, occurred in Ha Tay province in 1992. In a petition to provincial authorities, 65 people from one village claimed commune leaders took land that belonged to their village and gave it to an adjoining village. Moreover, they argued, they need the land more than their neighbors do because they are primarily farmers whereas people in the other village have alternative ways of making a living. When one of the petitioners' fellow villagers began ploughing part of the disputed area, local authorities detained and "oppressed" him (*ap buc*). They also complained that commune officials were selling some of their land. Their petition pleaded for provincial authorities to right these wrongs and allow them to form a separate cooperative "in order to ensure the lives of our people."[24]

Newspapers have reported several similar cases of villagers organizing themselves and going over the heads of local authorities. Some accounts mention that villagers have even used guns, including "AK" rifles, to retake disputed land by force and hold authorities at bay.[25] The most startling story comes from Nam Ha province. For several months beginning in mid 1991, a sizable group of people essentially took control of their village. They displaced officials approved by higher authorities and established their own government. In the process, several villagers had become so agitated that they pelted some officials' houses with hundreds of clay roofing tiles. Part of what galvanized the villagers was their desire to retrieve land that, in the 1960s, had been assigned to an adjacent village (which was part of a different commune as well). At one point several villagers cornered a commune official, took him to the village's community house, and refused to let him go until he signed their petition, which demanded that district officials recognize their claim to the disputed fields. Meanwhile, 300 fellow villagers, pounding on drums and setting off firecrackers, began to destroy boundary markers along the disputed land, provoking a free-for-all fight with the neighboring villagers. During that fray, villagers beat up several cadre and confiscated rifles from local security police who had rushed to the scene. Later, after district offices rejected their petition, villagers refused to give up because they had been "duped," according to the newspaper, into believing their claim was legitimate and lawful (*Dai Doan Ket* 7-16 April 1993:6). The villagers refused to pay land taxes and began following many local laws and customs that are "against the law." Ultimately, district and commune officials were able to regain control of the village. But the animosities lingered. In July 1992, when coming through the village looking to buy fish, a man from the rival area was beaten to death by three of the rebel leaders. Those leaders were subsequently arrested and sentenced: one to twenty years in prison, one to life imprisonment, and one to death.

In addition to their desire to retrieve village land, those people were also motivated by distrust and hostility toward local authorities, particularly due to corruption, including the mishandling of land. One important reason why rebel leaders were able to attract considerable popular support, concluded the journalist who investigated the incident, was that their allegations of corruption and abuse of authority against local leaders of the Communist party and various Fatherland Front organizations had sufficient credibility to "expunge" people's faith in the local officials. This plus the fact, according to the writer, that party organizations had become lifeless go a long way to explain why party cadre did not nip the problem in the bud and were powerless to stop it from growing (*Dai Doan Ket* 7-16 April 1993:6).

Across the country, officials who are abusive, are corrupt, and use their positions for personal and familial advantages greatly disturb citizens ("Report on Voters" 1993), including villagers for whom the improper use of land by local party and other officials is particularly aggravating considering how precious land is in most parts of the country. Newspapers frequently mention, though with few details, that villagers in many regions complain that cooperative and commune officials have given to relatives and friends or kept for themselves the use rights to prime land; have sold land use rights without proper consultation and without disclosing where the proceeds went; and have built their own houses on land that was intended for community projects. Aggravation over such abuses of authority has created considerable discontent among peasants and provoked innumerable quarrels and bloody fights (Dang Phong's chapter, this volume). Occasionally, evidence surfaces of villagers taking initiatives to expose and protest against such behavior. Some have submitted their written complaints to newspapers for publication. For example, residents of Vung Tau in the south and of rural districts of Hanoi publicly charged authorities with illegally selling land and rice drying areas to companies and individuals (*Nong Dan* 5 April 1993:8, 15 June 1993:8, 20 August 1993:8). Villagers have also organized petition campaigns against particular officials. For example, villagers (including some local officials) in a commune in (then) Ha Son Binh province for years, beginning in 1985, persistently wrote letters and filed petitions against the commune's Communist party secretary. Their complaints provoked a series of investigations by district and provincial authorities into allegations that the party secretary, who was in line for a National Hero award, had created a secret fund from public monies and encroached on land for his own use, among other offenses. In this case, the official was exonerated in 1989 (*Nong Dan* 5 May 1989:3ff, 20 June 1989:6ff). But in another, more recent case, complaints and petitions from several villagers prompted an investigation by the district government that found the party secretary, chairman, and other People's Committee officials of a commune in Gia Lam district east of Hanoi guilty of illegally selling land, though it is not clear if they personally benefited from the sales (*Nhan Dan* 22 October 1992:1ff, 8 July 1993:1ff).[26]

Besides the misuse of land, villagers have protested against other forms of abuses by authorities. People have accused police and public security officers of using excessive force and of brutality. In the southern province of Minh Hai, for example, villagers objected to law enforcement officials who had beaten a duck thief to the point of unconsciousness (*Nong Dan* 15 August 1993:4). More frequent are accusations of embezzlement and other improper use of public property. For example, in 1993 villagers in Thanh Tri district, Hanoi, were disgusted with local cadre who had been selling positions on the cooperative's management committee and prime plots of land along the roadway. People even suspected that officials had skimmed off for themselves several million dong that had been reserved for grave stones honoring the local war dead. Since people's efforts within the commune to hold these officials accountable had failed, they were hoping higher authorities would intervene (*Dai Doan Ket* 8-14 May 1993:6). In 1992, villagers in an area of Thai Binh province in the north had become so frustrated with corruption that they initiated their own investigation. They found the chairman of the commune guilty of embezzling funds from public works projects. Alarmed at this action, district officials launched their own inquiry, which confirmed the villagers' finding (*Nhan Dan* 6 November 1992:3).

The most dramatic confrontation I am aware of in this regard occurred in 1989. People in a village in Thanh Hoa province in northern Vietnam had been disgusted for some time with corruption by commune officials. Efforts to change the situation had brought no results. In fact, things worsened, as district officials pressured people to stop making allegations of misbehavior. In early 1989, villagers chose, by an election, the leaders of the two production groups within the village. When commune and district officials rejected these choices, villagers were "indignant" and refused to change their minds. Things came to a head in late June 1989 when eleven investigators and public security officers who had come to arrest several villagers, including the two elected leaders, for criminal and civil offenses. The officials were suddenly surrounded by a huge crowd of shouting, angry villagers, who prevented them from arresting anyone. Instead, the officers found themselves trapped. The crowd would not let them leave. When district and commune authorities sent in security police to rescue the eleven officers, "thousands" of villagers fought back, using sticks, bricks, and anything else they could find. The security police found themselves overwhelmed; several were even disarmed by swarms of people. The security police retreated, leaving the villagers still with five "captives" — three security police and two investigators. How this confrontation was resolved is unknown as I have found no further reports. The one available account, which criticizes party officials in the commune and district for being out of touch with local people's needs and sentiments, ends by presenting the citizens' three demands, which they wanted met before they would release the five officials they still held: drop all criminal charges against the villagers; immediately dismiss the chairman of the commune, the chairman of the cooperative, the local public security chief, and several top district officials; and conduct a thorough investigation of "problems regarding the economy, democracy, public accountability, and justice in the commune and village" and "organize democratic elections by which trusted people are chosen to be village leaders..." (*Nong Dan* 5 August 1989:1ff).[27]

However unusual, this case illustrates several actions found in other examples discussed in this section that express villagers' initiatives and concerns. People organize petitions and other appeals, asking officials to pay attention to their problems and help them resolve disputes. Frequently such pleas are pitched over the heads of village and commune authorities to higher ones. Occasionally villagers organize to confront the state and its agents by, for instance, refusing to pay land taxes, unilaterally attempting to secede from the local cooperative, challenging the integrity of authorities, and denying the legitimacy of state approved leaders. There have even been local uprisings against state authorities. Perhaps embedded in some of this activity is an attempt to reassert a measure of village identity and autonomy. Though not discussed here, one can imagine countless conversations, discussions, and meetings as rural residents deliberate and debate among themselves how to deal with problems concerning land use, governance, and other matters. Arguments sometimes erupt into fights and violence between fellow villagers, between people in neighboring villages, and between citizens and authorities. Also practices outside the law have emerged. Among the most common are buying, selling, pawning, and accumulating land use rights; the hiring of farm laborers; and tenancy. Sometimes such practices violate local custom or what is thought by many local people to be proper, assessments exemplified by minority group villagers who are at odds with lowlander newcomers in the area and peasants who dispute how officials misuse land and other community property.

Anti-Corruption Campaigns and the New Land Law

I cannot demonstrate well that the kinds of events discussed above have influenced changes in laws and policies. But I can suggest that rural interests — speaking in part through the kinds of activities just summarized (and probably through officially approved channels not discussed here) — have been heard by various parts of the state apparatus and in some respects have made an impact. This is not to say that the state is always a sympathetic listener or that its replies satisfy what rural people want. Moreover, the state's many parts frequently speak and act differently, rather than in unison, just as rural interests are diverse and sometimes contradictory. Many parts of the state in recent years, however, seem to be trying to address corruption and certain problems regarding land use and in so doing may be attempting to take into consideration what is happening in rural communities.

Since the late 1980s, there has been an official campaign against corruption and smuggling (which often involves the connivance, if not direct involvement, of officials). For many Vietnamese the results have been unimpressive. National Assembly representatives and even higher officials have complained that the campaign is not terribly effective.[28] And villagers sometimes scoff that the worst offenders are beyond reach unless, as one villager quipped to me, "they arrest themselves." Yet the campaign is not hollow. Between 1990 and 1992, close to 20,000 people, including seven vice-ministers, were punished for corruption. In 1992 alone, there were nearly 3,000 official cases of corruption for which 1,900 people were prosecuted. State authorities that year also identified 50,000 cases of smuggling (Heng 1993:356). In the first three months of 1993, courts nation-wide handled 380 cases of corruption and smuggling (*Lao Dong* 16 May 1993:3).

Turley (1993b:330, 333) has suggested that the stimulus for this drive against corruption and smuggling came from "below," which for him means the lower realms of the state (especially party) apparatus itself. This would limit influences to those percolating up through the party hierarchy, Fatherland Front organizations, and tiers of the bureaucracy. I can well imagine that those do feed into the decision making and implementation processes. But also plausible is that actions outside official institutions intersect. Put another way, it seems rather implausible that petitions which villagers' prepare and deliver to district and provincial authorities, peasants' unilateral investigations and condemnations of officials, crowds of angry villagers surrounding police and other officials, and occasional standoffs between villagers and authorities have made no impression on party and government leaders at various levels. More likely these events have stirred officials to make some credible responses. In fact, according to sources used in the previous section, peasant actions have influenced the behavior of local state officials. Higher ranking authorities have disciplined lower ranking ones because citizens' complaints were found to be valid. Authorities have also been restrained in their use of force when dealing with agitated, even rebellious peasants who are extremely angry about local party secretaries, commune chairmen, and public security officers' abuse of power. Indeed, Carlyle Thayer suggests, what helped to motivate the Communist party leadership to do something about corruption were public protests in late 1988 by peasants, including some carrying banners denouncing "local mandarins" (1992:354).

With regard to the land law, pressure was growing by 1990 to revise the 1988 legislation in order to legalize some popular practices, curb or decisively eliminate others, and generally deal better with the country's new circumstances in the era of economic renovation and de-collectivization. Pressure came from potential foreign investors, lenders, and assistance donors who argued, for instance, that existing law and administrative procedures did not provide the security to land that a market economy required. There was also a growing realization within the party, bureaucracy, and various levels of government, as officials tried to contend with conflicts and problems regarding land, that the existing framework and rules were rapidly being outstripped by adaptations to new market forces. Many of the problems confronting these authorities were a consequence of what villagers themselves were doing and demands they were making.

Among the most pressing were the increasingly common practices of buying and selling land use rights, using land as collateral for loans in the informal credit sector, lending use rights to someone else, transferring use rights to heirs and others, and accumulating large amounts of land.[29] The law either did not address these matters or deemed them illegal. Yet they were so common that officials on the scene could rarely stop them, not to mention that some officials themselves engaged in such practices. Trying to handle these issues by improvised administrative guidelines was proving more and more difficult and created considerable diversity from one locality and province to the next. An office of the party's Central Committee concluded in September 1990, after summarizing these and other problems regarding land use and administration following the 1988 official endorsement of family farming, that the country needed to "supplement and revise several provisions of the Land Law in order to bring it in accordance with practice and reality in our nation." The report specifically identified the need to "affirm by law the rights of those using land, including inheriting, mortgaging, and transferring" their land use rights (Vietnam, Communist Party 1990:6).

While some people in the state opposed such revisions to the 1988 Land Law, fearing that would undermine the land redistribution done during the revolution, more seemed by 1991 to agree that changes were required. According to a document summarizing the main views in various quarters of the state, a few supported complete privatization of land (Vietnam, Tong Cuc Quan Ly Ruong Dat 1991). One well-placed party member I met in late 1992 who held this opinion, which he acknowledged was a minority one, reasoned that, among other advantages, privatization would avoid what he saw as an impending crisis. Because many landholders, he said, especially in the south, firmly believe that they already own their fields, most peasants would be extremely mad if the state were to tell them otherwise. To the extent there was any support for privatization, however, it faded when the Constitution, as amended in 1992, reaffirmed that land and other natural resources in Vietnam are owned by "the entire people." Another position, also made impracticable by the revised Constitution, was to allow each farming household to own a limited amount of private land.

The most common view by 1991, according to the document, was to leave "the people" as the owners of all land and the state as its manager, but revise the law to spell out the rights of land use, which should include, among other things, the right to transfer land to someone else and allow such transferring to involve money. Most with this view wanted to specify conditions under which a land user could transfer use rights; a few said simply to legalize the transferability of use rights, period.

What emerged in the new law, passed in July 1993, is that "Households and individuals to whom the state has assigned land have the right to exchange, transfer, rent, inherit, and mortgage land use rights" (Land Law 1993:3.2).[30] Elsewhere the law elaborates these rights (74-78) and itemizes conditions under which one cannot transfer them, such as when the land is in dispute or lacks pertinent legal papers (30).[31] By contrast, the 1988 law restricted the transferring of land use rights to occasions such as a farming household moving into or out of the cooperative and the death of the person holding the use rights (Land Law 1988:3, 16, 48, 49). June and August 1992 drafts for a revised law refer somewhat vaguely to mortgaging land use right as one among other methods of transferring use rights; the August draft also allows the renting of use rights. Later, the April 1993 draft said that people may transfer use rights to others and leave it to heirs, but it does not discuss mortgaging or renting.[32] Such vacillations indicate that these matters were among the "seething issues" discussed in the National Assembly before a consensus crystallized to face up to the reality of land transfer practices in the countryside.[33]

While the National Assembly was the principal formal institution for debating a revised land law, other circles of the state were also involved and the matter was discussed in many parts of society. The April 1993 draft, which is what the National Assembly was working with by that time, was published in *Nhan Dan*. The newspaper invited readers to submit suggestions and opinions, several of which it published between April and June. Before and during those months leading up to the National Assembly's final deliberations in June and July 1993, local government officials, Peasant Association chapters, and other organizations held meetings where people discussed and debated proposals for revising the law.

The new law contains other changes pertaining to some of the practices and conflicts discussed earlier. One concerns selling and buying land use rights, something that was not addressed in the 1988 law. A June 1992 draft (10, 39.4), though never using the words "buy" and "sell," details how one person or household might transfer use rights to another by agreeing on a "value" and paying 5 per cent of that amount as a fee to the state to finalize the deal. Such a discussion does not appear in the April 1993 draft, which only refers vaguely to taxes to be paid when transferring use rights (28.1.c; 72.5). That draft also "Strictly forbids the buying and selling of land..." (6). It also stipulates that the state will determine land values for purposes of computing taxes (2). But *Nhan Dan* readers and discussions in meetings elsewhere in the country argued that it was contradictory to allow transferring but forbid buying and selling since the latter was a common, indeed logical, method by which to transfer use rights (*Nhan Dan* 20 April 1993:3, 23 April 1993:1ff, 3). Many also argued that it was foolhardy for the state to try to reserve for itself the power to set land values. The state needs to recognize, said the president of the Veterans Association in Hai Hung province, that the market will set land values — people will buy and sell use rights and the state cannot stop it (*Nhan Dan* 3 May 1993:3). Similar views were voiced by delegates to the National Assembly, though many also disagreed (*Nhan Dan* 13 July 1993:1). The outcome is that the 1993 Land Law does not stipulate that the state will set prices, nor does it forbid the buying and selling of land use rights. Indeed, the law has no discussion about buying and selling. It only speaks of "transferring" (*chuyen nhuong*). People who transfer their use rights must pay a tax, but the law seems to leave future laws to determine how that tax will be calculated (79.4). Apparently, lawmakers have finessed the issues of selling and pricing use rights. By neither endorsing nor forbidding the selling of use rights, the law leaves that open as a possible method for transferring them. Similarly, by neither saying the state shall determine land values nor indicating how else land use values will be determined, the law in effect allows the market to do the job.

Considerable deliberation was given to the conditions attached to use rights, especially the number of years per contract and amount of land per household. Regarding time limits, opinions reported in the *Nhan Dan* newspaper ranged from less than twenty years on annually cropped land and 50 on perennially cropped and forested lands to no specific time limit at all. The latter position proposed to allow a household to farm its assigned fields indefinitely unless it violates other terms of the contract, such as using the land for other purposes (*Nhan Dan* 20 April 1993:3). The dilemma, which was especially evident in reports about National Assembly deliberations, was wanting to assure peasants a long time period so that they will invest in and care for the land while simultaneously leaving the state sufficient leverage to retrieve the land (*Nhan Dan* 2 July 1993:1ff, 3 July 1993:1ff). The decision was to allow twenty years for annually cropped land and aquaculture and 50 years for perennially cropped land, with the possibility of renewal at the end of the first contract (Land Law 1993:20). The government is required to define limits for other types of lands.

The 1993 law has several provisions concerning land accumulation. Two articles, apparently aimed especially at people who try to retrieve fields they once owned, forbid encroaching on land that has been assigned to someone else or for other purposes (6) and reject efforts to reclaim land that the Democratic Republic of Vietnam, the Provisional Revolutionary Government in southern Vietnam, and the Socialist Republic of Vietnam previously confiscated and redistributed (2.2). Another article, around which there was considerable debate inside and outside the National Assembly, limits the amount of annually cropped land a family may hold. While there seems to have been a consensus for a more-or-less equitable distribution, particularly in densely populated areas, some people argued that the size limit should be as high as ten hectares in order to encourage "efficient" and "economical" production. Southerners especially favored five hectares or even more while northerners said about two (*Nhan Dan* 2 July 1993:1ff, 3 July 1993:1ff, 14 July 1993:1). The June 1992 draft (40) proposed different amounts for three kinds of land in northern and southern regions. Apparently this proved too cumbersome and controversial; the April 1993 draft simply says two to three hectares, according to local conditions. The final law puts the upper limit at three hectares per household for annually cropped land, with specific limits in each locality to be defined by the government (44). The maximum for other types of agricultural and aquaculture areas is to be defined later.

The final point to highlight about the 1993 Land Law is that it appears to reduce the resources and authority of the commune and cooperative. A partial manifestation involves land for welfare and other community purposes within the commune. Some villagers and local officials wanted the area to be at least 10 per cent of agricultural land or even to permit each commune to determine the amount. Others, though, wanted the area sharply reduced and strictly managed because, as a statement from the Peasant Association reports, such land has often been used for corrupt purposes by local officials and usurped by former landlords (*Nhan Dan* 23 April 1993:3). The National Assembly, where debate reflected such concerns (*Nhan Dan* 2 July 1993:1ff), approved 5 per cent of agricultural land for community purposes but left vague the level of government that will determine how exactly that area should be used (Land Law 1993:45).

The diminished role of communes and cooperatives (or production groups) is clearer with regard to assigning land and resolving disputes. The 1988 Land Law listed communes, cooperatives, and production groups among the units to which the state could assign land use rights (1, 13.4). The 1993 law, however, says land use may be assigned to individuals, households, and state offices (1). It does not mention communes, cooperatives, or production groups. It only adds that land may be assigned to "political" and "economic" organizations, which possibly could include some cooperatives. Moreover, the 1993 law gives people's committees at the district, district capital, and city levels — *not* the commune level — the power to assign land use to households and individuals (24.2). Similarly, the law allows commune officials to handle the paper work for the *exchange* of land use rights but only district officials may process the *transfer* of use rights from one household or other economic unit to another (31). The fact that an early draft (Land Law Draft 4 1992:39.3) had allowed more power to the commune on these matters suggests that lawmakers had changed their minds, perhaps because of growing doubts about the ability of commune officials to keep records straight and to deal adequately with potentially volatile conflicts. Regarding land disputes, the 1988 law instructed communes to solve land conflicts between individuals while the district should resolve disputes between organizations such as villages (21). The 1993 law, however, urges communes to work with local Fatherland Front groups to find peaceful solutions to land conflicts. Failing that, districts — *not* communes — and even higher levels of government are responsible for settling disputes (38.2). Also the courts, which are not discussed in the 1988 law, may get involved.

What this diminution in responsibilities and authority of communes and cooperatives may mean is that the state is trying to come to terms with those institutions' frequent weaknesses and inadequacies as administrative units with regard to land management. That plus numerous provisions in the new law regarding procedures for classifying land, creating and maintaining land records, and handling land disputes may help to reduce instances of arbitrary behavior by local officials and improper usage of land resources — matters about which many villagers and others have complained.

Creeping Pluralism

Even at the height of state economic planning and control, there were social, economic, and political activities in Vietnam that the state did not authorize. For starters, there were numerous "black markets." And, as I have indicated in the second section of this paper, many cooperatives in the 1970s seemed to conform to the state sanctioned model but in fact worked in different ways, which local people themselves had devised. "Pluralism" in the sense of multiple sources of social, political, and economic practices beyond the reach of the state has been around Vietnam for some time. But for a long while its movement was akin to a snail — a slow, sliding motion usually under the cover of darkness and quick to withdraw into its shell at the first sign of danger. Recently, pluralism has been "creeping," to use Porter's expression (1993:164), having now a less sluggish and nocturnal nature, being perhaps more like the creeping of vines — multi-tendriled, expansive, and responsive to sunlight. What blossoms or fruits these vines will put forth remain to surprise us. But fairly certain is that they will grow more rapidly, probably becoming more hardy and costly to uproot.

I have highlighted considerable unauthorized political activities in the countryside, which to a significant degree are manifestations of tensions, concerns, and interests of villagers in various parts of the country. And I have suggested that such behavior has prompted parts of the state to respond, often in ways that suggest that they are trying to take into account what villagers are expressing. Sometimes peasants and other rural people deliberately try to get the attention of, influence, and even confront state agents. Other actions may not be aimed that way but, nevertheless, seem to make an impression on authorities. Villagers' resistance to collectivization and their buying and selling of land use rights were not necessarily done in hopes of getting the state to change laws and policies or authorize people's adaptations, but the cumulative effect of their actions — together, no doubt, with other influences — was precisely that.

In recent years, an amazing number of new rural organizations have sprung up — an estimated 30,000 by December 1992, which are "essentially voluntary and organized by the population directly..." (Fforde 1993:73). They include many local credit associations, which lend to peasants vital farming capital that the state's banking system, though improving in this regard, is not capable of lending. Other organizations build and maintain irrigation systems, provide mutual aid, and construct roadways and other infrastructures. And across the country there has been a resurgence of community religious groups, often formed around village pagodas, temples, and meeting houses.

Religion is the basis of the largest non-state organizations and the ones most conspicuously at odds with the state authorities in recent years, as Thayer's chapter in this book elaborates. While the issues are numerous, a central one is the United Buddhist Church's insistence that the state recognize its right to exist as an independent organization. Meanwhile, tensions have also intensified between several Catholic Church leaders and state officials, also over matters to do with claims for autonomy from the state and other contested views of human rights.[34] Probably everyone on all sides of these confrontations expects that if these religious organizations can secure more independence from state intrusion, other types of organizations will likely follow.

Meanwhile, some organizations of the state's Fatherland Front show signs of putting daylight between themselves and the Communist party and other parts of the state. For rural areas, an interesting one to watch is the Peasant Association (*Hoi Nong Dan*), which has many village, commune, and town chapters and main offices in Hanoi and Ho Chi Minh City. Many observers as well as villagers see this organization primarily as a promoter of Communist party and government policies and thinking, with the addition in recent years of becoming a disseminator of technical information about agriculture and livelihood projects (Dang Ngoc Quang and Buse 1992:65, 105). Too often, writes one acerbic critic, peasants must say only good things, may not criticize, and have to endure district and commune authorities "treading on their necks" (*uc hiep*) while Peasant Association chapters do little or nothing. The organization only exists in name, the critic says; it lacks real substance because in many areas local officers of the association are also the local authorities of the state (*Dai Doan Ket* 21 May 1993:1ff). Local officers of the association have also been accused of encroaching on public land and other forms of corruption (*Dai Doan Ket* 14 May 1993:6).

Ending the discussion here, however, would be to miss substantial aspects of the association. Its own officials have criticized themselves and the organization for inadequately representing the peasantry and being insufficiently innovative and energetic about trying to help to improve villagers' conditions. That only 20 per cent of the peasantry are members, said the association's national vice-president, is indicative of its weaknesses (*Nong Dan* 20 June 1993:2). National leaders have also faulted party and government officials for treating peasants unfairly, ignoring peasants' views, and ordering villagers around rather than listening and seriously discussing matters with them. Association leaders have objected to "party committee echelons" picking Peasant Association leaders.[35] Meanwhile, association representatives and publications have sounded like advocates for issues important to many rural people. In particular, they have been asking the government to subsidize the price at which producers sell their rice, increase the volume of low-interest loans to peasants, implement programs that will create more rural employment, improve education facilities in the countryside, and work with the association to build a welfare fund for elderly peasants (*Ha Noi Moi* 13 October 1992:3; various issues of *Nong Dan*). Also the association's newspaper has been a chief avenue by which villagers and journalists criticize and report, frequently in considerable detail, corruption, abusive authorities, and the harsh living conditions in rural areas.

Notes

* I gratefully acknowledge the Center for Cooperative Vietnamese Studies at the University of Hanoi, Nguyen Quang Ngoc of that Center, and the Research School of Pacific Studies of the Australian National University for supporting and assisting my research. I am also thankful to Allison Ley for helping me to gather relevant materials from libraries in Canberra, to Kristin Pelzer and Bruce Koppel for sharing with me some materials, and to Dao The Tuan, Adam Fforde, David Marr, Doug Porter, Steve Sénèque, Carlyle Thayer, Thaveeporn Vasavakul, and Vo-Tong Xuan for their encouraging comments on

earlier drafts.

1. Theda Skocpol (1979:29-31) and Joel Migdal (1988:19-20) are my guide for conceptualizing "the state" as a set of policy making, administrative, policing, and military organizations with a central leadership that attempts to make binding rules for the nation, monopolize the authoritative use of violence, and defend itself and nation's territory against international intruders and domestic rivals. Having those purposes, the state has its own interests which may indeed be different from other sectors within the nation and in the international state system. The extent to which a state can project and defend its interests, its parts be coordinated by the central leadership, and its leaders and agencies be widely regarded as the nation's legitimate authorities can fluctuate considerably over time and from one part of society to another. Hence a state's strengths and weaknesses vary; and the state can be strong in some respects while weak in others. Also, though "state" is a singular noun, "the state" is rarely a singular actor. The degree of coherence among its many motions and voices is one important, though not the only, measure of a state's strength. Broadly speaking a state is "weak" if it is but one of many large social organizations, but having little ability to marshall resources and set parameters for society as a whole. A very "powerful" state, on the other hand, has those abilities. A powerful state, however, is not necessarily a "strong" state. To be strong, a state must also have considerable legitimacy among most sectors of society.

2. Also see Gareth Porter's book (1993:118-26 *passim*; 153, 161). Though Porter emphasizes the first interpretation discussed here, he presents evidence that is compatible with the fourth and suggests that unanticipated, non-official societal influences on state agencies have occurred. His situation suggests that analysts are not necessarily locked into one of the four positions I have identified.

3. For an argument that this is what occurs in China, see Kelliher (1992:esp. 233-253). Also suggestive here are other studies on China that demonstrate a dynamic interaction at the sub-provincial and village levels as peasants, party cadre, and other state officials try to accommodate and manipulate, negotiate and maneuver, often having different, even conflicting interests. For example, see Chan, Madsen, and Unger (1984); and Oi (1989).

4. Interviews in ten communes within a 30 kilometer radius of Hanoi, October 1992 and more interviews in two of those during April-May 1993; Beresford 1989:143-153; Ngo Vinh Long (1993:168-169).

5. Interviews with officials in Hanoi, September 1992; Tran Duc (1991:18, 21); Nguyen Duc Nhuan (1983:371-372).

6. Quang Truong 1987:188, also ch. 8 *passim*; Ngo Vinh Long 1988:163-173; Beresford 1989:113-115.

7. Comments by Vo-Tong Xuan during the ANU Vietnam Update conference, Canberra, 3 December 1993, and during my interview with him, 1

December 1993. Also see Vo-Tong Xuan's chapter in this book.

8. This is the range of figures reported in "Sau 30 Nam" 1990:48; Fforde 1989:218; and Nguyen Huy 1991:130-131.

9. From the team leader's elaboration, "foot dragging" seems to be the best translation of his term *lan cong*. The dictionary defines it as deliberately working lazily or not working (*cung nhau co tinh lam viec chay luoi*), adding that is a form of struggle for the interests of workers in capitalistic enterprises (*mot hinh thuc dau tranh doi quyen loi cua cong nhan trong cac xi nghiep tu ban chu nghia*), an ironic statement in this context. *Tu Dien Tieng Viet* (Hanoi: NXB Khoa Hoc Xa Hoi, 1988). Also see Luong 1992:197, 202-205; Fforde 1989:127-128.

10. Interviews in a commune of Gia Lam district, Hanoi, April 1993; and *Nong Nghiep Ha Bac* 1978, no. 3:9-10.

11. Tran Duc 1991: 25, 29; Diep Dinh Hoa et al. 1993:75-76; and Cung Co Hop Tac Xa 1981:esp. 66-67. The latter refers to experiments in the provinces of Nghe Tinh, Vinh Phu, Ha Bac, Ha Nam Ninh, Ha Son Binh, Hai Hung, and Hai Phong. Diep Dinh Hoa, et al., write about a village in Thai Binh province.

12. Interviews with officials in Hanoi and several communes, September and October 1992.

13. Interview with Doan Duy Thanh, Hanoi, 17 September 1992. Thanh was party secretary of Hai Phong at the time of these modifications and was involved in encouraging them. He has written some about the experience (Doan Duy Thanh 1985:58, 103-104, 227).

14. This is how some in government and the Communist party, when looking back on the 1980s, characterized the situation to me in 1992 and 1993. Similarly, a recent book, one of whose authors, Dang Tho Xuong, works in the Economic Committee of the Central Committee, says that "sneaky contracts" had become widespread. The Communist party had to resolve this, the authors say, not by trying to abolish household-based production but by coming to terms with it (Chu Van Lam, et al. 1992:78-79).

15. See examples in the southern province of Dong Thap (*Nhan Dan* 2 Nov. 1992:3; 3 November 1992:3; 5 July 1993:3), the central region near Hue and in Quang Nam-Da Nang (*Nhan Dan* 27 April 1993:3; 31 May 1993:2); and Thai Binh in the Red River delta (*Nhan Dan* 23 September 1992:3). A document of the Tieu Ban Tong Ket Phat Trien (1993:pt.2) highlights several active cooperatives in various regions. An impressive cooperative I have visited several times is in Da Ton (Gia Lam district, Greater Hanoi).

16. Vien Xa Hoi Hoc 1991:34-35; Pham Van Phu 1990:21; Do Nguyen Phuong 1991:40.

17. Such sentiments resonate well with Francesca Bray's conclusion that the commune or collective is too large for rice growing but "the family farm is too small to stand alone" (1991:212).

18. Vietnam, Communist Party 1993:pt.3, item 3; Do Muoi 1993:pt.3; Vo

Van Kiet 1992:49.

19. *Nong Dan* 15 August 1993:1ff. Also see account of a case in Cam Ranh, *Nong Dan* end of July 1993:9.

20. For a useful analysis of lingering problems in these interior parts of Vietnam, see Evans 1992.

21. *Nong Dan* end of Aug. 1993:5, 25; Vietnam, Communist Party 1990:1, and 1 appendix.

22. The ten communes I visited in 1992 and 1993 suggest that there is considerable variation in distribution methods and factors taken into consideration. One report referred to the diversity as "anarchic" ("For the Second Time" 1992:23).

23. I am drawing on my visits in 1992 and 1993 to ten communes in the Red River delta. Some similar features are noted in Cruz et al. 1993:89, 91; Tran Duc 1991:40-41; and articles in *Nhan Dan*, such as 16 May 1993:14. Luong (1992:212-213) discusses three categories of land, the first seeming to be similar to the "first land fund" and the other two combined being similar to the "second land fund."

24. Petition, dated Dec. 1992, attached to "Phieu Huong Dan" of the Ha Tay People's Committee, 14 January 1993.

25. See reports from Ha Bac, Thai Binh, and Vinh Phu provinces and rural Hanoi areas in *Nong Dan* 5 January 1989:6,20, April 1989:1ff, 5 June 1989:6, 5 August 1989:3, 20 October 1989:1ff, 5 May 1993:11. There may be accounts in 1990-92 issues of this paper, which I have yet to read.

26. Local authorities have reportedly used monies from the illegal sale of land to finance schools, roads, electrification, and other community services ("For the Second Time" 1992:24).

27. A similar confrontation, I have been told, occurred in Nghe An province in September 1993. Throngs of villagers "arrested" several officials, including public security officers, and held them for several days. Army soldiers were sent to the vicinity, though were not used. Apparently the matter was settled through peaceful negotiations. The main issue that had aroused the villagers was taxes imposed by local officials. What kinds of taxes is not known. According to another source, special taxes devised by district and commune officials have become numerous and have created considerable discontent among rural people in many areas (Dang Phong's chapter, this book). A Peasants Association report, according to Fforde (1993:72), found that a "farming family must make some 28-40 'contributions' a year, of which 15-20 are without any sound basis."

28. Vice-premier Phan Van Khai (1993), speaking to the National Assembly on 16 June 1993, said that "The struggle against corruption and smuggling is achieving only limited effect." Prime Minister Vo Van Kiet (1992:55), however, speaking to the same body on 9 December 1992, deemed the accomplishments so impressive that "...there are grounds for the removal of

all skeptical feelings" regarding the state's "ability to carry out this struggle to the end." For a pessimistic survey of the situation, see Nguyen Van Canh (1990).

29. Interviews with three well-informed party members, Hanoi, September 1992.

30. The "3.2" notation refers to article 3, paragraph 2 in the law. Similar notations will be used when citing the 1988 Land Law and drafts leading up to the 1993 law. This analysis is restricted mainly to matters pertaining to agricultural lands with some attention to other rural lands. Provisions regarding urban land are not included.

31. Transferring, renting, mortgaging, etc., of land use rights is limited to the duration of the contract. Once the lease has expired, the land in question, theoretically, can be assigned by offices of the state to another household or economic unit. The length of a contract is discussed later in this section.

32. Land Law Draft 4, 1992:9, 10, 37, 39, 41, 43; Land Law Draft 7, 1992:2.3, 5, 24, 27-31; Land Law Draft April 1993:5, 27, 29.

33. The quote is from a *Nhan Dan* account of National Assembly deliberations (2 July 1993:1ff). Also see *Nhan Dan* 28 June 1993:1ff.

34. Sources on these matters involving the Unified Buddhist Church and the Catholic Church include an AFP story in FBIS-EAS-92-250, 29 December 1992:74-75; Thich Huyen Quang 1992; "Arrest and Protest in Hue: Background Documents," *Vietnam Journal*, Spring-Summer 1993; *Nhan Dan* 31 May 1993:4, *FEER* 13 May 1993:26, 5 August 1993:26-28; *Washington Post Foreign Service* 19 October 1993; "Human Rights in Vietnam: An Interview with Father Chan Tin," *Eglises d'Asie* June 1993; and *Guardian Weekly* 29 August 1993:14.

35. Pham Bai, Chairman of Collective Peasants Association, the former name for the Peasant Association, in "Scientific Conference" 1990:5.

References

Beresford, Melanie. 1988. *Vietnam: Politics, Economics and Society.* London: Pinter.

_____. 1989. *National Unification and Economic Development in Vietnam.* London: Macmillan.

Bray, Francesca. 1991. "Rice Economies: The Rise and Fall of China's Communes in East Asian Perspective," in Jan Breman and Sudipto Mundle, eds., *Rural Transformation in Asia.* Pp. 195-217. Delhi: Oxford University Press.

Chan, Anita, Richard Madsen, and John Unger. 1984. *Chen Village.* Berkeley: University of California Press.

Chu Van Lam. et al. 1992. *Hop Tac Hoa Nong Nghiep Viet Nam: Lich Su, Van De, Trien Vong* [Agricultural Cooperativization in Vietnam: History, Problems, Prospects]. Hanoi: NXB Su That.

Cruz, Gladys. A. et al. 1993. "Equitability," in Le Trong Cuc and A. Terry Rambo, eds. Pp. 83-93.

Cung Co Hop Tac Xa. 1981. "Cung Co Hop Tac Xa San Xuat Nong Nghiep Day Manh Cong Tac Khoan" [Reinforce Agricultural Production Cooperatives, Speed Up Contract Work]. A Ministry of Agriculture Report, in Le Thanh Nghi, *Cai Tien Cong Tac Khoan Mo Rong. Khoan San Pham De Thuc Day San Xuat Cung Co Hop Tac Xa Nong Nghiep.* Pp. 32-79. Hanoi: NXB Su That.

Dai Doan Ket [Great Unity]. Newspaper of the Fatherland Front.

Dang Ngoc Quang and Kent Buse. 1992. "Rural Household Support and Household Economy: Feasibility Study." Hanoi: Mennonite Central Committee Vietnam.

Diep Dinh Hoa et al. 1993. "Autonomy and Solidarity," in Le Trong Cuc and A. Terry Rambo, eds. Pp. 53-82.

Do Muoi. 1993. "Address to the Communist Party of Vietnam Central Committee's Fifth Plenum, 3-11 June 1993." BBC Monitoring Service, internet, Vietnam News, 18 and 20 June 1993.

Do Nguyen Phuong. 1991. "May Van De Thoi Su. Cap Bach Rut Ra tu Nong Thon, Nong Dan, Nong Nghiep Hai Hung" [Some Current Urgent Matters from the Hai Hung Countryside, Peasantry and Agriculture]. *Xa Hoi Hoc* 2:39-44.

Doan Duy Thanh. 1985. *Hai Phong trong Chang Duong Dau cua Thoi Ky Qua Do* [Hai Phong in the Initial Stage of Transition]. Hai Phong: NXB Hai Phong.

Evans, Grant. 1992. "Internal Colonialism in the Central Highlands of Vietnam." *Sojourn* 7(August):274-304.

FEER. Far Eastern Economic Review.

Fforde, Adam. 1989. *The Agrarian Question in North Vietnam, 1974-1979: A Study of Cooperator Resistance to State Policy.* Armonk, NY: M. E. Sharpe.

_____. 1993. *Vietnam: Economic Commentary and Analysis.* (Canberra: ADUKI), no. 3, May.

"For the Second Time, the Peasants of Ha Bac Province Are Real Masters of their Fields." 1992. *Economic Problems*, No. 18 (Oct.-Dec.):23-26. Translation of an article from *Nhan Dan* 27-28 April 1992.

Hanoi Moi, daily Hanoi newspaper.

Heng, Russell Hiang Khng. 1993. "Vietnam 1992: Economic Growth and Political Caution." *Southeast Asian Affairs 1993*, 353-363.

Hien Trang. 1990. "Hien Trang ve Quan He San Xuat Trong Nong Thon" [The Situation Regarding Production Relations in the Countryside]. Typescript manuscript, Hanoi, 8 August. A draft of a report done for the Communist Party's Central Committee.

Kelliher, Daniel. 1992. *Peasant Power in China: The Era of Rural Reform, 1972-1989.* New Haven: Yale University Press.

Kerkvliet, Benedict J. Tria. 1990. *Everyday Politics in the Philippines.* Berkeley: University of California Press.

_____. forthcoming. "Village-State Relations in Vietnam: The Effect of Everyday Politics on De-Collectivization." *Journal of Asian Studies.*

Land Law. 1988. "Luat Dat Dai," in *Luat Dat Dai va Huong Dan Thi Hanh.* Hanoi: NXB Phap Ly, 1992, 3-25.

Land Law. 1993. "Luat Dat Dai ." Hanoi: NXB Chinh Tri Quoc Gia.

Land Law Draft 4. 1992. "Luat Dat Dai Du Thao 4." 18 June. Typescript.

Land Law Draft 7. 1992. "Luat Dat Dai Du Thao 7." 10 August. Typescript.

Land Law Draft April. 1993. "Luat Dat Dai Du Thao," published in *Nhan Dan* 5 April 1993, 2ff. An English translation was published in FBIS-EAS-93-076, 22 April 1993, 50-59.

Lao Dong. Daily newspaper published in Ho Chi Minh City.

Le Trong Cuc and A. Terry Rambo, eds. 1993. *Too Many People, Too Little Land: The Human Ecology of a Wet Rice-Growing Village in the Red River Delta of Vietnam.* Honolulu: Program on Environment, East-West Center.

Luong, Hy V. 1992. *Revolution in the Village: Tradition and Transformation in North Vietnam, 1925-1988.* Honolulu: University of Hawaii Press.

Migdal, Joel S. 1988. *Strong Societies and Weak States: State-Society Relations and State Capabilities in the Third World.* Princeton: Princeton University Press.

Ngo Vinh Long. 1988. "Some Aspects of Cooperativization in the Mekong Delta," in David Marr and Christine White, eds., *Postwar Vietnam: Dilemmas in Socialist Development.* Pp. 163-173. Ithaca: Southeast Asia Program, Cornell University.

_____. 1993. "Reform and Rural Development in Vietnam: Impact on Class, Sectoral, and Regional Inequalities," in Turley and Selden, eds. Pp. 165-207.

Nguyen Duc Nhuan. 1983. "The Contradictions of the Rationalization of Agricultural Space and Work in Vietnam" (trans. by Miriam Atlas). *International Journal of Urban and Regional Research* 7:363-379.

Nguyen Huy. 1991. "Hop Tac Hoa va Phuong Huong Dieu Chinh Qua Trinh HTH trong Thoi Gian Toi o Nuoc Ta" [Cooperativization and the Direction of the Cooperativization Readjustment Process in Our County's Near Future], in Pham Nhu Cuong, ed., *Mot So Van De Kinh Te cua Hop Tac Hoa Nong Nghiep o Viet Nam.* Pp. 125-173. Hanoi: NXB Khoa Hoc Xa Hoi.

Nguyen Van Canh. 1990. "A Party in Decay: The New Class and Organized Crime," in Thai Quang Trung, ed., *Vietnam Today: Assessing New Trends.* Pp. 23-35. New York: Crane Russak.

Nhan Dan. Daily newspaper of the Central Committee, Communist Party of Vietnam.

Nong Dan. The full title is *Nong Dan Viet Nam,* a newspaper published usually twice a month by the Peasant Association [*Hoi Nong Dan*].

Nong Nghiep Ha Bac. [Ha Bac province Agriculture]. A journal published by the Agricultural Committee of Ha Bac province.

Oi, Jean. 1989. *State and Peasant in Contemporary China: The Political Economy of Village Government.* Berkeley: University of California Press.

Pham Van Phu. 1990. "Da Dang Hoa Kinh Te va Doi Moi Chinh Sach Giai Cap o Nong Thon" [Diversifying the Economy, Renovating Policies, Classes in the Countryside]. *Nghien Cuu Kinh Te* 6:19-22.

Phan Van Khai. 1993. "Report to the Ninth National Assembly's Third Session, 16 June 1993." BBC Monitoring Summary of World Broadcasts, internet, 23 June 1993.

Porter, Gareth. 1993. *Vietnam: The Politics of Bureaucratic Socialism.* Ithaca: Cornell University Press.

Quang Truong. 1987. *Agricultural Collectivization and Rural Development in Vietnam: A North/South Study, 1955-1985.* Amsterdam: Vrije Universiteit te

Amsterdam.

"Report on Voters' Views on Economy, Society, and Culture." 1993. Voice of Vietnam, 18 June. From BBC Monitoring Service, 29 June.

"Sau 30 Nam." 1990. "Sau 30 Nam Hop Tac Hoa Nong Nghiep: Doi Song Nong Dan va Van De Quan Ly San Xuat Nong Nghiep Hien Nay [After Thirty Years of Agricultural Cooperativization: Current Peasant Living Conditions and Agricultural Production Management Problems] in Nguyen Luc., ed., *Thuc Trang Kinh Te Xa Hoi Viet Nam Giai Doan, 1986-1990.* Pp. 27-60. Hanoi: Tap Chi Thong Ke.

"Scientific Conference on the 'Problem of Democracy in Vietnam — The Actual Situation and Proposals.'" 1990. *Tap Chi Cong San*, February, 39-49. JPRS-ATC-90-008, 1 Oct. 1990, 2-9.

Skocpol, Theda. 1979. *States and Social Revolution.* Cambridge: Cambridge University Press.

Thayer, Carlyle A. 1992. "The Challenges Facing Vietnamese Communism." *Southeast Asian Affairs 1992,* 349-364.

Thich Huyen Quang. 1992. "'From the Heart Letter' to Buddhist Faithful." 24 September.

Thrift, Nigel and Dean Forbes. 1986. *The Price of War: Urbanization in Vietnam 1954-1985.* Sydney: Allen and Unwin.

Tieu Ban Tong Ket. 1993. Tieu Ban Tong Ket Phat Trien Nong, Lam, Ngu Nghiep Nong Thon va Chuan Bi Hoi Nghi Nong Nghiep Toan Quoc cua Chinh Phu. 1993. "Mot So Nhan To Moi Nong Nghiep va Nong Thon" [Several New Factors in Agriculture and the Countryside]. April.

Tran An Phong and Cao Duc Phat. 1991. Tran An Phong and Cao Duc Phat. "Nhung Van De Kinh Te cua Ho Gia Dinh Nong Dan Hien Nay" [Current Economic Problems of Peasant Households]. *Xa Hoi Hoc* 2:10-13.

Tran Duc. 1991. *Hop Tac Xa va Thoi Vang Son cua Kinh Te Gia Dinh* [Cooperatives and the Resplendent Period of the Family Economy]. Hanoi: NXB Tu Tuong Van Hoa.

Turley, William S. 1993a. "Party, State, and People: Political Structure and Economic Prospects," in Turley and Selden, eds. Pp. 257-276.

_____. William S. 1993b. "Political Renovation in Vietnam: Renewal and Adaptation," in B. Ljunggren, ed., *The Challenge of Reform in Indochina.* Pp. 327-347. Cambridge, MA: Harvard Institute for International Development, Harvard University.

Turley, William and Mark Selden, eds. 1993. *Reinventing Vietnamese Socialism.* Boulder: Westview.

Vien Xa Hoi Hoc. 1991. "Su Chuyen Doi Co Cau Xa Hoi o Nong Thon Dong Bang Bac Bo trong Dieu Kien Kinh Te Moi" [The Transformation of Social Structure in the Northern Rural Plains under New Economic Conditions]. *Xa Hoi Hoc* 1:22-40.

Vietnam, Communist Party. 1990. Agricultural Committee of the Central Committee. "Bao Cao Tinh Hinh Tranh Chap Ruong Dat o Nong Thon Hien Nay" [Report about the Current Agricultural Land Conflict Situation in the Countryside]. 27 September.

_____. 1993. Central Committee, Fifth Plenum Resolution, "Tiep Tuc Doi Moi va Phat Trien Kinh Te Xa Hoi Nong Thon" [Continued Socio-economic Renovation and Development in the Countryside]. *Nhan Dan* 1 July 1993:1ff. (English translation provided by BBC Monitoring Service: Far East, e-mail transmission, Vietnam News, 14 July 1993.)

Vietnam, Tong Cuc Quan Ly Ruong Dat. 1991. "Tai Lieu Dung Trong Hoi Thao Chuyen De Che Do So Huu Dat Dai o Viet Nam Hien Nay" [A Document for the Special Seminar "The Land Ownership System in Vietnam Today]. January, 5pp.

Vo Van Kiet. 1992. "Report on Socioeconomic Conditions to the Ninth National Assembly's Second Session on 9 December." FBIS-EAS-92-239, 11 December, 71-3, and 14 December, 48-56.

White, Christine Pelzer. 1985. "Agricultural Planning, Pricing Policy and Co-operatives in Vietnam." *World Development* 13(January):97-114.

Womack, Brantly. 1992. "Reform in Vietnam: Backwards Towards the Future." *Government and Opposition* 27(Spring):177-189.

Woodside, Alexander. 1979. "Nationalism and Poverty in the Breakdown of Sino-Vietnamese Relations." *Pacific Affairs* 52(Fall):381-409.

4

The Economy and the Countryside: The Relevance of Rural Development Policies

Adam Fforde & Steve Sénèque

Rural Economic Conditions — Competing Explanations

Vietnamese agriculture continues to employ the great mass of the Vietnamese population. However, the position it can and should take in economic development remains subject to debate. This chapter will examine current developments in the economy and the countryside in the light of both their effects upon what remains a large and rather poor group of people, as well as implications for future research. Debate is healthy and normal. It is also a first step to developing a framework for analyzing policy and future trends.

Agricultural policy in Vietnam has gone through two main reforms, and appears now to be going through a third. Directive 100 in 1981 initiated a first stage in decentralization of power to farm households and away from the producer cooperatives. This was significant but limited in impact. Then in 1988 Resolution 10 introduced further changes that amounted to a full scale de-collectivization in some parts of the country, whilst in others cooperatives lost most of their power. (For more detail on these two policies see Vo-Tong Xuan's chapter, this volume.) The year 1993 saw the Party Central Committee fifth plenum focus upon rural development problems; the year also saw passage of the new land law, as well as government decrees on extension work, reform of state businesses in agriculture, rural credit, and land allocation.[1] These latest measures present elements of a normal set of rural development policies. Until now, however, the main meaning of government and party policy has been to do with the basic issue of de-collectivization, and only in 1993 — more than a decade after the first steps in rural reform — can such ideas be seen expressed in detailed policy. This presents the conundrum addressed in this chapter: in the absence of supportive policies, real rural income growth in Vietnam has reportedly been high. What is the basis for this, and what has it meant for the rural population?

In the inter-Congress party conference of January 1994, indus-trialization and modernization were presented as the main goals of development policy for the remainder of the decade. The project priorities of the November 1993 Donor's Conference confirmed this thrust to accelerate growth through an urban and industrial focus. Such a clear statement of sectoral priorities is of importance in a country that remains both as poor and as rural as Vietnam. In this, debate can be seen already to be well developed, and resting upon very different analyses of conditions in the rural areas.

We identify a number of different strands in this discussion:

1. The "optimistic about markets" and "pessimistic about policy" position: markets work, and state policy is not very important.

Central to this position is the notion that the rural economy is undergoing a dynamic process that is rather independent of state policy, once given the commitment to abandoning the old central-planning model. The positive forces of the market, once unleashed, lead to greater diversification and a reduction in poverty levels. They also result in social differentiation that is in essence positive, in that it is not at root a process leading to impoverishment and the creation of a landless group, but essentially a means to more efficient resource allocation. In this process, the contribution of government has been — by withdrawing from direct intervention in economic activities — to free up the rural economy, granting family farms high levels of autonomy and, by opening up domestic and foreign trade, stimulating rural incomes growth and diversification. This analysis places little emphasis upon either the negative effects upon growth of the ongoing involvement of local authorities in the rural economy, or the possibility of underlying structural reasons for the instability of cash crop production and marketing. This view basically accepts the positive role of unregulated markets, and sees the existing pace of development as satisfactory.[2]

A variant of this position is highly skeptical of the capacity of local authorities actually to implement "developmentalist" state policies, arguing that discussions of optimal policies are relatively incon-sequential.

2. The "optimistic about regulated markets" and "optimistic about policy" position.

According to this way of thinking, Vietnamese urban and industrial growth processes in the 1990s are likely to be very strong, and will need to be balanced by a sound and healthy process of socio-economic development in the rural areas. Growth will depend upon rapid increases in popular savings which must come in large part from the rural areas. Believing that the rural economy is still weakly developed, this approach focuses upon constraints. Under conditions where farm product markets are apparently highly competitive, stress is placed upon such problems as: continued obstacles to the unrestricted entry of capital into crop processing and export marketing, and the non-implementation of the New Deal for agriculture promised by Resolution 10 in 1988.[3] It also points to the slow and distorted pace of development of state rural credit, extension services, and other elements of a normal rural development support strategy. This approach then identifies the need for government to move to create better markets, for example through appropriate rural infrastructural work and by improving entry and exit in areas such as crop processing and exports, and also for government to move faster in actively developing rural support services.[4] This position has necessarily to assume that "developmentalist" policies have some hope of implementation.

3. The "pessimistic about both markets and policy" position.

This stance argues that the market oriented reforms have had a series of important, negative, and interlinked social effects that have been widely ignored as a result of various "blindnesses" — gender and "economism" being the most important. The reduced role of collectives is seen as having greatly increased the load upon women, whilst pushing them out of participation in important social fora. Publicly funded health and education services have deteriorated, again eroding women's room for maneuver. Furthermore, this position argues that the positive role of the market has created a powerful process of social differentiation that, whilst at present still containable, will inevitably lead to a polarization of rural society as opportunities for the landless fail to grow sufficiently fast. This position points to the slowdown in urbanization and the sheer weight of rural numbers that urbanization and industrialization (at rates that the environment will be capable of absorbing) would have to absorb. Under this analysis, the present relative calm is superficial, and major rural social problems will emerge in the mid 1990s.[5]

The chapter by Tran Thi Van Anh and Nguyen Manh Huan in this volume points up many of the complexities involved in any simple notion of what constitutes rural development policy in Vietnam: the continued use of cooperatives in some areas to pressure the rural population; the land conflicts; and the pressures upon women. The chapter by Ben Kerkvliet also shows the bubbling social disorder.

The position of the present authors is somewhat skeptical. As economists we tend to be optimistic about the role of markets, but as observers of the realities of Vietnamese rural life,[6] and the activities of the party-state apparatus at the local level, we experience a certain pessimism regarding the implementability of developmentalist policies. Nevertheless, we are sufficiently "institutionalist" in our economics to feel that under appropriate conditions the state can and should play a positive role in making markets work well. At the same time, we find the present lack of research into Vietnamese rural development — compared with other topics — is itself both revealing and rather disquieting. Overseas, there are few economists working on the area outside of Harvard University and the Australian National University, and even there this is far less extensive than research, for example, into finance and industry. In Vietnam, a number of institutes are busy, but the relationships between them seem weak. However, the recent large national research program into problems of rural development (KX-08) has thrown up some very interesting work.[7] There may be a need to assist with structuring the debate, partly by bringing into formal analysis certain "political economy" issues, and also partly by applying analytical rigor so as to isolate areas where further empirical work is needed.

The following section looks at current trends from an empirical and economic point of view. The concluding section attempts to relate these to the explanations outlined above.

Recent Trends

In this section, we present the trends evident in the Vietnamese economy as they pertain to agriculture and the countryside since the last agricultural reforms were implemented in 1988 and the implementation of a major economic restructuring program in 1989, which effectively abandoned central planning along with the end of "two-track" pricing. The majority of the statistical evidence presented in this survey is derived from official Vietnamese sources. However, other sources are also used and these include a number of recent surveys by international agencies.

The Macroeconomy and Agriculture

Stabilizing the Economy — Positive Measures Adopted and Implemented by the State and Vital for Agricultural Growth. In 1989, after a decade-long gestation, Vietnam made the final commitment to transform its economy to a market oriented economic system.[8] It embarked on an ambitious program of stabilization by implementing tight fiscal and monetary measures; liberalizing trade, including a devaluation of its currency; and, foremost, liberalizing its market. Furthermore, access to Soviet foreign assistance, shrinking from 1988, was effectively cut off by 1990 and the paucity of western aid seeping in to Vietnam meant that it embarked on this ambitious economic transformation program with very little foreign help. Despite this constraint, among many others, Vietnam has achieved some creditable gains and the economy has shown rather fast growth.

Between 1985 and 1988, the Vietnamese economy grew at 5.7 per cent (*Nien Giam Thong Ke — 1988*).[9] By comparison, between 1989 and 1992 the economy grew at an impressive 8.4 per cent on average (see Table 4.1). This was despite loss of foreign assistance that had been worth nearly US$1 billion annually during the mid 1980s. The initial impact of the reforms was a sudden surge in output, especially agriculture, increasing GDP by 8.0 per cent in 1989 and then 11.1 per cent in 1990.[10] However, the subsequent sharp falls in foreign assistance between 1989 and 1991 had a dampening effect on Vietnam's economic growth, pulling it back to 6.0 per cent in 1991. By 1992, Vietnam had adjusted to the supply shock of the Soviet aid cuts, and

TABLE 4.1: GDP Growth and Share by Economic Sectors (per cent)

Item	1988	1989	1990	1991	1992	Average 1989-1992
GDP Growth by sectors:	5.1	8.0	11.1	6.0	8.3	8.4
Agriculture	3.9	6.4	11.2	2.2	6.3	6.5
Industry	3.3	2.3	10.7	9.9	12.6	8.9
Services	8.9	2.7	10.6	8.2	8.5	7.5
Construction	-3.1	2.0	17.7	5.2	4.2	7.3
Share of GDP by sectors:	100	100	100	100	100	100
Agriculture	39.2	40.3	40.3	38.9	38.2	39.4
Industry	18.3	18.8	18.7	19.4	20.2	19.3
Services	39.2	37.3	37.1	37.9	38.0	37.6
Construction	3.3	3.6	3.8	3.8	3.6	3.7

Note: In constant 1989 prices/local currency.

Sources: *Tai Khoan Quoc Gia o Viet Nam 1986-1990 (VIE 88/032 Project) 1992; Nien Giam Thong Ke — 1992.*

with further efforts by the state to manage fiscal and monetary policies more tightly and allow the emerging market economy to play the major role, the economy posted a GDP growth rate of 8.3 per cent. The GDP growth rate for 1993 is expected to exceed 8 per cent.[11]

On the savings and investment front, credit must be given for Vietnam's efforts to mobilize domestic savings. Over the period it has managed to replace foreign savings with domestic savings. In 1989 foreign savings inflow was 9 per cent of GDP, while domestic savings was a mere 2 per cent of GDP (World Bank 1993). The severe cutback in foreign assistance meant that the responsibility was on the government to provide a solution. Its effort to consolidate the budget by exercising some fiscal restraint and to create positive real interest rates by tightening monetary policy had an immediate impact. Although the tight policy environment was relaxed slightly between 1990 and 1991, evident from the rate of inflation discussed below, the continuation of tight policies in 1992 saw domestic savings up to 10.5 per cent of GDP, compared to foreign savings which were down to 1.6 per cent of GDP.

A notable feature of this process is that the level of investment in Vietnam did not fall over the period 1989 to 1992. Instead it slowly crept from 11 per cent to 12 per cent of GDP (World Bank 1993), hence the strong response to domestic savings meant that Vietnam was able to maintain domestic investment despite cuts in foreign assistance. This aspect of Vietnam's investment, however, does not reflect the fact that total recorded investment is rather low for sustaining growth of 7-9 per cent annually. There is a need to further increase both savings and investment.[12] In China it is usually argued that much of this came in the early 1980s from farmers' savings out of buoyant real incomes.

On the public finance side, the fiscal measure of reducing bank finance of government expenditure has achieved several positive results. In effect, the budget deficit was reduced from 11.4 per cent in 1989 to 3.8 per cent in 1992 (World Bank 1993). However, most of this increase in government revenue comes from the revenue earned in oil exports and not from a broad base tax collection system. A fundamental negative consequence of Vietnam's effort to cut back spending and consolidate its budget is that public investment programs have been seriously curtailed. Infrastructure, especially rural roads, telecommunications, and irrigation, so necessary to Vietnam's economic growth process, is in vital need of development and poses a major developmental constraint if not addressed seriously (SPC and FAO 1993). However, in 1993 the fiscal deficit rose to around 8 per cent of GDP.[13]

The most significant achievement of the strict fiscal and monetary measures implemented in Vietnam has been the cessation of rampant inflation and the creation of a conducive environment for its emerging market economy. Inflation, which was as high as 393.8 per cent through most of the year, was dramatically reduced to 34.7 per cent by the end of 1989 as a consequence of the initial impact of the economic measures. Although there was a resurgence of inflation in 1990 (67.4 per cent) and 1991 (67.6 per cent), inflation was brought under control to 17.6 per cent by 1992 as policies were pushed through, and has been reined in to an impressive 5.2 per cent for 1993 (*Nien Giam Thong Ke — 1992*; AFP 20 October 1993).

Lastly, on the trade side, the notable achievements have been a limited diversification and rapid growth of exports (see Table 4.2). The growth rate of exports (current prices) in 1989 and 1990 was extremely high, at 87 per cent and 24 per cent respectively. This reflects the low base from which it was emerging, and increases in rice and crude oil sales. This rate slowed to 19 per cent by 1992 and in 1993 total dollar exports are thought to have increased by 14 per cent (AFP 20 October 1993). In contrast, import growth rates have been low, especially for the speed at which the Vietnamese economy has been developing. As a result, Vietnam's balance of trade deficit fell dramatically from US$1,718 million in 1989 to US$30 million in 1992; trade figures for the first nine months of 1993 suggest that after bottoming out in 1992 the trade balance deficit is on the rise, apparently due to a surge in imports of 30 per cent. Given the high levels of capital inflows, this is quite natural.[14]

It is undeniable that Vietnamese economic performance since 1989 has been far better than most economists would have predicted. Despite the clearly positive effects of "getting it right" in terms of macro-policy, the truth is almost certainly more complicated and the precise reasons for this success are not well understood and usefully subject to debate. "*Post hoc ergo propter hoc*" arguments tend to ignore the powerful accumulation processes that had emerged prior to 1989, as well as the important parameter and non-systemic changes that also took place around that time. The period 1989-93 was a time of rapid institutional transformation leading to greater economic efficiency. But it is worth pointing out, for example, that the rapid growth in rice output owed much to technical advances (and a substantial increase in the sown area in the Mekong as various infrastructure projects came on-stream), whilst exports have greatly benefited from crude oil.

Despite the uncertainties, it is clear that the transformation process is far from over and that it is important that the government continue to get the basic macroeconomy "right." Thus a continued commitment by

TABLE 4.2: Trade Balance (current US$ millions)

Item	1988	1989	1990	1991	1992	1993[a]	Average 1989-1992
Trade Balance	-1,718	-620	-348	-251	-31	-220	-313
Imports	2,757	2,566	2,752	2,338	2,506	2,200	2,541
Exports	1,038	1,946	2,404	2,087	2,475	1,980	2,228
Growth Rates:							
Imports	na	-0.07	0.07	-0.15	0.07	na	-0.02
Exports	na	0.87	0.24	-0.13	0.19	na	0.29
Exports by Sectors:							
Agriculture	587	1,017	1,149	1,089	na	na	na
Heavy industry[b]	67	355	617	697	na	na	na
Light industry and others	385	574	638	301	na	na	na
Share of Exports:							
Agriculture	0.56	0.52	0.48	0.52	na	na	na
Heavy industry	0.06	0.18	0.26	0.33	na	na	na
Light industry and others	0.37	0.30	0.27	0.14	na	na	na

a   For the first nine months of 1993.
b   Includes petroleum products.

Sources: Agence France Presse 20 October 1993; *Nien Giam Thong Ke — 1992*; *Nien Giam Thong Ke — 1990*.

the state is required if the trends are to be sustained. Low inflation needs to be maintained in order to preserve the incomes of wage earners and encourage the incentives of small businesses emerging all over Vietnam. This will not be easy given the underlying weakness of the Vietnamese economy and the very great demands placed upon state resources by the development effort (Ljunggren 1993). In the same vein, the government should also maintain a liberal trade policy. Economic openness and a realistic exchange rate can be expected to promote healthy competition, and also stimulate production for export with the potential for improving production and resource efficiency.

Agriculture in the Macroeconomy. Macroeconomic analysis says much about the relative success of agriculture in recent years. It shows rather powerful growth that is not, as yet, broadly based. Structural change is significant — the country is industrializing. However, the aggregate data hides important inter-regional and inter-personal differences.   It also tells us little directly about the underlying institutional reality. These are discussed in later sections.

By any developing country standard, the performance of the agricultural sector in Vietnam's economy has been strong, growing in real terms at an annual average rate of 6.5 per cent since 1989 (see Table 4.1). However, when compared to other productive sectors, agriculture's growth has generally lagged behind industry, services, and construction which grew respectively at 8.9 per cent, 7.5 per cent, and 7.3 per cent over the same period. Focusing on the trend in the share of GDP for different production sectors, we find that since 1989-90 agriculture's share has declined in real terms from 40.3 per cent to 38.2 per cent in 1992 (see Table 4.1).

In a recently published report by the SPC and FAO, prepared for the Donor Conference in early November 1993, it was estimated that agriculture's sectoral share should continue to decline slowly over the next ten years to a level equivalent to 35 per cent of GDP; and that agriculture's contribution to real GDP growth would not change significantly, declining from 32 per cent to 30 per cent over the period.[15] In general, it is inevitable in the development process of developing economies that the agricultural sector face the phenomenon of secular decline (Timmer 1988). However, the slow rate of decline in the case of Vietnam indicates the importance that agriculture must take in its development process. We shall return to this issue.

Turning to the growth patterns in gross agricultural output (see Table 4.3),[16] we find the general picture mixed; but we shall qualify this picture. Agriculture, especially crop output, grew significantly in 1988 (4.3 per cent) and 1989 (7.4 per cent). These strong growth patterns can be attributed to the "unleashing of productive efforts" brought about as a result of the changes to agricultural management and the responsibility system in agriculture implemented through Resolution 10 in 1988. In addition, the stimulatory effects of the economic reform program of 1989 and favorable climatic conditions in 1988 and 1989 have also contributed to this growth. Food crop production, notably rice, was quick to respond, growing by 11.3 per cent in 1988 compared to both cash crop and livestock outputs which fell. In 1989 food crop output maintained a high growth rate and both cash crop and livestock output recorded positive growth rates.

In contrast, agricultural output growth declined severely in 1990 (1.5 per cent) and 1991 (2.9 per cent). However, note that the gross agricultural output growth rate of 1.5 per cent for 1990 (Table 4.3) differs dramatically from the GDP growth rate of the agricultural sector of 11.2 per cent (Table 4.1).[17] Although the lower gross agricultural output growth rate in 1991 is admissible given the fact that agricultural production was marred by unfavorable weather conditions in the north and the Red River delta region and by pest problems in the Mekong delta region, the low growth rate for gross agricultural output in 1990 seems highly dubious. It is our suspicion that the gross output figures reported in the most recent General Statistical Office publication (*Nien Giam Thong Ke — 1992*) have not been revised for the year 1990.[18] Although the volume of food crops fell by 0.1 per cent in 1990, we suspect that food crops have been undervalued. It is our opinion that the overall pattern of growth for 1990 is better reflected by the agricultural component of GDP in Table 4.1 (11.2 per cent). In addition to the positive effects of the reform process, the fact that Vietnam maintained a reasonable level of fertilizer imports in 1990 makes the higher growth figure for 1990 more credible than the lower figure.[19] Continuing the analysis we find that crop output growth fell to 3.7 per cent in 1991 but then recovered in 1992 to 9.4 per cent. Livestock output followed a similar trend.

On the trade side of agriculture, the breakdown of exports by sectors indicates that the share of agricultural exports is on a slowly decreasing trend. Whilst in 1988 the share of agricultural exports was 56 per cent, by 1991 it had fallen to 52 per cent. The share of light industrial goods and handicrafts (much of which is sourced from the Vietnamese countryside) in exports shrunk rapidly, falling from 37 per cent in 1988 to 13 per cent in 1991. In contrast, the share of heavy industrial goods in exports for the same period rose rapidly from 6 per cent to 33 per cent. However, heavy industrial goods include crude oil production, which makes up a large component of this export category. The rapid increase in the volume of crude oil exports indicated in Table 4.4 explains why other export sectors are shrinking. In 1992, crude oil represented almost 30 per cent of the value of total exports and for the first six months of 1993 almost 32 per cent (see Table 4.4).

Despite the small decline in the share of agricultural exports in total exports, these represent a major proportion of export revenue in Vietnam. Within this category, rice dominates all other agricultural exports. Since the reform process in 1989, Vietnam has reversed its position from being a net importer of food to being the third largest net exporter of rice in the world. The volume of rice exports has been significant, and in line with the government's active policy of exporting over one million tonnes of rice each year. In 1992 rice exports accounted for almost 16 per cent of the value of total exports and for the first six months of 1993 almost 17 per cent. Rice not only generates an important export revenue with which to finance imports, but also a source of government revenue in terms of the export duty it generates for the state. This duty varies between 3 per cent to 10 per cent depending on the quality of the exported rice (SPC and FAO 1993).

TABLE 4.3: Gross Output Growth in Agriculture (at constant prices) (per cent)

Item	1988*	1989*	1990*	1991**	1992^a**
Total Agricultural Output	4.3	7.4	1.5	2.9	8.3
Crop output:	7.5	7.8	1.0	3.7	9.4
Food crops^b	11.3	9.9	-0.1	2.0	na
Cash crops^c	-0.3	3.1	3.8	7.2	na
Livestock^d	-4.4	6.3	3.2	0.7	5.0
Food crops^e	7.6	9.9	-0.1	2.3	9.1

* Calculated in constant 1982 prices.
** Calculated in constant 1989 prices.
a 1992 figures are estimates (General Statistics Office, Hanoi).
b Includes all grains and tuber crop converted to a paddy equivalent.
c Includes vegetables, beans, fruits, and industrial crops.
d Also includes sea and fresh water produces.
e Quantity of paddy equivalent production.

Source: Nien Giam Thong Ke — 1992.

In comparison to rice, the export value of other crop exports has been small. This relative failure is striking. Since 1989, the export of cash crops such as rubber, coffee, groundnuts, fruits, and vegetables has been increasing only slowly — with the exception of tea (see Table 4.5). The loss of markets in eastern Europe and the former Soviet Union (through the Council of Mutual Economic Assistance) is one reason for the slow growth; however, other factors such as heavy state monopolization of the cash crop sector (barriers to entry); poor quality of produce; low investment in production, lack of value-added processing; poor and ineffective marketing and distribution; and low international prices are equally important. In addition to the significance of crude oil and rice exports, the third most important export item is seafood products which has grown significantly over the period, accounting for 12 per cent of total export revenue in the first six months of 1993.

In sum, it is evident that agriculture as a whole has benefited greatly from the economic reforms implemented in 1988-89. Agricultural production, notably in the food crop sector, has expanded well beyond the national population growth rate of 2.3 per cent, implying that Vietnam has achieved and maintained self-sufficiency in

TABLE 4.4: Export Commodities (current US$ millions)

Commodity	1992	% of Exports	1993[a]	% of Exports
Total Exports	2,455.0	100.0	100.0	100.0
Oil	725.6	29.6	381.5	31.3
Rice	390.3	15.9	207.2	17.0
Frozen seafood	303.0	12.3	150.5	12.3
Coffee	85.2	3.5	43.3	3.6
Rubber	57.3	2.3	24.0	2.0
Groundnuts	33.5	1.4	20.3	1.7
Fruits and vegetables	27.0	1.1	7.6	0.6
Tea	13.7	0.6	4.3	0.4

a   First six months of 1993.

Source: Aduki Pty Ltd.

TABLE 4.5: Exports of High Value Primary Produce (thousand tonnes)

Commodity	1988	1989	1990	1991	1992
Oil	na	1,514.3	2,616.7	3,917.0	5,400.0
Rice	91.2	1,420.4	1,624.4	1,032.9	1,950.0
Rubber	38.0	57.7	75.9	62.9	75.0
Groundnuts	na	38.5	70.7	78.9	70.5
Tea	14.8	15.0	16.1	8.0	12.5
Coffee	33.8	57.4	89.6	93.5	98.0
Frozen seafood	31.2	47.9	45.7	58.3	78.5*

Sources: Nien Giam Thong Ke — 1992; Nien Giam Thong Ke — 1990; * Aduki Pty Ltd.

food production since 1989. Furthermore, the strong performance in food crop production has meant that large marketable surpluses have been mobilized for the international market, making Vietnam the third-largest rice exporter in the world. Given the relative size of agriculture in the national economy, and the importance in Vietnam's food policy for generating sufficient, if not surplus, food balances, the positive response to economic reforms in the agricultural sector points to the overall success of the past few years. That a large number of people, previously hungry for many months a year, now eat rice, is an achievement of historical significance. However, the rising inter-regional differences and the rapidly emerging pattern of social differentiation requires further discussion. What are the social costs of this success, and how sustainable is it likely to be?

Trends in Agriculture

Food Availability and Income Generation

The creation of a national rice market in 1987-89 has provided an important opportunity for farmers in the areas where the comparative advantage is not in wet-rice production. With increased market access (helped by the opening of the Chinese border in 1989), the ready supplies of cheap Mekong rice in markets has eased farmers' worries about subsistence supplies and costs, and encouraged diversification. However, this is not the end of the story.

Despite Vietnam's self-sufficient position in food production and its ability to export vast quantities of rice, food consumption remains critically low in many parts of the country. An indication of this fact is provided by comparing staples production per capita with a basic food consumption level across different regions of Vietnam. Meeting consumption needs is an important task in alleviating rural poverty. This can be achieved not only from improving food crop production in food deficit regions, but also from developing other production activities. In the presence of low and inadequate food production, incomes sourced from other activities enable rural households to make up shortfalls in their own food production by purchasing food. The level of income, therefore, determines the ability of the rural household to feed itself.

In addition, the capacity of the household to earn an income outside the food sector will depend on the extent of rural development which includes the level of agricultural, market, and rural infrastructural development. These issues are taken up in the following sections.

If we accept 260 kilograms of paddy as the minimum consumption standard per person per year (roughly providing some 2,300 kcal per capita per day),[20] then comparing this with the per capita staples production across Vietnam (see Table 4.6), it is clear that food production is well below the food consumption requirement in many regions. Amongst the regions most affected by food production shortages are the Northeast southern, Northern mountain and Midlands, Central highlands, and North central coast regions. The area with the lowest per capita staples production is the northeast southern region, which includes Ho Chi Minh City. Food crop production there has fallen significantly since 1988, and by 1991 declined to half of the yearly subsistence requirement (see Table 4.6). This fall reflects a fast shift out of staples cultivation and into higher valued crops in a region facing excellent markets, and lying close to the most rapid processes of urbanization and industrialization in the country. By contrast isolated areas such as the northern mountains, evident in Map 4.1, but also the midlands and the central highlands regions, have experienced a general decline in per capita staples production. Within the north central coastal region per capita staples production stagnated over the period 1988 to 1991. In the latter regions, food production generally remains 10-15 per cent below subsistence needs. Capacity for development of cash crops in these areas is limited by distance from markets. Furthermore, it appears that the level of non-rice food crop production per capita has not varied much when compared to the level of paddy production per capita. However, annual changes in production for both paddy and non-rice food crop indicate that the latter is more variable and on a declining trend (see Table 4.7). This implies that non-rice food crops have diminished as an alternative source of food consumption for these food deficient areas. This points to rising real incomes.

Agronomically, the northeast southern region is better suited to the cultivation of tree crops, particularly rubber, coffee, and pepper. In 1991, this region accounted for almost 79 per cent of the national rubber production, 40 per cent of the coffee production, and 63 per cent of the pepper production (SLTKNN 1992). Other important cash crops are sugar cane and tobacco. In addition to the income that cashcrops generate, the proximity of the region to the markets of Ho Chi Minh City presents the opportunity for rural households to derive an income through activities outside the food crop sector. In the other food deficit regions, cash crops production also contributes to household incomes, especially in the highland regions where tea, cotton, and coffee are important, in addition to forestry products. In the north central coast region, on the other hand, fishery and livestock production are important sources of alternative incomes.[21] In contrast to the northeast southern region, other food deficit regions are generally located further from important central markets such as Hanoi in the north and Ho Chi Minh City in the south. Given that the proximity to markets and a strong cash crop sector in trees presents households in the northeast southern region with opportunities to earn an income outside of food crop farming suggests that food consumption in that area may not be deficient.

In other regions of Vietnam per capita incomes diversification has advanced so that food crop production does not so greatly constrain

TABLE 4.6: Food Crop Production per Capita by Region

(i) Food crop production per capita by region (kilograms per person)

Region	1988	1989	1990	1991	1992
Mekong delta	535.3	631.9	658.2	703.1	
North and Midlands	247.5	268.9	230.0	200.0	231.9[a]
Red River delta	287.7	314.4	294.5	256.5	
North central coast	219.3	225.7	226.0	222.1	
South central coast	268.8	281.5	274.0	289.8	528.2[b]
Central highlands	237.6	238.1	223.7	225.7	
NE southern region	143.5	134.1	160.5	129.0	
Entire Vietnam	307.3	332.2	324.4	324.9	349.4

(ii) Paddy production per capita by region (kilograms per person)

Region	1988	1989	1990	1991	1992
Mekong delta	525.7	622.0	649.5	695.5	
North and Midlands	176.7	194.6	166.6	133.8	188.5[a]
Red River delta	248.9	274.4	259.8	225.5	
North central coast	171.5	181.4	185.8	180.6	
South central coast	227.2	239.9	234.8	250.0	498.8[b]
Central highlands	148.0	158.0	148.6	160.5	
NE southern region	105.3	106.2	129.9	101.6	
Entire Vietnam	266.8	293.3	290.2	289.9	311.5

(iii) Non-rice food crop production per capita by region (kilograms per person)

Region	1988	1989	1990	1991	1992
Mekong delta	9.6	9.9	8.7	7.6	
North and Midlands	70.8	74.3	63.4	66.2	43.4[a]
Red River delta	38.8	40.0	34.7	31.0	
North central coast	47.8	44.3	40.2	41.5	
South central coast	41.6	41.6	39.2	39.8	29.4[b]
Central highlands	89.6	80.1	75.1	65.2	
NE southern region	38.2	27.9	30.6	27.4	
Entire Vietnam	40.5	38.9	34.2	35.0	37.9

a North Viet Nam all provinces north of, and including, Thua Thien Hue province.
b South Viet Nam all provinces south of Thua Thien Hue province.

Sources: Nien Giam Thong Ke — 1989, 1990, 1992.

112

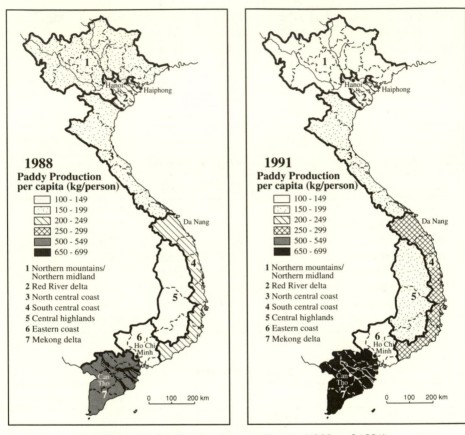

MAP 4.1: Paddy Production per Capita (1988 and 1991)

TABLE 4.7: Annual Growth in Food Crop Production by Region

(i)   Annual growth in food crop production by region (per cent)

Region	1988	1989	1990	1991	1992	Average 1989-1992
Mekong delta	17.8	16.5	6.5	8.9		
North and Midlands	7.7	10.0	-13.6	0.8	23.8[a]	
Red River delta	16.3	7.4	-4.4	-15.7		
North central coast	0.6	2.2	2.7	0.6		
South central coast	0.1	3.5	-0.4	8.1	2.5[b]	
Central highlands	7.1	6.1	-2.6	4.5		
NE southern region	6.3	-2.9	-7.6	8.3		
Entire Vietnam	11.5	9.9	-0.1	2.3	10.0	5.5

(ii)   Annual growth in paddy production by region (per cent)

Region	1988	1989	1990	1991	1992	Average 1989-1992
Mekong delta	17.9	16.8	6.7	9.2		
North and Midlands	7.0	11.5	-13.4	-6.9	26.0[a]	
Red River delta	16.9	8.4	-3.4	-16.0		
North central coast	1.2	5.1	5.1	-0.4		
South central coast	2.6	4.3	0.1	8.8	2.6[b]	
Central highlands	6.2	13.0	-2.5	11.8		
NE southern region	6.3	4.8	-5.6	5.5		
Entire Vietnam	12.6	11.7	1.2	2.1	10.0	6.3

(iii)   Annual growth in non-rice food crop production by region (per cent)

Region	1988	1989	1990	1991	1992	Average 1989-1992
Mekong delta	8.3	1.7	-9.8	-11.3		
North and Midlands	9.5	6.2	-13.8	21.0	15.2[a]	
Red River delta	12.7	1.3	-11.6	-13.3		
North central coast	-1.5	-7.8	-6.9	5.5		
South central coast	-11.7	-1.2	-3.5	3.6	2.2[b]	
Central highlands	8.5	-5.4	-2.8	-10.2		
NE southern region	6.3	-24.1	-15.3	20.3		
Entire Vietnam	5.0	-2.5	-10.2	4.6	10.8	0.7

a North Viet Nam all provinces north of, and including, Thua Thien Hue province.
b South Viet Nam all provinces south of Thua Thien Hue province.

Sources: *Nien Giam Thong Ke — 1989, 1990, 1992.*

food consumption. In the Red River delta and south central coast regions, per capita food production has generally been adequate and these regions have sometimes managed to produce modest surpluses. In the Red River delta, however, both paddy and non-rice production were affected in 1990 and 1991 (see Table 4.7), primarily by bad weather, which diminished the region's marketable surplus production. The Mekong delta is the only region in Vietnam that maintained a significant and positive rate of annual growth in paddy production between 1988 and 1991. Although the level of growth settled to around 9 per cent in 1991 from its initial surge of about 17 per cent in 1988-89, this level is outstanding and reflects the capacity with which the Mekong delta has been able to respond to new economic conditions (see Table 4.7). On average, the per capita food crop production in the Mekong delta exceeds the basic subsistence standard of 260 kilograms per person by almost 2.7 times. There is no doubt that Vietnam's large rice exports originate from the huge marketable surpluses of this region. It is worth noting, however, that the Mekong is vulnerable to adverse shifts in the rice price, for a distinguishing feature of the delta is that non-rice food crop production per capita is marginal in comparison to the rest of the country. The sharp decline in the level of non-rice food crop production (see Table 4.7) indicates the Mekong delta's growing specialization in rice production.

Although a regional breakdown of food crop production is not yet available for 1992 at the time of writing, some information is available on the levels of food crop production by north/south distinction.[22] The national food crop production per capita for 1992 is above the previous two years (see Tables 4.6 and 4.8). Both rice and non-rice food crop production rose dramatically between 1991 and 1992, respectively 10 per cent and 10.8 per cent, at the national level. With a sharp increase in food crop production of 10.1 per cent, it is expected that the per capita food consumption for food deficit areas should improve over 1992. This is especially true for north Vietnam where production levels increased dramatically. Paddy and non-rice food crop production were up 26 per cent and 15 per cent respectively over 1991, thereby yielding an impressive 24 per cent increase in food crop production for north Vietnam. Food crop production in south Vietnam, by comparison, grew marginally at 3 per cent, paddy at 3 per cent and non-rice food crops at 2 per cent. Furthermore, provisional food crop production estimates for 1993, indicate that the trend is likely to be positive but not as strong as the previous year. The national level food crop production is expected to rise by only 1.2 per cent. The apparent reduction in the annual food crop production growth rate stems from the expectation that production will fall by 2 per cent in the south. However, the north

TABLE 4.8: Food Crop Production by Region

(i)   Food crop production by region (in '000 tonnes paddy equivalent)

Region	1987	1988	1989	1990	1991	1992	1993
Mekong delta	6,576	7,743	9,024	9,608	10,464		
North and Midlands	2,296	2,474	2,720	2,350	2,367	9,702[a]	10,250[a]
Red River delta	3,433	3,994	4,289	4,101	3,457		
North central coast	1,891	1,902	1,945	1,998	2,011		
South central coast	1,819	1,821	1,884	1,876	2,027	14,513[b]	14,250[b]
Central highlands	525	563	597	581	607		
NE southern region	1,023	1,087	1,056	976	1,057		
Entire Vietnam	17,563	19,583	21,516	21,489	21,990	24,215	24,500

(ii)   Paddy production by region (in '000 tonnes)

Region	1987	1988	1989	1990	1991	1992	1993
Mekong delta	6,447	7,604	8,883	9,480	10,351		
North and Midlands	1,650	1,766	1,969	1,702	1,584	7,885[a]	8,450[a]
Red River delta	2,955	3,455	3,744	3,618	3,038		
North central coast	1,470	1,488	1,563	1,642	1,635		
South central coast	1,500	1,539	1,606	1,607	1,749	13,705[b]	13,450[b]
Central highlands	330	350	396	386	432		
NE southern region	750	797	836	789	833		
Entire Vietnam	15,103	17,000	18,996	19,225	19,622	21,590	21,900

(iii) Non-rice food crop production by region (in '000 tonnes paddy equivalent)

Region	1987	1988	1989	1990	1991	1992	1993
Mekong delta	128	139	141	128	113		
North and Midlands	646	708	752	648	783	1,816[a]	1,800[a]
Red River delta	478	539	546	483	418		
North central coast	421	414	382	356	375		
South central coast	319	282	278	269	278	808[b]	800[b]
Central highlands	196	212	201	195	175		
NE southern region	273	290	220	186	224		
Entire Vietnam	2,460	2,583	2,519	2,263	2,368	2,624	2,600

a North Vietnam all provinces north of, and including, Thua Thien Hue province.
b South Vietnam all provinces south of Thua Thien Hue province.

Sources: Nien Giam Thong Ke — 1989, 1990, 1992.

should maintain its positive growth rate but at the more modest rate of 5.6 per cent. These figures indicate that south Vietnam is losing the momentum it had in food crops in the period 1989 to 1991.

The strongest response to the new economic system has been primarily in the Mekong delta. However, the push for diversification strategies in other regions suggests that family farms there may be about to show surprisingly rapid increases in production based upon almost opportunistic responses to market developments, for instance in China (see Dang Phong's chapter this book).

Besides the low level of production in the food deficit regions, another common feature is the low level of incomes available to purchase food. Incomes of the poor in these regions differ greatly. For example, the National Farm Household survey conducted by the GSO in 1989-1990 reports that the average monthly income per person in Hau Giang province in the Mekong delta region was almost 50 per cent greater than that of the average person in Hoang Lien Son province in the northern mountains region or almost 30 per cent greater than those in Binh Dinh province on the south central coast (SLTKNN 1991; Nguyen Van Tiem 1993).

Preliminary estimates from Vietnam's Living Standards Measurement Survey (LSMS), reported in World Bank (1993), give another indication of income differences between various regions of Vietnam. Amongst the poorest regions are the northern mountains and midlands, the central highlands and the north central coast regions which have a per capita GDP of under 350,000 dong (US$75) in 1989 prices. Following this are the Red River delta and south central coast regions which have per capita GDP of 350,000-450,000 dong (US$75-96), and finally the Mekong delta and the northeast southern region, including Hanoi and Hai Phong in the north, which have a per capita GDP between 450,000 and 1,278,000 dong (US$100-275). These figures largely correlate with the level of per capita food crop production reported earlier, with the exception of the northeast southern region which is amongst the richest regions in Vietnam for the reasons also cited earlier. These figures clearly indicate the vast gaps between regions, but also indicate the severity of income constraints suffered by the rural population living in remote parts of the country.

At the national level, Table 4.9 indicates that the gap between the richest and poorest group widened between 1989-1990 and 1990-1991. Although, the information provided in Nguyen Van Tiem (1993) suggests that this income gap decreased to 7.7 in 1992, this figure should be treated cautiously given Tiem's income classification which does not correlate with the GSO classifications. Whichever direction the income distribution gap is trending in Vietnam, one factor is evident;

the income gap is very large between different rural regions.[23] Therefore, in the absence of productivity increases in food deficit regions, the lack of income seriously constrains the ability of households to feed themselves.

Indeed, low rural incomes seriously constrain the demand for food, and it is likely that in the food deficit regions of Vietnam that the demand for staple foods faces a high income elasticity. Therefore, households are likely to increase their demand for rice consumption with an improvement in rural income in these regions. This position differs significantly with the food surplus regions, especially the Mekong delta where cereal and vegetable consumption is already high (Tu Giay 1991). According to the World Bank (1993), additional growth in rice production will come from areas other than the Mekong delta where productivity and modern input use are presently quite high by international standards. With this view, Vietnam's ability to continue high levels of rice exports will be affected in the near future when increased rural incomes imply increased rice demands domestically. Of course, this outcome will depend on augmenting rural incomes.

In the event of rapid increases in rural incomes, another possibility is that the level of consumption of high value food items such as meat, poultry, and seafood products will rise as incomes rise, especially in the Mekong delta region and in other regions with improved food crop production per capita (SPC and FAO 1993). Increases in meat demand bears considerable importance to the use of food crops in Vietnam. Other than direct human consumption, non-rice food crops in most parts of the country are used primarily as animal feed. In view of the general declining trend in non-rice food crop production in Vietnam, a continued decline will lead meat producers to use rice as an alternative feed. According to World Bank (1993) estimates, the present use of paddy as animal feed is between 5-15 per cent of total paddy

TABLE 4.9: National Average Income Distribution Indicators for 1989-1990 and 1990-1991 (in current value)

| | Net Income per Person per Month (dong) | | |
	Rich	Poor	Ratio
1990	39,930	5,467	7.3
1991	56,461	5,368	10.5

Sources: So Lieu Thong Ke Nong Nghiep 35 Nam (1956-1990) 1991; Nguyen Van Tiem 1993.

production. On a rough estimate, this represents an amount of feed equivalent to 36-108 per cent of Vietnam's rice export in 1992 (1.95 million tonnes). Although this is a broad range, there is no dispute that this is a large volume of paddy being fed to animals when many parts of the country are suffering food shortages. Therefore, based on present conditions, paddy as an animal feed could become sensitive to farm supplies (own price effect), the prices of livestock products (complementary price effect), and competing feeds (substitution price effect).

Markets — Some Observations. As a consequence of Vietnam's stabilization efforts, rice prices in major markets of the country (Hanoi and Saigon) during 1989 and early 1990 were fairly stable, varying within a band of 600-800 dong per kilogram (see Figure 4.1). However, rice prices rose rapidly from mid 1990 to the end of 1991 because of a small resurgence in inflation in 1990 and 1991. Between 1992 and early 1993, rice prices generally fell across the country, in line with the fall in inflation to 17.6 per cent for 1992, as a result of renewed measures by the state to stabilize the macroeconomy. However, since early to mid 1993 prices in major markets have been on the rise and are currently around 2,200 dong per kilogram. Given that inflation in Vietnam decreased to 5.2 per cent in 1993, implying that the general level of prices is rising around 0.43 per cent per month, rice prices are rising faster than other goods. In fact relative to rice prices, agricultural input prices, such as urea, have been falling (see Figure 4.3). As sufficient quantities of rice are available domestically, after rice is exported, rising rice prices indicate that rice demand is increasing, but if rural poverty is significant and particularly severe in many parts of Vietnam, there is little indication that the poor are in a position to increase their demand of rice for consumption. Most probable is the use of rice as animal feed and in production of foodstuffs and alcohol, in the more prosperous regions.

The quality of markets around the country is a key issue. The ability of farmers to produce profitably depends greatly upon their access to good markets. This covers a number of areas:

1.   The degree of monopsony ("gouge") in product markets: do farmers have to sell to buyers who can use their market power or some other mechanism to keep prices lower than they would be under competitive conditions?
2.   The extent to which the transport and distributional systems are competitive, offering good services to farmers who want to get their produce to the final purchaser.

3. The extent to which sectors adding value (such as crop processing) possess competitive structures, with low barriers to entry and exit.
4. The nature of and access to overseas markets. Is the export business competitive, with entry easy for newcomers, so that farmers' costs in gaining access to world markets are kept low and profitable markets found that permit exploitation of Vietnam's comparative advantages?

These are complicated issues, and they are not easy to research. There is considerable anecdotal evidence that, whilst immediate product markets are rather competitive, many others are not. This tends to reduce the productive efficiency of the sector as a whole. For example, according to the authors of the SPC and FAO (1993:41) report, Mellor and Qureshi:

> ...Vietnam has a marketing margin of about 30-40 per cent in rice trade when the similar margin in Thailand is only 10 per cent.... The pervasive monopolies in processing and distribution of output and inputs should be important reasons for high marketing margins. The state enterprises' contribution to government revenues is huge (and) an important consideration for the government in its decision not to dismantle the state-owned enterprises in agricultural trade. The adverse effects on efficiency and suppression of farmers' incentives should nevertheless convince policy makers to review the adverse current situation urgently.

Although free markets coexisted with Vietnam's central planning system prior to reforms, their role in resource allocation was not only discouraged but also limited as the state attempted to gain control of certain markets, especially food crops. Since 1989 market forces have determined the prices of commodities; the question is, however, whether entry barriers and other distortions have allowed prices to accurately reflect relative scarcities. Based on these prices, producers make decisions concerning the level of consumption of various commodities. However, the efficiency with which markets signal prices varies significantly between regions and major centers, and with respect to their level of development. It is striking how in Vietnam the level of regional development generally reflects the ease of access to markets, both domestically and internationally.

The different characteristics of markets for different commodities in the same region also affects the ability of agricultural producers to allocate resources efficiently. One of the present authors argues that in

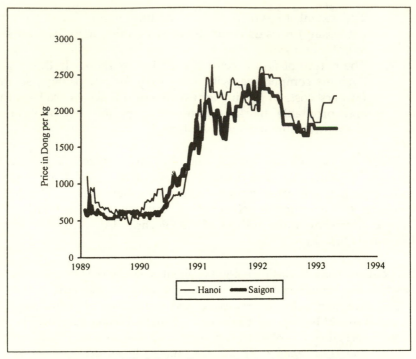

FIGURE 4.1: Milled Grain Prices in Major Markets of Vietnam

Source: Aduki Pty Ltd.

the case of farm households in the Red River delta, where rice markets are well established and more competitive than markets in cash crops (such as garlic and onion) and non-rice food crops, households are more efficient in allocating resources when producing rice as opposed to other crops (Sénèque 1993). Although this should be qualified by noting that households have more (technical) experience in cultivating rice than a cash crop such as garlic on a large scale,[24] better knowledge of cultivation methods implies that resources are used more efficiently.[25]

Figure 4.2 presents the ratio of rice and urea prices between Hanoi and Saigon. The variability in the price ratio between the two markets is greater for rice than urea; however, rice prices appear to be higher in the north. In general, higher prices in the north reflect the level of rice production in the region, as well as the cost of transportation for supplying northern markets from food surplus regions. Seasonality between the south and the north affects the price ratios. In particular, this is noticeable for rice in the first half of the year for 1989 and 1990.

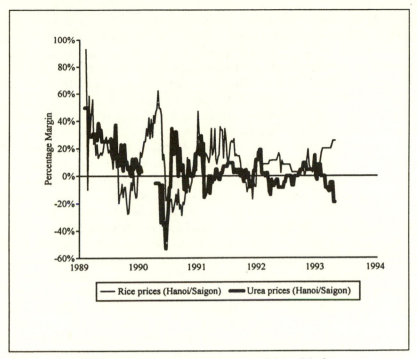

FIGURE 4.2: Price Ratios Between Major Markets

Source: Aduki Pty Ltd.

At this time of the year rice is abundant in the south relative to the north. This position reverses towards the end of the year when rice becomes scarce in the south relative to the north. However, because of the improvement in the distribution system through the introduction of the market system and the strong performance in agriculture since the implementation of reforms, the fluctuation in the price ratios for rice and urea between the Hanoi and Saigon markets diminished consistently over 1991, 1992, and 1993, suggesting improvement in the efficiency of the national market.

Figure 4.3 shows the variation in the ratio of urea to rice for each market. The amount of rice required to buy one kilogram of urea is an important indicator of the terms of trade facing rice farmers. North and south have followed similar paths. As urea is predominantly imported, this trend suggests that both markets have a similar degree of international access. The cut off of Soviet assistance in 1990, which up to then was Vietnam's primary supplier of chemical fertilizers, appears clearly in Figure 4.3 when the scarcity of urea relative to rice increased sharply. However, Vietnam's quick response to deal with the sudden shortage of fertilizer is indicated in Figure 4.3 by the equally sudden fall in the relative scarcity of urea to rice, as well as by the fact that paddy production, which uses most of Vietnam's chemical fertilizers, increased by 1.2 per cent in 1990 (see Table 4.7). Between 1991 and 1993, the ratio between urea and rice prices remained moderate, fluctuating in a band from 0.75 to 1.25. However, since the beginning of 1993 the relative scarcity of urea to rice has declined to a ratio around 0.70. Similarly, estimates of the urea to paddy ratio calculated at border prices and adjusted for marketing costs, indicate a declining trend: the ratio fell from 2.24 to 1.43 between 1989 and 1992 (SPC and FAO 1993:40-41).

If the urea to rice price ratio gives an indication of the rural-urban terms of trade, then the trend appears to indicate that the terms of trade have improved for agricultural producers across Vietnam. This is evident when considering that the urea-rice exchange ratio set by the state in the mid 1980s was typically 2:1. This improvement in the terms of trade would suggest an increase in the amount of fertilizer used by farmers. In contrast, the SPC and FAO report suggests that a declining ratio implies that farmers' incentives for efficient fertilizer use have weakened over time. However, the report qualifies this remark by giving emphasis to infrastructural availability, credit constraints, and technological opportunities amongst other factors determining farmers' fertilizer use.

Despite their limited and sometimes distorted development in many regions and for certain commodities, however, markets have clearly opened new opportunities for farmers and others in the countryside. In an effort to verify national level statistics on agricultural production and dispel the belief held by some western observers that agriculture has been slow to grow in Vietnam's recent economic success, Dang Phong's chapter provides numerous examples where farm households have left rice farming and turned to other production activities in the wake of new market opportunities. He is certainly correct in his assertion that agriculture has grown anything but slowly since the reform process began in 1988-1989, at least at the national level. His many examples of rural households, both in food deficit and food surplus regions, striking it rich illustrates the common feature that markets are important in the livelihood of those turning to other production activities as alternative sources of income for purchasing food. However, at the regional level varying conditions and opportunities have meant that those benefiting from the new set of conditions, namely the introduction of the market and the transformation process itself, are those regions that were to begin with and/or have become better integrated into the market.

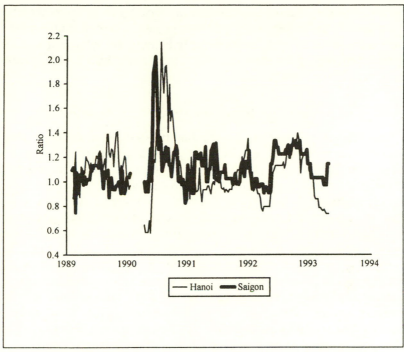

FIGURE 4.3: Ratio of Urea to Milled Rice Prices in Major Markets

Source: Aduki Pty Ltd.

What implications can we draw from these general trends for food production and the general welfare of nearly 80 per cent of Vietnam's population living in the countryside? If food crop production, especially rice production slows down in the Mekong region, then rice exports will not only fall from their present level but domestic supplies will also be affected, unless rural conditions are improved. As rapidly rising incomes in urban centers and prosperous rural regions placed increased demand on high value consumption goods, especially meat products, a deterioration in non-rice staples production would further exacerbate a slowdown in rice production, as rice was used as an alternative animal feed. Such an effect would drive domestic rice prices upwards. The implications for food deficit regions, especially poor and remote regions, are grave if household incomes remain low. But because food demand in Vietnam is hindered by low incomes, given the current physical and market conditions facing Vietnam's countryside, especially the food deficit regions, new opportunities to raise rural incomes will not come from cultivating food crops alone. Rural households will need to diversify production in order to augment their incomes which, in turn, allows them to increase food demand, that further stimulates food production. This, in turn, is viable only if there are good markets. The role of the market in improving rural incomes will be a crucial factor in alleviating rural poverty.

Removing Constraints on Agricultural Development

Underdeveloped agriculture is inherently linked to rural poverty in Vietnam. As mentioned earlier, many parts of Vietnam suffer from both food and income shortages. For these regions, simultaneous access to food purchases and sale of goods and services for income will be dependent upon market access. Similarly, markets allow rural households to access information and resources vital in augmenting production. Underdeveloped rural markets, however, hinder the ability of rural households to gain access to goods and services that allow them to develop agriculture and to break from their impoverished low-income position. Poor market access is a consequence of poor physical infrastructure and rural linkages. It is also an outcome of local monopoly and entry barriers imposed by weak institutional development (see the remarks by Mellor and Qureshi on p.119 above). These factors constraining agricultural development are now explored.

Infrastructure. It is well recognized that weak and inadequate infrastructure is a major impediment to agricultural development, market development, and poverty alleviation (SPC and FAO 1993; World Bank 1993; SRV and UNDP 1993). The SPC and FAO report (1993:44-46) recommends that rural roads, including associated investment in rural electricification and telecommunications, be ranked before research, irrigation, and the availability of credit as a major project facilitating agricultural growth. The World Bank (1993:143, 204), sees irrigation as a major priority, over rural services and credit in facilitating agricultural development, but also recognizes the importance of rural transportation links in alleviating poverty, amongst other factors such as: credit, education, social services, and support for informal farmer "self-help" groups. Although the actual priority attached to various types of infrastructure differs slightly between reports, there is no doubt that rehabilitation and development is urgently required in both central and rural transportation, electricification, telecommunications, and irrigation.

State investment in Vietnam is funded from different budgetary levels: central and local (most importantly the provinces). The evidence provided in Table 4.10, indicates that total state investment in the economy fell only marginally between 1988 and 1989, increased substantially during 1990 and 1991 at around 11 per cent, and fell dramatically by 19 per cent in 1992. This trend largely coincides with the fiscal measures adopted in 1989 and 1992 to cut subsidies to the state sector. The share of the transportation and communication sectors consistently increased from 13 per cent in 1989 to 21 per cent in 1991 and, by comparison, the share of industry fluctuated around 40 per cent. It is evident, however, that the obvious loser over the period is the agricultural (and forestry) sector, which experienced a fall in its share of total state investment in real terms.

Although state investment in the transportation and communication sectors is not available by regions, information presented on total local level state investment in Table 4.11 indicates that at the local level, state investment was generally more volatile for the poorer areas where it suffered sharp falls in investment. This is particularly noticeable for the north central coast area which in 1991 experienced a fall of 15 per cent in local state investment.

Regarding agricultural infrastructure, investment in irrigation has been rather mixed. Total state investment between 1988 and 1989 grew by 0.2 per cent and during 1990 by 33 per cent. During 1991 it fell by 10 per cent (*Nien Giam Thong Ke — 1992; 1990; 1989*). The outcome for 1992 is likely to be in line with the sharp fall in state investment at both central and local levels.

It is evident that a consequence of the economic policy measures undertaken since 1989 has been an unstable investment program in physical infrastructure: either sharp rises or sharp falls at both the central and regional levels. While the state has increased investment in infrastructure over the period, this has been from a low base.[26] The relatively large share of state investment going to industry, presumably to finance many loss-making state owned enterprises, reflects the position the state adopts in relations to developing much needed infrastructure in the countryside.[27]

The de-centralization process, on the other hand, has pushed the burden of financing infrastructure maintenance and development from the center to the provincial and even the district levels. The extent to which provincial governments have been able to manage this transformation generally depends on the province's wealth as well as on what the province decides to do with whatever resources it has. Here the position taken towards local state businesses can be very important, with significant implications for the nature of local markets. As most parts of rural Vietnam comprise poor provinces, investment in developing rural infrastructure has suffered. This factor poses a serious problem to the development of agriculture and the general welfare of isolated rural communities because markets remain uncompetitive due

TABLE 4.10: State Investment

(i) Fixed investment by sectors (billion dong — 1982 prices)

Sector	1988	1989	1990	1991	1992
Gross fixed investment	16.8	17.5	19.6	21.8	17.6
Industry	7.8	8.7	7.4	9.4	
Agriculture and forestry	3.8	2.7	3.4	3.4	
Transportation and communications	2.3	2.8	3.9	4.5	
Construction and others	2.9	3.3	4.9	4.5	

(ii) Sectoral share (per cent)

Sector	1988	1989	1990	1991	1992
Gross fixed investment	100	100	100	100	100
Industry	0.46	0.49	0.38	0.43	
Agriculture	0.23	0.16	0.17	0.16	
Transportation and communications	0.13	0.16	0.20	0.21	
Construction and others	0.17	0.19	0.25	0.21	

(iii) Annual growth (per cent)

Sector	1988	1989	1990	1991	1992
Gross fixed investment	4.9	4.4	11.8	11.1	-19.1
Industry	11.7	11.3	-14.3	26.7	
Agriculture	19.0	-28.5	22.6	1.6	
Transportation and communications	22.7	23.7	39.9	14.1	
Construction and others	-26.9	13.9	47.0	-8.6	

Sources: *Nien Giam Thong Ke — 1992; Nien Giam Thong Ke — 1990.*

TABLE 4.11: Local State Investment by Region (in constant value)

(i) Local level state investment by region (billion dong — 1982 prices)

Region	1988	1989	1990	1991	1992
Country	6.00	5.22	7.32	8.69	5.7
Regions:					
North and Midlands	0.72	0.83	0.96	1.39	na
Red River delta	1.29	1.18	1.55	1.82	na
North central coast	0.85	0.59	1.41	1.20	na
South central coast	0.62	0.55	0.72	0.89	na
Central highlands	0.25	0.32	0.33	0.42	na
NE southern region	1.05	0.86	0.97	1.39	na
Mekong delta	1.22	0.89	1.37	1.57	na

(ii) Annual growth rate of local level state investment by region (billion dong — 1982 prices)

Region	1989	1990	1991	1992
Country	-13.0	40.2	18.7	-34.6
Regions:				
North and Midlands	14.9	15.9	45.5	na
Red River delta	-8.4	31.3	17.4	na
North central coast	-31.1	140.7	-14.9	na
South central coast	-10.9	31.1	23.1	na
Central highlands	28.7	4.5	25.4	na
NE southern region	-18.2	13.2	43.1	na
Mekong delta	-26.9	52.7	15.0	na

Sources: Nien Giam Thong Ke — 1992; Nien Giam Thong Ke — 1990.

to lack of information; agricultural implements remain primitive; and monetary incentives remain weak because certain consumer goods require electricity (eg., pumps, threshers, radios, fans, televisions, etc.) when electricity is either inadequate or unavailable. Teachers, as well as health workers, from urban areas have no incentive to work in such communities.

A program of infrastructural investment, therefore, has the potential to access many remote regions of Vietnam, develop markets, and facilitate agricultural development. But equally as important, a major public rural roads project such as that proposed by the SPC and FAO report (1993:46-59) with an estimated expenditure of US$250 million per year over a projected period of ten years, would bring with it certain positive elements for mitigating poverty in many rural regions, at least in the short term, while providing a long term rural growth solution. The SPC and FAO rural road building proposal claims it could reach up to as many as 1.0-1.5 million or 10 per cent of rural families.

Rural Development Institutions

Under normal conditions, successful modern developing countries tend to put in place a variety of rural activities designed to stimulate the rural economy. Land reform has been an important element of successful and rapid development in East Asia.[28] Other elements of a normal rural development policy include: extension, credit, and support for farmers' organizations. Here we will deal with the last two, but will note in passing that Vietnam still lacks an effective extension system, and in those areas that still have cooperatives what does exist is still focused upon cooperatives rather than farmers.

Credit. The acquisition of modern inputs and technology that increases agricultural productivity is dependent on credit access. Rural credit is important in expanding the food crop, cash crop, and livestock sectors in agriculture. However, rural credit should provide for the financial needs of many other activities surrounding agriculture — for example, the many small businesses that provide inputs and consumer goods to farmers and market farmers' output, including small businesses such as those processing agricultural produce into foodstuffs, producing handicrafts, and various trades (carpentry, brick making, brick laying etc.). These small businesses are in a position to expand rural employment and stimulate agricultural development. In short, the lack of liquidity seriously constrains farm households from expanding production, and this is further exacerbated when the small traders that farmers depend on to access inputs are also constrained by the lack of credit.

As part of its economic reform package, Vietnam restructured its banking system to serve the emerging market economy in 1990. The Vietnam Bank of Agriculture (VBA) was established to provide short and medium term credit to rural public institutions, as well as to farmers and the emerging private sector. However, the VBA did not start lending to farmers until mid 1991. Since then, the activities of VBA have increased rapidly. In 1992, half of VBA's lending came from deposits, including private deposits which made up 10 per cent of the total lending of the VBA; private sector lending at the end of 1991 was 7 per cent of its portfolio and by the end of 1992 had increased to 26 per cent (World Bank 1993:149). The rate of default on credit collection from small borrowers was an impressive 2 per cent. The outlook for 1993, from the bank's projection, suggests that private sector activity should continue to expand rapidly (World Bank 1993:149).

Does the VBA reach all those in the countryside? The World Bank (1993:150) claims that due to a shortage of lending funds, the VBA was only able to provide short term credit to about 10 per cent of the potential private rural borrowers. Furthermore, the World Bank estimates that even if modest agricultural growth is to be sustained, the annual credit requirements of the rural sector will be between US$2.5 and US$3.0 billion. With a current loans portfolio of US$236 million, VBA loans only amount to a mere 8-9 per cent of the rural sector's financial needs. Clearly, the VBA has not played a significant role in the successful agricultural performance to date. The fact that agricultural growth averaged 6.5 per cent over the period 1989-1992 suggests that the rural sector has found the necessary funds to finance working capital. In fact, most working capital is financed from private savings and informal credit networks. This highlights several factors: the extent of the shortfall in required funds being financed outside the banking system is enormous; the ability of farm households to meet their financial needs from their own savings indicates a lack of confidence in the public banking system or lack of access to the banking system; and the reliance on an informal credit market not only appears to be common practice but is widely practiced. In many cases, informal credit becomes a key mechanism for land concentration (Rutherford 1992).[29] Thus any effective analysis of rural capital markets must examine the role of informal credit, which is clearly of great importance.

Farmers' Organizations. One of the most interesting aspects of current trends in the Vietnamese rural economy is the increasing arrival upon the scene of autonomous farmers' organizations. Although such organizations have been documented (see Chu Van Lam 1992) further research is necessary in order to effectively determine the scope and efficiency of this newly emerging institutional arrangement. Nevertheless, they are actively encouraged by the party (see the speech by Party Secretary Do Muoi at the November 1993 conference of the Peasants Association). They appear to be designed to address the wide range of institutional gaps left from the legacy of collectivization. They cover areas such as marketing, joint production, credit, transport, and so on. They tap into the extensive informal credit market, and they exploit the considerable capacity for organizational innovation that appears to be a national characteristic when presented with locally profitable opportunities for public goods production. They by-pass the existing formal structures.

Formal structures in the rural economy are, in some quarters, dismissed as being simply a set of exploitative interlocking systems. In the so-called "triangle," there are three groups:

1. The party-state personnel at the local level.
2. The economic organizations, such as cooperatives, state farms, state trading companies, etc.
3. The functional state organizations, such as the local VBA, the police, security forces etc.

At the local level, it is certainly the case that the result can be a strong interlocking "triangle" of party, state, and private interests that will treat additional resources (state credit, aid funds, etc.) as a resource to be used for the group's benefit. This can greatly inhibit normal "developmentalist" activities and NGO tactics will tend to reflect this. This is not to say, however, that in certain areas dedicated civil servants and enlightened local leaders cannot be found. However, the problem helps to explain the slow penetration of private capital into cash crop processing and the maintenance of high observed marketing margins.[30] As we have seen the party supports both these groups and the farmers' countervailing strategies. What has not yet happened is any strong state action against these interferences with the normal operation of the market.[31] The pattern of state investment priorities alluded to by the SPC and FAO report suggests that there are stronger forces at work here.

There clearly exists a number of methods for accelerating Vietnamese rural development. In many parts of rural Vietnam, improving weak and inadequate rural infrastructure in terms of roads and telecommunications, including electricity supplies, has the potential to simultaneously facilitate agricultural and market development. Furthermore, addressing limitations in farm services and extensions and credit availability has the capacity to improve agricultural productivity and related rural activities. Unshackling agriculture from these constraints, in turn, should play a major role in improving rural incomes and provide a positive step towards alleviating rural poverty.

Conclusion

The evidence drawn from the macroeconomic data, with all its well known shortcomings, is striking. It shows just how strong the positive and negative forces unleashed by dismantling a centrally planned system can be. It argues that the key issue in explaining real income growth, both regionally and between different households, is to do with the nature of market access, and the sorts of markets to which access is gained. Rates of agricultural GDP growth of 5-6 per cent are relatively high, and to be welcomed.

However, the analysis has considerable shortcomings. In the absence of sufficiently detailed and focused research into the determinants of economic change at the micro level, arguments (ours included), tend to rely upon *a priori* reasoning. For example, there are strong theoretical reasons for believing that price reforms and market liberalization are the reasons for the favorable post 1989 performance. A more institutional position, on the other hand, would stress the accumulation that had been going on in the rural areas prior to 1988, and thus view the effects of 1989 as being more a product of better markets and higher incomes — in other words, less systemic in origin. The basic issue is lack of empirical research.

Certain things can be said, however, about the role played by policy. Whatever praise is granted to the government for the post 1988-89 performance, few would attribute this to the elements of a normal rural development program: extension, credit, etc. If policy had any effect, it was macro-liberalization and stability and micro-de-collectivization, rather than conventional rural development policies. The question then arises, because the 1993 measures appear precisely designed to fill that gap, what impact and relevance might they have. Here it is worth recalling that Resolution 10 in 1988 did offer a "New Deal" for agriculture, but that the macroeconomic aspects of this were not implemented. The question has to be asked — what has changed to make the rural development support elements of the 1993 measures more implementable than those of 1988? We have indicated, as have other authors in this volume, that underlying the political economy of the rural areas is the tendency for farmers to go it alone, setting up their own autonomous organizations in juxtaposition to official bodies. These and other matters mean, at the least, that arguments questioning the capacity of the state to implement policies in rural areas must be taken seriously. The nature of the current debate itself, therefore, suggests that the second position we outlined at the beginning of the chapter has to confront these arguments. Why be "optimistic about policy"? It is perhaps sufficient to argue that such policies, if implemented, are needed and would have a positive effect — but only perhaps.

With regard to the role played by markets, the range of arguments seems to be less contradictory. The macroeconomic picture argues that the unleashing of market forces is not only a major cause of rural development, but that the extent and nature of that market development explains differences between regions. Market pessimism is therefore less acceptable than "policy pessimism".

It would follow that further improvement of the economic analysis would require greater attention to the nature of Vietnam's rural markets. There is considerable evidence that many rural markets leave much to be desired — note the remarks by Mellor and Qureshi about the wide difference between rice marketing margins in Vietnam and Thailand. And regarding rural institutions, we come up against signs of strong forces acting to reduce the quality and efficiency of rural markets: the strong processes of land loss; and the local "club" based upon interlocking party-state structures (the "triangle" mentioned above) through which state and party policies must operate at the local level.

These two issues are likely to be closely linked. However, whilst it is clear that these are significant problems, we do not know just how significant. Their potential economic impact, however, could be great, leading to social unrest and political turmoil. And, if so, the task of overhauling the formal institutional framework of the rural areas would be extremely difficult to accomplish. Carried to an extreme, it would be appropriate to paint a high proportion of apparently "developmentalist" rural activities as being in essence little more than "rent-seeking," with important implications for national economic development as well as economic policy. However, the economic success to date argues that, if there is a "club" then, like many other Vietnamese institutions, it is a rather weak "club" which intelligent and well-organized farmers can maneuver around. But in a narrow context, it is still costly and wasteful to have to do so. Economic performance would probably have been better if the problem had not existed.

It is useful to accept that the picture is not clear. One reason for this is the lack of a rigorous and widely accepted analysis of trends during the 1980s. This would enable us to gauge better the arguments about the role of local party state structures, and so assess the likely meaning and impact of rural development policy. At the present state of knowledge it is hard to choose between positions in the current debate noted in the Introduction. In an economy still so dependent upon rural conditions as Vietnam's, there are many reasons to be concerned. Yet it is striking how, in the period 1988-93 the absence of much of the normal apparatus of rural development does not seem to have mattered — perhaps not yet. It is also striking how many, though not all, of the issues that such state policies are intended to meet are capable of local solution (for example, credit, technological innovation, marketing, etc.). Furthermore, entry barriers can be struck down, as simply another "fence" to be broken. Probably much will depend upon the extent to which the mass of the population retains the land access rights which the combinations of history and de-collectivization has granted them. Almost all textbooks on East Asia seem to argue that land reform, whether in Japan, Taiwan or wherever, was a key element in the early success of economic development. And any land reform will be accompanied by measures to contain concentration of land. In this area, it is interesting to reflect upon whether the Vietnamese Communist Party's refusal to grant private property rights in land in the 1993 Land Law should be viewed as a recognition of such issues, or as a support for one basis of the "triangle," or perhaps as both?

In concluding it is useful to recapitulate the three positions:

1. The "optimistic about markets" and "pessimistic about policy" position: markets work and state policy is not very important.
2. The "optimistic about regulated markets" and "optimistic about policy" position.
3. The "pessimistic about both markets and policy" position.

On the one hand, our analysis supports the first and last positions in that there are grounds to be pessimistic about the implementability and positive value of rural development policies in Vietnam. On the other hand, it encourages optimism about the role of markets, and thus supports the first and second positions. On the whole, therefore, it upholds the first position: Vietnamese rural development, thanks to the growth of markets, is thus likely to continue to be strong; rural development policy (aside from sectoral reforms and relevant aspects of economy wide policies) will not be greatly relevant.

Notes

1. See Nguyen Cong Tan 1993.

2. Whilst any allocation of particular analysts will naturally risk criticism, Dang Phong's chapter in this book represents this position.

3. Communist Party 1988; "Bao Cao (du thao) So Ket Tinh Hinh Thuc Hien Nghi Quyet 10 cua Bo Chinh Tri ve Doi Moi Quan Ly Kinh Te Nong Nghiep" 1989. Note that according to the latter the reason why the Resolution in practice became little more than the micro reform of cooperatives (important as that was), was to do with the fact that the Resolution originated in the Economics and Propaganda Departments of the Party Secretariat, but was implemented by the Party/State apparatus as a whole. Taken with overt criticisms of the quasi-exploitative activities of some rural cadre in the media in the run-up to the Resolution, this points to certain differences within the party on the way to deal with the rural areas. Note also that whilst the June 1993 fifth

plenum of the Central Committee continued with its support for cooperatives in those areas that still have them (mainly the north and center of Vietnam), the November conference of the Peasants Association called for redoubled efforts to accelerate rural development. It also both supported the cooperatives left over from the old system whilst encouraging the emergence of autonomous peasant collective organizations.

4. The report written for the FAO and SPC by Professor J.W. Mellor and Sarfraz Qureshi (SPC and FAO 1993) takes this position. See also Vo-Tong Xuan and Timmer (1990).

5. This view is increasingly common amongst many NGOs. For example — Stuart Rutherford (1992). Similar notions, referring almost to a "Red Bourgeoisie" in the rural areas, could be found in the official media prior to Resolution 10. See also Kaufman and Sen (1993).

6. See, for example, Nguyen Khac Truong's novel *Manh Dat Lam Nuoi Nhieu Ma* (1991). It describes a commune where all of the formal party/state structures are simply fronts for the generations-old rivalries between various families.

7. For example, item 05 of sub-project 01 "Tong Hop, Phan Tich Dien Hinh, Nhan To Moi o Nong Thon" [Round-up and Analysis of New Forms and Factors in the Rural Areas], and Chu Van Lam 1992. The former work stresses the rapid and creative growth of farmers' own autonomous organizations quite outside the formal party/state structures. Party General Secretary Do Muoi's speech to the Peasants' Association Conference in November 1993 clearly stated that these trends were positive and to be supported, whilst also supporting the existing cooperatives.

8. See Adam Fforde and Stefan de Vylder (in progress), and Fforde (1992).

9. This growth rate refers to the Gross Social Product which differs from Gross Domestic Product, in that amongst other differences the former does not include the service sector.

10. These are the latest figures — the earlier, unrevised, data showed rather lower growth rates for 1990 and 1991.

11. Recent estimates by the World Bank project a growth rate of 8.2 per cent; however, the Asian Development Bank forecasts a more moderate projection of 7.5 per cent by comparison. We believe that the Vietnamese economy will show a growth rate of over 8 per cent.

12. There are arguments that statistical under-recording of investment in 1992 was considerable (VECA 1993:45-46). Based upon some rather simple estimates, this concluded that domestic private savings in 1992 were at some 17.5 per cent of GDP, compared with 11 per cent in 1990, rising to near 22 per cent in 1993. On the same basis total investment in 1993 is around 17 per cent of GDP.

13. VECA 1993:49.

14. ODI disbursements had reached near $700 million a year by 1992 — VECA 1993:41.

15. The SPC and FAO estimates are based on conservative growth figures for each major sector of the economy and within different sub-sectors of the agricultural sector (SPC and FAO 1993:14-16).

16. Gross output differs from GDP in that the latter only includes intermediate consumption (payment to factors), hence, GDP represents the income derived from the production activity since it is gross output minus intermediate consumption. Gross agricultural output was used in this category since a breakdown of agricultural GDP was not available.

17. This could suggest a sharp increase in the efficiency of non-factor resource utilization, with cost savings appearing as faster factor income growth, as a result of the micro reforms and abolition of price controls and subsidies.

18. In general, the quality of Vietnamese statistics has been improving over recent years, but care is still warranted when making judgment based on national account figures. Only since 1992 has Vietnam adopted the United Nations System of National Accounts. Although national account figures have been revised as far back as 1986 for some categories (GDP, Gross Output, National Income) and these have been reported in some of the most recent publications of the General Statistical Office, it appears that the reporting of growth figures based on Vietnamese national accounts by major international institutions are not "up to date" and even based on unrevised statistics since they vary between each other. Take, for example, four recent reports: an IMF working paper (May 1993), the SPC and FAO report (September 1993), a UNDP (SRV) report (September 1993), and the World Bank country report (September 1993) all reports differ from our growth rate which is based on the most recent publications reporting GDP estimates. Note that both the UNDP and SPC and FAO reports were prepared for the Donor Conference in November 1993, and that the most recent national accounts data were published in Hanoi in March 1993.

19. In fact chemical fertilizer imports increased from 1.840 million tonnes in 1989 to 2.085 million tonnes in 1990 (*Nien Giam Thong Ke — 1992*).

20. The figure of 260 kilograms is based on the estimate of monthly subsistence consumption of 13 kilograms of milled rice provided in Nguyen Van Tiem (1993:34). We have used a 13 month lunar year, and the paddy to milled rice conversion rate of 0.65, to arrive at 260 kilograms per person per annum.

21. Dang Phong's chapter in this book provides an interesting anecdote, whereby farmers have taken to raising deer, apparently with extremely high returns (up to US$100-500 per animal) but also with high capital outlays.

22. North Vietnam includes the Northern mountains and Midlands, Red River delta, and North central coast. South Vietnam includes the South central coast, Central highlands, Northeast southern, and the Mekong delta regions.

23. In Ngo Vinh Long's (1993) study of class differentiation in the Vietnamese countryside, the author asserts that the situation has worsened since the economic reforms began.

24. Relative to rice, garlic has only been recently grown commercially in some parts of Hai Hung province in the Red River delta. At the time when the observations were made, there was considerable state involvement in cash crop marketing especially for garlic.

25. In the literature, efficiency can be separated into technical efficiency and allocative efficiency. Kalirajan and Shand (1988) have shown that technical efficiency generally facilitates economic efficiency. That is to say, the better a farmer applies scarce resources (eg., timely application of fertilizers and correct method of application) the better is the quantity applied (ie., the least amount of input to yield the greatest amount of output). The product of both technical and allocative efficiencies is economic efficiency.

26. Road density area (km/km^2) in Vietnam is amongst the lowest of all low-income developing countries and is worse off than some countries with similar per capita GDP (World Road Statistics, International Road Federation, Washington D.C. cited in SPC and FAO 1993).

27. Mellor and Qureshi, the consultants for the SPC and FAO report (1993) also mention similar views. According to them, the importance that the government places on rural infrastructure investment can be weighed up by a recent workshop on Public Investment held in Hanoi. Apparently, rural infrastructure was virtually left unmentioned.

28. Little, Scitovsky, Scott (1970); Chenery, et al. (1974); Fei, Ranis and Kuo (1979).

29. For the classic statement on "interlocking markets" see Bhaduri (1973).

30. The mechanisms used by this interlocking group to obtain resources include, apart from straight corruption, such economic "distortions" as pressurizing incoming foreign investors to carry out joint ventures with state economic units belonging to the local authority, use of the "contract" system in cooperatives to ensure supply of cash crops at appropriate prices to local state trading companies, processors etc. Whilst little studied, there is abundant evidence for such behavior in NGO reports and the official mass media, as well as, less directly put, in academic studies.

31. It is worth recalling here that the debates over the New Constitution about the position of province leaders were heated, but resulted in little change to the status quo, within which such important members of the nomenclatura are still locally appointees, subject only to the approval of the Head of Government.

References

Aduki Pty. Ltd., Canberra, private collection.
Agence French Press (AFP) (20 October 1993).

"Bao Cao (du thao) So Ket Tinh Hinh Thuc Hien Nghi Quyet 10 cua Bo Chinh Tri ve Doi Moi Quan Ly Kinh Te Nong Nghiep" [Draft Report on the Results of the Implementation of Resolution 10 of the Politburo in Agricultural Economic Management Reform]. 1989. Mimeo, Hanoi.

Bhaduri, A. 1973. "A Study in Agricultural Backwardness under Semi-Fuedalism". *Economic Journal* 83:120-137; 'Reply', 89:420-221.

Chenery, H.B. et al. 1974. *Redistribution with Growth.* London: Oxford University Press.

Chu Van Lam, et al. 1992. *Hop Tac Hoa Nong Nghiep Viet Nam — Lich Su — Van De — Trien Vong* [Agricultural Cooperativization in Vietnam — History — Problems — Hopes]. Hanoi: NXB Su That.

Communist Party. 1988. *Nghi Quyet Bo Chinh Tri ve Doi Moi Quan Ly Kinh Te Nong Nghiep (10)* [Resolution of the Politburo No. 10 on the Reform of Agricultural Economic Management]. Hanoi: NXB Su That.

Fei, J., G. Ranis, and S.W.Y. Kuo. 1979. *Equity with Growth: The Taiwan Case.* London: Oxford University Press.

Fforde, A. 1992. "The Institutions of Transition from Central Planning — the Case of Vietnam." Seminar Paper, Dept of Economics, Research School of Pacific and Asian Studies.

Fforde, A. and S. de Vylder. (in progress). *From Plan to Market: The Vietnamese Transition from 1979 to 1994.* Boulder: Westview.

Kalirajan, K. and R.T. Shand. 1988. "Causality Between Technical and Allocative Efficiencies: An Empirical Testing." *Journal of Economic Studies* 19(2):3-17.

Kaufman, J. and G. Sen. 1993. "Population, Health, and Gender in Vietnam: Social Policies under the Economic Reforms," in B. Ljunggren, ed. Pp. 233-258.

Lipworth, G. and E. Spitaller. 1993. "Viet Nam — Reform and Stabilization, 1986-92." IMF Working Paper, WP/93/46 May.

Little, I.M.D., T. Scitovsky, and M.F.G. Scott. 1970. *Industry and Trade in some Developing Countries.* London: Oxford University Press.

Ljunggren, B. ed. 1993. *The Challenge of Reform in Indochina.* Cambridge, MA: Harvard Institute for International Development, Harvard University Press.

Ngo Vinh Long. 1993. "Reform and Rural Development: Impact on Class, Sectoral, and Regional Inequalities", in W.S. Turley and M. Selden eds., *Reinventing Vietnamese Socialism: Doi Moi in Comparative Perspective.* Pp. 165-208. Boulder: Westview Press.

Nguyen Cong Tan, ed. 1993. *Chu Truong Chinh Sach cua Dang, Nha Nuoc ve Tiep Tuc Doi Moi va Phat Trien Nong Nghiep Nong Thon* [Lines and Policies of the Party and State on the Continued Renovation and Development of Agricultural and the Rural Areas]. Hanoi: NXB Nong Nghiep.

Nguyen Khac Truong. 1991. *Manh Dat Lam Nuoi Nhieu Ma* [The Land of People and Ghosts]. Hanoi: NXB Hoi nha van.

Nguyen Van Tiem. 1993. *Giau Ngheo Trong Nong Thon Hien Nay* [Rich and Poor in the Countryside Today]. Hanoi: Agricultural Publishing House.

Nien Giam Thong Ke (NGTK) — 1988 (Statistical Year Book 1988). 1990. Hanoi: Statistical Publishing House.

_____ — *1989 (Statistical Year Book 1989)*. Hanoi: Statistical Publishing House 1991.

_____ — *1990 (Statistical Year Book 1990)*. 1992. Hanoi: Statistical Publishing House.

_____ — *1992 (Statistical Year Book 1992)*. 1993. Hanoi: Statistical Publishing House.

Rutherford, S. 1992. *Visit Report — A Peasant Economy Readjusts in a District of Northern Vietnam*. Hanoi: ActionAid.

Sénèque, S.J. 1993. "The Household Crop Production System in Quoc Tuan," Department of Economics, Research School of Pacific and Asian Studies, Australian National University. Mimeo.

So Lieu Thong Ke Nong Nghiep 35 Nam (1956-1990) (SLTKNN) [35 Years of Agricultural Statistics 1956-1990]. Hanoi: NXB Thong Ke.

So Lieu Thong Ke Nong, Lam, Ngu Nghiep Viet Nam (1976-1991) (SLTKNN) [Statistical Data on Agriculture, Forestry and Fisheries (1976-1991)]. 1992. Hanoi: NXB Thong Ke.

SPC and FAO (State Planning Committee and the Food and Agriculture Organization). 1993. *An Agriculture-Led Strategy for the Economic Transformation of Vietnam: Policy and Project Priorities*, Contribution to the Preparation for the Round Table Meeting of Donors, September.

SRV and UNDP (Socialist Republic of Vietnam and United Nations Development Programme). 1993. *Vietnam: A Development Perspective*, Prepared for the Donor Conference, Hanoi.

Tai Khoan Quoc Gia o Viet Nam 1986-1990 (VIE 88/032 Project), [System of National Accounts of Viet Nam 1986-1990]. 1992. Hanoi: Statistical Publishing House.

Timmer, C.P. 1988. "The Agricultural Transformation" in H. Chenery and T.N. Srinivasan eds., *Handbook of Development Economics* (Vol 1). Pp. 276-331. Amsterdam: North Holland.

Tu Giay and Ha Huy Khoi. 1991. *Public Health Aspects of Nutrition in Vietnam*. Hanoi: The National Institute of Nutrition.

VECA (*Vietnam Economic Commentary and Analysis*). 1993. Number 3 (April). Canberra: Aduki Pty Ltd.

Vo-Tong Xuan and C.P. Timmer. 1990. *Development Discussion Paper No. 351 AFP*. "A Food Policy for Vietnam," Harvard Institute for International Development, Mass., July.

World Bank. 1993. *Viet Nam Transition to the Market*. The World Bank, Country Operation Division, Country Department I, East Asia and Pacific Region.

Interior of home of settler family, Ba Ria-Vung Tau.

Labouring in paddy fields, Mekong delta.

Negotiating traffic, Hanoi.

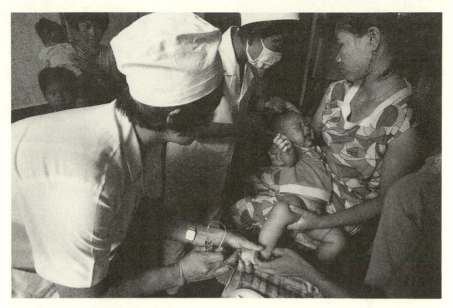

Community health clinic, Ben Tre.

Mother and daughter, Lao Cai.

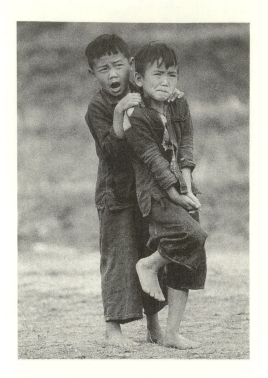

Two boys watching sport,
H'Mong minority group.

Mother and son, Ba Ria-Vung Tau.

Women fishing, Vung Tau.

Community at work on hand-dug well, Lao Cai.

5

The Peasant Household Economy and Social Change

Dao The Tuan *

Introduction

Since the initiation of agricultural de-communalization in the early 1980s and its more recent acceleration by new land reforms, rural people in Vietnam have experienced great social changes. During this period, the peasant household economy has become the most important mode of production. This chapter describes some of these changes, identifies current problems faced by peasant households, and discusses them in the context of economic differentiation among households.

In 1981, the household began to be reconstituted as the major unit of agricultural production in place of the farm cooperative. Households were allocated specific plots of land for management under a contract system. The cooperative still held a monopoly over the provision of inputs and the marketing of outputs. In 1988, however, with the enactment of Resolution 10, household property rights were strengthened. Under this reform, although the state retained ownership of the land, households were allocated the right to use land in exchange for paying a tax. By 1992, six million of the seven million hectares of agricultural land were farmed under direct household use rights, although the specific arrangements varied from place to place. In July 1993, the revision of the land law allowed for the extension of tenure of use rights to at least twenty years and, more importantly, made provision for the transfer of use rights. It is against this background that the issues of the development of the peasant household economy are discussed.

In order to monitor rural change and inform policy development, several surveys have been conducted since 1988 by the Agrarian

Systems Department of the Vietnam Agricultural Science Institute. In addition, a large-scale survey was conducted by Vietnam's General Statistics Office in January 1990, which gathered data for 1989. This survey included 6,457 households in seventeen villages in five provinces. A similar survey was conducted in 1993, presenting data for 1992. In 1992, the National Research Program on Rural Development also coordinated a major peasant household survey which sampled more than 2,000 households in fourteen provinces representing seven regions of Vietnam.

The results of these surveys are used here to construct a cursory view of the changing profile of economic differentiation of peasant households in Vietnam. Those who have conducted research in Vietnam are no doubt aware of the vagaries which often thwart household data collection particularly with respect to income, hence the following analysis should be interpreted as exploratory and tentative. For example, the survey data for 1989 were collected in a way somewhat different from the method used for the 1992 data. Furthermore, the surveys conducted by various research groups are not always comparable as the methodologies vary. Although regional comparisons in particular years are possible, longitudinal comparisons using data from different sources and different provinces should be treated cautiously.

Regional Differentiation of Average Income
Per Capita in Peasant Households

Vietnam is divided into seven economic regions (see Map 5.1). Among these regions, only two (the deltas of the Red River and the Mekong River) are plains; other regions have both plains and mountainous areas, especially two regions (the Northern mountains and Midlands and the Central highlands) which consist mostly of sloping areas. The first region includes both mountainous and midlands areas of northern Vietnam, so frequently it is divided into two subregions. Figure 5.1 and Table 5.1 present net per capita income data in 1989 and 1992 from household surveys conducted in 1990 and 1993 in various provinces representing five regions of Vietnam (the North central and Eastern south are missing). For the purposes of comparison, income has been converted to 1992 values. The table indicates that net per capita income increased in all regions following the 1988 land reform although the rate was faster in some regions than others.

Those provinces with lower population densities, commodity production, and more opportunities for alternative employment in the non-agricultural and service sectors had higher average incomes per

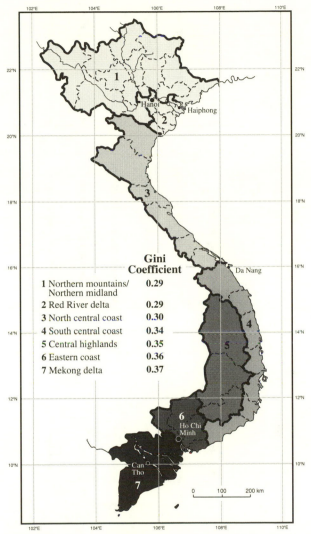

MAP 5.1: Household Economic Differentiation 1993

Source: General Statistics Office, 1994.

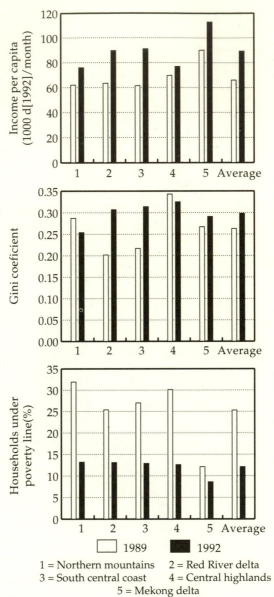

FIGURE 5.1: Household Income

TABLE 5.1: Results of Surveys on Household Income

| Region | Province | Year | Income per Capita per Month (1,000 dong) | | Gini Co-efficient | Households under Poverty Line |
			Actual Price	1992 Price	(%)	(%)
Northern mountains	Yen Bai	1989	18.8	62.0	0.287	31.9
		1992	75.9	75.9	0.254	13.2
Red River delta	Nam Ha	1989	19.2	63.3	0.202	25.4
		1992	89.7	89.7	0.307	13.1
South central coast	Binh Dinh	1989	18.6	61.4	0.217	27.0
		1992	91.1	91.1	0.314	12.9
Central highlands	Dac Lac	1989	21.1	69.6	0.343	30.1
		1992	76.9	76.9	0.325	12.6
Mekong delta	Can Tho	1989	27.3	90.0	0.267	12.1
		1992	113.0	113.0	0.291	8.6
Average		1989	20.0	66.0	0.263	25.3
		1992	89.3	89.3	0.298	12.1

Note: Both 1989 and 1992 surveys were made by the General Statistics Office.
The poverty line is defined as income equivalent to 20 kilograms of rice per month per person.

capita. In 1989 net income per capita was highest in the Mekong delta region; the lowest income per capita region was the South central coast region, where the average was 68 per cent of income of the former. By 1992, incomes had increased with the Mekong delta still representing the highest income per capita region; the lowest incomes were now in the Northern mountains region representing 67 per cent of the Mekong delta average.[1] That the difference between the highest and lowest scarcely changed indicates that the regional income gap has not varied significantly during the last few years. Compared to the Mekong delta, average per capita incomes in the Red River delta and South central regions improved faster, than that of the mountainous and highland regions. The co-efficient of variation between regions in 1989 is 16.6 per cent and that of 1992 is 16.8 per cent. In summary it appears that regional differentiation has not changed since the introduction of the 1988 land reform.

Economic Differentiation Among Households Within Regions

Net per capita incomes were used in conjunction with quintile calculations from the 1989 and 1992 data surveys in order to calculate the Gini co-efficient between income groups of the different regions.[2] The percentage of people under the poverty line is also calculated (Table 5.1).[3] These data indicate that in 1989, inequality between individual net incomes was least in the Red River delta, although the average income was below the entire sample's average. Inequality was greatest in both the Central highlands, which had an above average income level, and the Northern mountains region, which had below average income levels. The Mekong delta had the highest average income and a low percentage of poor, yet inequality was only just above average — perhaps because the market economy in this region was the most developed in the country. The 1989 survey data suggest that rich households were those with greater access to factors of production (i.e., land, labor, and capital). They were more often engaged in intensive agriculture together with a variety of activities such as gardening, permanent crop cultivation (e.g., growing tea, rubber, and coffee), aquaculture, forestry, processing, service (agricultural inputs, transportation, and marketing), and making handicrafts.

Data for 1992 indicate that although average incomes were greatest in the Mekong delta, inequality there is also one of the highest. The region's percentage of poor households, however, is relatively low. The Northern mountains region has the lowest average income, relatively low inequality, and the highest percentage of poor households. The

South central coast region showed a relatively high average income, together with increased inequality and a medium percentage of poor households.

Comparing the Gini co-efficients from 1989 to 1992, it appears that the degree of economic differentiation has increased on average for the country from 0.263 (1989) to 0.298 (1992). But the percentage of the poor decreased from 25.3 to 12.1. More specifically, since the introduction of the 1988 land reform, inequality has increased in all regions with the exception of the mountainous and highland areas. Furthermore, economic differentiation between households in northern and central parts of the country increased faster than in the south.

Alternative Typologies for the Analysis of Economic Differentiation of Peasant Households

More detailed surveys were conducted under the auspices of the Vietnam Agricultural Science Institute (VASI) between 1989 and 1992 in the northern regions and in 1992 in the Mekong delta in order to ascertain an appropriate typology for the analysis of economic differentiation of peasant households. Data were collected in 21 communes over ten provinces representative of seven regions. The methodology of data collection over the seven regions was consistent and it is thought that these data are reliable. For the northern regions, data were collected by researchers who have been based for many years in three rural development stations. In the south the data were collected by many institutions participating in the National Research Program on Rural Development.

After comparing different methods of typology, we found that the typology by production objective held the greatest explanatory value. This typology can show the level of households in the process of their evolution from subsistence to commercial farming. Certainly there is a consistent relationship between different typologies: the self-sufficient farmers are poor, have less production factors, and cannot diversify their economic activities, while commercial farmers tend to be the opposite.

The typology of production objectives was constructed according to the method illustrated in the Appendix to this chapter. Applied to all the surveyed villages, it distinguishes the different types of peasant households in seven regions of Vietnam. The typology describes the range of households' production objectives:

1.   "Consumption only" — that is, they are self-sufficient and may be either:

      (a) food deficient (i.e., consume more food than they produce),

      (b) reproduction deficient (i.e., the financial balance is negative because expenditure is greater than gross annual income), or

      (c) reproduction sufficient (i.e., the financial balance is positive but the objective is still consumption).

    2.   "Both consumption and the market" defined as self-sufficient and commercial households.

    3.   "The market" including households engaged mainly in the production of commercial commodities.

Survey results show that the richest villages are in the Mekong delta with relative high levels of differentiation, followed by the Eastern south where inequality is highest (Table 5.2). Gini co-efficients in these surveys are lower than in the previous surveys because the data include only agricultural households. Poorest households are in the more mountainous areas and in the coastal regions, a profile that coincides with previous surveys. Medium income and highest equality are observed in the Red River delta. Although the percentage of households within each production objective type varies by village even within the same district, it is possible to draw general conclusions from the data. First, the percentage of commercial farmers is greater in the Mekong delta than the Red River delta and conversely, more than 60 per cent of households in the Red River delta produce only enough for their own consumption. Nevertheless, producers in the Red River delta are not deficient in food. The food deficit households are concentrated in the more mountainous areas and the central coast; that is, not surprisingly, they are primarily in the poorest regions. More specifically, in the Red River delta, the proportion of self-sufficient households is still very high (Table 5.2). By contrast, in the Mekong delta, well over half the households in half the villages surveyed were producing considerably for the market. At the same time, a high proportion of households produce only for their own needs. In other words, differentiation appears in the Mekong delta between households who produce only for their own needs and those who produce for the market. The percentage of households with dual objectives, suggesting a transitional stage from self-sufficiency to commercialization, is curiously low.

In summary we can see that the majority of Vietnamese peasants are very poor and still engage heavily in subsistence farming. Households in the plains doing commercial farming are more prominent in the south, which is also richer. Given this overall condition, differentiation among households is still very low. The main task of rural development

TABLE 5.2: Types of Households by Productive Objective

Region	Consumption Only			Consumption and Market (%)	Market (%)	Gross Income (1,000 dong/cap)	Gini Co-efficient
	Food Deficient (%)	Reproduction Deficient (%)	Reproduction Sufficient (%)				
Northern mountains:							
Yen Nhan, Bac Thai	0	0	24	38	38	845	0.12
Tan Lap, Bac Thai	0	0	10	67	23	1,085	0.15
Ngoc Phai, Bac Thai	0	0	55	33	11	1,134	0.15
Dong Vien, Bac Thai	28	0	0	38	34	1,403	0.15
Northern midlands:							
Hop Thinh, Vinh Phu	27	32	0	22	18	873	0.14
Gia Khanh, Vinh Phu	0	16	37	36	11	872	0.13
Honag Hoa, Vinh Phu	17	10	27	22	31	780	0.17
Red River delta:							
Cong Hoa, Hai Hung	0	0	28	32	35	1,352	0.13
Quoc Tuan, Hai Hung	0	64	15	18	3	1,405	0.11
Thai Tan, Hai Hung	0	0	48	10	42	1,479	0.10
Thanh Binh, Hai Hung	0	13	54	25	8	1,345	0.13
Song Ho, Ha Bac	0	1	52	0	46	1,026	0.15

(continues)

TABLE 5.2: Types of Households by Productive Objective (continued)

Region	Consumption Only			Consumption and Market (%)	Market (%)	Gross Income (1,000 dong/cap)	Gini Co-efficient
	Food Deficient (%)	Reproduction Deficient (%)	Reproduction Sufficient (%)				
North central coast:							
Dien Chau, Nghe An	37	0	0	49	14	1,052	0.18
South central coast:							
Phuoc An, Binh Dinh	38	31	25	0	5	847	0.15
Central highlands:							
Easup, Dac Lac	54	21	21	0	4	575	0.16
Eastern south:							
Phu Ngoc, Dong Nai	0	0	74	0	26	3,006	0.23
Phu Hoa, Dong Nai	0	65	4	0	31	1,773	0.19
Mekong delta:							
Thuan My, Long An	42	2	0	45	12	1,197	0.20
Hoa Khanh Dong, Long An	0	30	20	12	36	1,981	0.16
Tan Thanh, Long An	0	0	30	6	64	2,684	0.18
Cai Lay, Tien Giang	0	33	0	0	67	3,426	0.24

Source: Based on surveys by the Vietnam Agricultural Science Institute, 1989-1992.

in Vietnam at the present time, therefore, is to help peasants to change from subsistence to commercial farming.

By looking at more details in the 1989-1992 surveys of the VASI and doing the statistical analysis explained in this chapter's appendix, we can achieve additional insight into the problem facing agricultural households in various regions (Table 5.3). In the mountains, food deficiency is a major cause of deforestation. Food production is done by shifting cultivation. The development of industrial crops, cattle husbandry, and reforestation requires high investment, which poor farmers do not have. Now in many areas, where forests are already destroyed, villagers are in a difficult situation, trying to survive by producing poor food crops and supplementing their incomes from the forest.

In midland and coastal areas, the problem of food deficiency is also severe due to difficult ecological conditions, so the percentage of food deficient households is relatively high. The development of industrial crops and cattle husbandry is limited by the lack of investment and markets.

In the plains, conditions are more favorable for food production, which explains why there are few food deficient farming households there. But the development of commercial rice production in the north is limited by the lack of land, and the expansion of cash crops and animal husbandry is restricted by the lack of inputs and markets. In the south, rice commercial farming is developed, but low rice prices cause many difficulties. The trend of diversification is constrained by the lack of markets.

The main constraint of self-sufficient farmers is access to credit. Poor farmers have great difficulties getting credit. The major constraint of more commercially-oriented farmers is the lack of markets. Credit and market institutions in the country are not yet sufficiently formed to support the development of the household economy.

Social Changes in the Rural Areas

In order to understand the social changes in the rural areas, the processes must be monitored over a longer period. Yujiro Hayami and Masao Kikuchi (1981) show that in Asian villages, strong population pressure causes changes in the agrarian structure which leads to the stratification of farmers. This general process is also occurring in Vietnam.

Over the past six decades, population in the rural areas has increased, even though Vietnam was at war for half this period and suffered heavy casualties. In the Mekong delta the rate of population

TABLE 5.3: Classification of Households in Some Typical Villages

Type[a]	Households %	Gross Annual Income[b]	Food Balance[b]	Financial Balance[b]	Consumption Value[b]	Commercial Value[b]	Production Objective[c]	Production Strategy[d]	Production Factors[e]	Constraints[f]
Northern mountains — Dong Vien commune — Gini co-efficient: 0.15										
1	28	633	-155	522	480	153	Consumption	ARF	lcw	capital
2	38	1,171	224	976	492	679	Cons+market	RAF	Lcw	capital, work
3	6	1,751	-178	1,207	722	1,028	Market	ARG	LCw	capital, work
4	16	1,983	249	1,721	472	1,510	Market	RAG	LCW	capital, work
5	12	4,710	932	2,517	484	2,526	Market	AFG	LCW	work
Average		1,403	177	1,164	500	903				
Middle region — Gia Khanh commune — Gini co-efficient: 0.13										
1	37	654	6	173	438	216	Consumption	RAV	lcw	capital
2	16	717	-13	-375	625	92	Consumption	ARN	lcw	capital
3	23	932	117	0	435	497	Cons+market	RAN	lcw	capital
4	13	1,646	423	267	570	1,076	Cons+market	RAF	LCW	capital
5	11	2,542	416	-136	1,078	1,464	Market	RAN	LCW	capital
Average		872	35	-127	507	3,621				
Red River delta — Thai Tan commune — Gini co-efficient: 0.10										
1	48	1,041	191	179	533	508	Consumption	RAN	lcw	capital
2	27	1,653	255	611	550	1,103	Market	ARN	LCW	capital
3	10	1,698	313	195	992	776	Cons+market	ARN	lCW	capital
4	8	1,841	765	852	578	1,262	Market	RAF	LCW	work
5	7	1,982	271	1,347	787	2,194	Market	ANR	LCW	–
Average		1,479	279	435	600	879				

TABLE 5.3: Classification of Households in Some Typical Villages

Type[a]	Households %	Gross Annual Income[b]	Food Balance[b]	Financial Balance[b]	Consumption Value[b]	Commercial Value[b]	Production Objective[c]	Production Strategy[d]	Production Factors[e]	Constraints[f]
South central — Phuoc An commune — Gini co-efficient: 0.15										
1	28	592	-224	-813	872	-280	Consumption	RAF	lcw	capital
2	7	773	-121	-1,849	1,724	-950	Consumption	RAF	LCW	land
3	29	818	126	-691	782	36	Consumption	RAF	LCW	capital, land
4	23	877	242	-204	462	415	Consumption	RAF	lcW	capital, land
5	5	2,407	261	212	850	1,557	Market	RAV	LCW	work
Average		847	37	-645	804	42				
Eastern south — Phu Hoa — Gini co-efficient: 0.19										
1	61	1,598	-258	285	962	637	Consumption	NIA	lcw	land
2	13	2,046	63	297	1,323	723	Consumption	NIR	Lcw	capital, land
3	16	4,959	-300	1,823	1,820	3,139	Consumption	INA	LCW	land
4	2	7,481	1,755	3,474	1,932	5,549	Market	IRA	LCW	capital
5	8	10,932	-227	6,113	1,952	9,142	Market	INA	LCW	work
Average		1,829	-147	301	1,109	720				

(continues)

TABLE 5.3: Classification of Households in Some Typical Villages *(continued)*

Type[a]	Households %	Gross Annual Income[b]	Food Balance[b]	Financial Balance[b]	Consumption Value[b]	Commercial Value[b]	Production Objective[c]	Production Strategy[d]	Production Factors[e]	Constraints[f]
Mekong delta — Hoa Khanh Dong — Gini co-efficient: 0.16										
1	26	786	-175	-346	599	187	Consumption	VAR	lcw	capital
2	20	1,574	-54	-416	1,053	520	Consumption	VAR	lcw	capital
3	4	1,610	220	-1,314	1,622	-12	Consumption	VRA	LCw	work, capital
4	23	2,297	127	344	750	1,547	Market	AVR	lCw	capital
5	12	2,622	453	-327	1,206	1,417	Cons+market	VRA	LCW	capital
6	13	4000	631	934	983	3,017	Market	VAR	LCW	capital
Average		1,981	119	-69	895	1,086				

a Type of production objective for households in each commune. The same number in different communes does not necessarily mean the same production objective or combination of objectives. For elaboration of this and other aspects of the table, see the annex for this chapter.
b Per capita, expressed in 1,000 dong (1992 prices).
c The production objective is estimated from a Cobb–Douglas function Y = f (C, M).
d R: rice, F: non-rice food crops, V: vegetables, I: industrial crops, G: garden, A: animal husbandry, F: forestry, N: non-agricultural activities.
e L: land, C: capital, W: work force. In uppercase, above average; in lowercase, below average.
f Constraint is determined by Cobb–Douglas function Y = f (L, C, V).

Source: Based on surveys by the Vietnam Agricultural Science Institute, 1989-1992.

increase was rapid — about 2.2 per cent per annum due both to natural increase and net migration which was over twice that of the Red River delta which was subject to net out-migration (Table 5.4 and Figure 5.2). At the same time, land available for agriculture has decreased by one-third in the Red River delta (-0.6 per cent annually) due to the use of land for activities such as housing, urbanization, and the construction of irrigation systems. Land availability increased only slowly in the Mekong delta (0.2 per cent annually) mainly by reclamation through irrigation works, especially in the Plain of Reeds and the Long Xuyen quadrilateral. Arable land available per capita has declined in both deltas and more rapidly in the Mekong due to the rapid increase in population. In 1990, agricultural land per capita was a little more than one-third of what it was in 1930 in the Red River delta (decreasing at 1.6 per cent a year) and a little less than one-third in the Mekong delta (decreasing at 2 per cent annually). Nevertheless, land availability for agriculture per person in the Mekong delta is more than three times that of the Red River delta.

Although land available for agriculture has decreased substantially in the north and only increased slightly in the south, production has increased dramatically in net terms due to an increased paddy yield per hectare of approximately 150 per cent over the sixty-year period. Currently, yield (tonnes per hectare) is higher in the Red River delta than in the Mekong River delta. Most importantly, paddy production per capita in both regions has increased which means that rice production is keeping pace with population growth. Nevertheless, in the Red River delta food production per capita is less than in the Mekong delta, which means that the gross income per capita from paddy production in the north is less than in the south.

In Vietnam, many institutional changes affected social conditions and agricultural production. In 1946-47, in the north and south, land which previously belonged to the French and French collaborators was redistributed and land rent was reduced. In the north during 1953-55, a radical land reform occurred and was followed during 1958-60 by collectivization. In the south, the 1955-56 land reform under the Ngo Dinh Diem government restricted the rent that could be charged to tenants and was limited to holdings that were 100 hectares or more. Again in 1970, land reform occurred both in territories controlled by the Provisional Revolutionary Government and by the Nguyen Van Thieu government. Following the liberation of the south, collectivization was introduced in 1978 but had little time to take root as de-collectivization began in 1981 with Directive 100 and continued throughout the whole country between 1980-1988.

TABLE 5.4: The Evolution of Agrarian Systems in the Two Largest Deltas in Vietnam

Region		Rural Population (million)	Arable Permanent (million ha.)	Land Density (m²/capita)	Food Crops Production (million tonnes)	Food Yield (t/ha.)	Food per Capita (kg)
Red River delta	1930	6.5	1.2	1,846	1.8	1.5	277
	1990	11.9	0.8	689	4.9	5.9	411
Growth rate (%)		(1.0)	(-0.6)	(-1.6)	(1.7)	(2.3)	(0.6)
Mekong delta	1930	3.2	2.0	6,250	2.6	1.3	812
	1990	11.8	2.3	1,949	9.6	4.2	816
Growth rate (%)		(2.2)	(0.2)	(-2.0)	(2.2)	(2.0)	(-0.01)

FIGURE 5.2: The Evolution of Agrarian Systems in the Two Deltas.

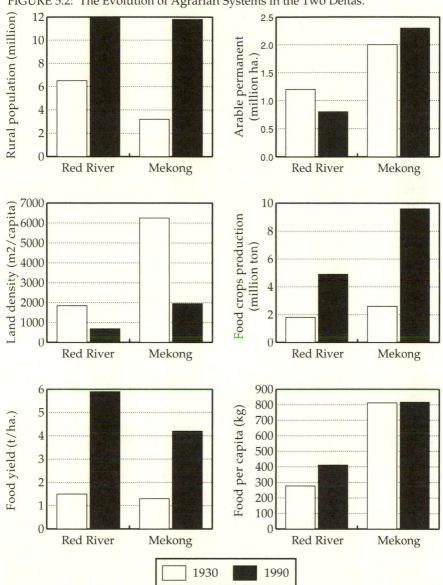

FIGURE 5.2: The Evolution of Agrarian Systems in the Two Deltas

Using the sporadic data available, an attempt is made in Table 5.5 and Figure 5.3 to establish the course of social change through an examination of farmers' net incomes and social equity represented by the Gini co-efficient for the two most important regions in the country over the 1930 to 1990 period. Average income was used together with data on income distribution to calculate the Gini co-efficient. However, a number of caveats affecting the interpretation of data need to be given at the outset. For comparative purposes, the average net income is calculated as kilograms of paddy per capita. Admittedly, the use of paddy as a deflator has some imperfections as the net prices for paddy have changed and vary from north to south. In the north, the Gini co-efficient for the collective period was based on the average income data and data on income distribution from some provincial statistics offices. Due to the lack of data on income distribution during the French period and in South Vietnam, the distribution of land was used as the equity criteria. These data suggest that average net incomes have increased in both regions over the sixty-year period with some periods of reduction probably due to disruption as a consequence of the wars. Furthermore, the rate of increase has been more rapid in the south leading to a 1990 regional income differential of 2:1, although one must bear in mind that the living costs are much higher in the south. Table 5.5 also illustrates that net social equity has increased in both regions over the period, although the more detailed data set for the north indicates fluctuations with an acceleration of equity following institutional reforms begun in the 1950s.

Two general and possibly contentious conclusions can be drawn from Table 5.5. First, it appears that in the north, the process of social differentiation among households resumed even during the period of cooperatives and collectivization in the 1960s. Families had the opportunity to produce their own household income even within the cooperative structure. It is estimated that household plots contributed 40-60 per cent of all production and that 60-70 per cent of farmers' income came from this and other household production (General Statistics Office 1979, 1982). Furthermore, access of families to the collective production was not fully equitable which exacerbated the process of differentiation. Second, social differentiation was alleviated both in the north and the south following institutional reforms, which frequently took the form of land redistribution. Other studies in Asia show that the process of social differentiation occurs in areas which are subjected to population pressure and production intensification (Hayami and Kikuchi 1981). Intervention through institutional reform is a method by which rural people's differential access to production factors can be regulated.

TABLE 5.5: The Evolution of Peasants' Living Standard and Social Equity in the Rural Areas in Vietnam

	Year	Average Net Income (kg paddy per cap.)	Gini Co-efficient
Red River delta	1930	584	0.43[a]
	1945	370	0.59[a]
	1954	501	0.35
	1957	568	0.07
	1965	596	0.15
	1970	570	0.26
	1978	680	0.25
	1990	692	0.25
Mekong delta	1930	782	0.87[a]
	1955	600	0.84[a]
	1966	866	0.80[a]
	1972	863	0.55[a]
	1981	1,009	0.30
	1990	1,259	0.35

a Gini co-efficient of land ownership.
The paddy price in the Mekong delta is about 80 per cent of that of the Red River delta.

Sources for Red River delta: Gourou (1936), General Statistics Office (1980, 1992), estimates from General Statistics Office (1971, 1979, 1982), and data of provincial statistics offices.
Sources for Mekong delta: Gourou (1940), Callison (1983), US Dept. of Agriculture (1973), Nishimura (1975), General Statistics Office (1982, 1992).

Vietnam's 1993 Land Law will undoubtedly have an impact on future social differentiation, although in what way is not clear at this stage. This latest institutional land reform, unlike those which have preceded it, does not require the re-allocation of unevenly distributed land. Rather, the most important component appears to be that now land use rights can be transferred, leased, inherited, and used as collateral. In other words, the new law sanctions the beginnings of a land market. During the discussion before the adoption of this law, some economists argued that this situation necessarily would lead to the concentration of land into the hands of some farmers while others either engaged in non-agricultural activities, such as the provision of rural services, or moved to the urban areas. However, this outcome is not obvious. In fact Hayami and Kikuchi (1981) found for other agricultural countries in Asia that the economic returns to land

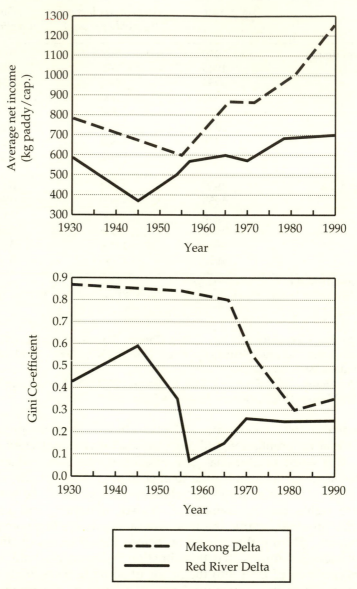

FIGURE 5.3: The Evolution of Peasants' Income and Social Equity

increased much faster than did economic returns to labor, consequently peasants were reluctant to give up their land. Furthermore, in Vietnam the opportunities for rural exodus are limited although this has not prevented urban migration in other industrializing economies.

The socio-economic changes which will occur as a consequence of the 1993 Land Law need to be examined in the context of the rapidly emerging market economy. On the one hand, privatization of agricultural services for providing inputs and marketing outputs may create income generating opportunities in the countryside which would alleviate the negative impact of landlessness. On the other hand the market mechanism of trading and the extension of credit may promote differentiation.

It appears that the most important constraint on rural development is the lack of alternative employment opportunities in order to increase rural incomes. The diversification of agriculture and the development of non-agricultural activities are limited by the lack of markets. The development of the internal market is restricted by the low purchasing power of farmers, and the external market is limited by the lack of increasing demand in the world market.

As was mentioned earlier, the most important constraint on the poor is access to credit whereas for the rich it is the market. In many areas associations are organized by peasants in order to remove these constraints. This tendency must be supported by the government and NGOs.

Appendix

A Method of Household Typology
Based on a Multivariate Statistical Analysis

Normally, in studies of the household economy, households are typologized according to income. In order to devise a typology that better reflects how households function economically in Vietnam, we at the Vietnam Agricultural Science Institute considered various typologies using different combinations of criteria, including:

- production objectives
- production factors
- structures of production
- level of income.

The typology which held the greatest explanatory value turned out to be one based on production objectives. This typology can show household levels in the process of evolution from subsistence to commercial farming. There is also a consistent relation between production objectives and different typologies. In particular, self-sufficient farmers are poor, have less production factors, cannot diversify their economic activities, while commercial farmers are the opposite. The typology of production objectives was constructed by using a cluster analysis method combined with grouping households around the mobile centers with the following criteria: the balance of food stuffs, the financial balance, the value of consumption, and the value of commercial surplus.

The result of this analysis allows us to distinguish among groups of households having different combinations of these criteria. For each group, data are presented on a per capita basis for gross annual income, food balance (i.e., total production of paddy and paddy equivalents of maize, sweet potato, and cassava minus consumption), financial balance (i.e., the gross annual income minus total expenditure), consumption value (i.e., the total value of all consumption) and commercial commodity value (i.e., the value of commercial surplus). For every group of households, the production objective is defined by calculating the function:

$Y = f(C, M)$ where: Y is the value of production
C is the value of consumption
M is the value of commercial surplus.

From this analysis, households can be categorized according to three production objectives:

- production for consumption only
- production for both consumption and the market
- production for the market.

Within the first type we can distinguish three subtypes using the food and financial balance:

- food deficient (having negative food balance),
- reproduction deficient (having negative financial balance),
- reproduction sufficient (having positive financial balance).

Furthermore, it is possible to ascertain the production activities that generate the greatest income for each type, in which:

> R is the production of rice
> F is the production of non rice food crops
> V is the production of vegetables
> A is animal husbandry
> N is non-agricultural activities.

After calculating the relative importance (i.e., above or below average for the village) of the major production factors of land (L), capital (C) and labor (W), the major constraint for each production objective type can be determined using the Cobb-Douglas function $Y = f (L, C, W)$.

Following is the example of the Thai Tan village in the Red River delta.

Result of Classification by the Method of Mobile Centers

Type	Households (%)	Gross annual income	Food balance	Financial balance	Consumption value	Commercial value
1	48	1,041	191	179	533	508
2	27	1,653	255	611	550	1,103
3	10	1,698	313	195	922	776
4	8	1,841	765	852	578	1,262
5	7	2,982	271	1,347	787	2,194
Average		1,479	279	435	600	879

Parameters of the Objective Functions

Type	Constant	Consumption value	Commercial value	Co-efficient of determination	Objective
1	0.79	0.61	0.37	0.90	Consumption
2	0.70	0.32	0.67	0.99	Market
3	2.62	0.36	0.36	0.97	Cons+market
4	0.74	0.30	0.68	0.99	Market
5	0.52	0.24	0.76	0.99	Market

Definition of subtypes with "consumption" objectives:

Type	(There are no households of the type with a negative food balance.)
1	The financial balance and the commercial value are negative: reproduction deficient.
2	The financial balance is negative but less than the commercial value: reproduction sufficient.
3	The financial balance is negative but more than the commercial value: reproduction deficient.

Parameters of Production Functions

Type	Constant	Land	Labor	Capital	Co-efficient of determination	Constraint
1	5.77	-0.11	-0.17	0.30	0.49	Capital
2	6.77	-0.15	-0.03	0.26	0.54	Capital
3	5.00	0.04	-0.07	0.32	0.46	Capital
4	9.08	0.17	0.46	-0.42	0.98	Labor
5	–	–	–	–	–	–

Some functions have relative low co-efficients of determination but from these functions we can see that the co-efficient of elasticity of capital is relatively high compared to other factors.

Notes

*   Special thanks to Professor Stephanie Fahey of the Victoria University of Technology for comments and help during the preparation of this chapter.

1.   This pattern is broadly similar to that reported in the Fforde and Sénèque chapter, this book, though the figures there are somewhat different from the ones here on account of different data sets.

2.   The Gini co-efficient or Gini concentration ratio is an aggregate measure of inequality and can vary anywhere from zero (perfect equality) to one (perfect inequality). In countries with highly unequal income distribution the Gini co-efficient lies between 0.50 and 0.70 while for countries with relatively equitable distribution, it is in the order of 0.20 to 0.35.

3.   The poverty line is defined as an income equivalent to the price of 20 kilograms of rice per month per capita (Center for Population and Labor Resource Research 1993).

References

Callison, C.S. 1983. *Land-to-the-tiller in the Mekong delta*. New York: University Press of America.

Center for Population and Labor Resource Research. 1993. "Doi va Ngheo o Viet Nam" [Hunger and Poverty in Vietnam]. Hanoi.

General Statistics Office, Vietnam.   1971, 1979, 1980, 1982, 1992. *Nien Giam Thong Ke [Statistical Yearbooks]*. Hanoi.

_____. 1991. *Nhung Van de Kinh Te va Doi Song qua Ba Cuoc Dieu Tra Nong Nghiep Cong Nghiep va Nha O* [Economic and Living Problems Through Three Surveys on Agriculture, Industry and Housing]. Hanoi.

_____. 1994. *Ket Qua Dieu Tra Tinh Trang Giau Ngheo o Viet Nam 1993* [Results of Survey of Rich and Poor in Vietnam 1993]. Hanoi.

Gourou, P. 1936. *Les Paysans du Delta Tonkinois*. Paris: Les editions d'art et d'histoire.

_____. 1940. *L'utilisation du sol en Indochine Francaise*. Paris: P. Hartmann.

Hayami, Yujiro and Masao Kikuchi.   1982.   *Asian Village Economy at the Crossroads*. Tokyo: University of Tokyo Press.

Nishimura H. 1975. "Farm management analysis and its problems of rice farming in the Mekong delta." *South-east Asian Studies* 13(1):127-145.

U.S. Department of Agriculture. 1973. *Agriculture in the Vietnam Economy*. Washington: Department of Agriculture.

6

Aspects of Agricultural Economy and Rural Life in 1993

Dang Phong

(translated by Viviane Lowe and Dang Xuan Thu)

In 1992 the Vietnamese economy made quite creditable progress overall: inflation fell, production increased considerably, and the country registered its first ever trade surplus. In 1992 Vietnam exported two million tonnes of rice.[1] By the end of January 1993 the country had exported another 500,000 tonnes, an accomplishment which has drawn praise from even the most critical of experts on Vietnam. Regarding the results, there is obviously a consensus.

When it comes to assessing the complex problems facing the economy, however, the breadth of opinion is much wider. Among the many questions I heard raised by researchers at conferences in Paris (December 1992), Brussels (January 1993), Amsterdam (February 1993) and finally Hanoi (March 1993) one stood out as of special interest theoretically and practically, from both a sociological and economical point of view. Why does agricultural development seem to be lagging behind development in the Vietnamese economy as a whole? And is it not the case that the farmer's standard of living has improved very little?

During the first weeks of March 1993 five fellow researchers and I conducted a series of rapid surveys in five Red River delta provinces: My Duc and Phuc Tho districts in Ha Tay, My Van district in Hai Hung, Gia Vien district in Ninh Binh, Hai Hau district in Nam Ha and Kim Boi district in Hoa Binh; in several provinces in the central part of the country: Trieu Phong district in Quang Tri, and Huong Son district in Ha Tinh; and several in the Mekong delta: Vinh Hung district in

Long An, Tri Ton and Thoai Son districts in An Giang. The objective of this rapid survey was simply to check for any major discrepancies in the economic data we already had collected at the national level and to see for ourselves how, in the countryside today, the liberalization of the market has solved the peasants' problems. This chapter presents some of the observations gathered during this study.

Income from Rice Production

In most of the southern villages visited, the majority of peasant households (four to five people) farm about one hectare of land. This level coincides with the average area of land per agricultural population for the southern delta region as a whole (12.6 million people for 2.8 million hectares of paddy land). About 25-30 per cent of these grow rice; about 18-20 per cent cultivate up to two hectares of paddy.

To calculate the costs and income involved in rice production in 1992 and winter 1993, let us assume that one hectare of land per family is the norm. In most of the southern provinces visited, with the exception of Can Tho, yields had attained an average of six tonnes per hectare per season (while the contracted level was only 4.5 tonnes per hectare per season). In An Giang province especially, quite a few areas and many individual households had achieved yields of ten tonnes per hectare and over, making the province the leading rice producer in the country. In 1992 An Giang's rural population of 1.425 million produced 1.75 million tonnes of rice, more than a tonne per person on average and a threefold increase since 1980 (520,000 tonnes). Assuming an average yield of six tonnes per hectare (or six tonnes per household), as is the case in Vinh Chang and Phu Hoa communes (Thoai Son district), the rice-grower's accounts are as follows: costs for seeds, ploughing, fertilizer, plant protection, irrigation, harvesting, and threshing total about three million dong (of which the cost of services is: irrigation 200,000, ploughing by tractor 200,000, threshing 200,000 and plant protection 100,000 dong). With the market price of paddy at 800-850 dong per kilogram, for each season on each hectare the producer can expect an income of about two million dong, the equivalent of more than two tonnes of paddy.[2] Though in Vietnam as a whole there are three rice seasons (main, winter, and spring), in reality, in any given area fields are usually only cultivated with rice during two seasons. Thus each year one hectare of rice returns an income of four million dong (almost US$400) or an income of about US$100 from rice for each agricultural worker. Given the prices and level of consumption of goods in rural Vietnam, this income places peasants far from the starvation level, but is still not enough for them to become rich or save their money. However, in light of the recent past, when famine and poverty were common occurrences, the present abundance of food represents a major step forward.

In addition to increased incomes from paddy, two other factors yet to be considered are the distribution of land and income earned outside of rice production.

Concentration of Land

Concentration of land is appearing quite strongly in the southern provinces and in some central provinces (in the north the trend is much less pronounced). By "concentration" I mean that some households gain land while others lose land. In the larger districts of An Giang, like Thoai Son and Tri Ton, the level of concentration is higher; in Thoai Son for instance, 23 per cent of households own two hectares or more. These families' income from rice production is sufficient to make them wealthy and allow them to save. With two hectares cultivated in two seasons, they can produce over 20 tonnes of rice, which earns them 10 million dong, enough not only for their daily needs but also to buy agricultural equipment. A number of households have thus been able to purchase pumps or threshers, and a few have even bought ploughs.

In the Plain of Reeds (Dong Thap Muoi) concentration of land is perhaps more extreme than anywhere else in Vietnam. In Vinh Hung district, the family of the district vice president owns as much as 100 hectares, while in every district in the area there are a few families with ten hectares or more. These families can be considered genuinely rich, and manage prosperous family enterprises. Income from rice is very high — for ten hectares it would be around 40-50 million dong per year — but as a rule, large landowners also engage in many other lines of business. For instance, while the vice president of Vinh Hung is kept busy with his work in the district, his wife runs the family business. In addition to their 100 hectares of land, they own a tractor and a thresher, a pump, a petrol station which services the entire area, and a truck. Another household, headed by Tran Van Thai, aged 32, owns eighteen hectares as well as a tractor which is rented out. Mr Thai does not plough himself but hires someone to do the job, according to the following contract: the tractor consumes 7.1 liters of petrol per hectare, for each hectare the worker receives 20,000 dong, meanwhile the fee to the landowner is 200,000 dong per hectare. After subtracting the cost of labor and petrol (14,000 dong per hectare), and wear and tear on the machine, the profit from each hectare ploughed is 150,000 dong. Every season, one tractor might service from 200 to 300 hectares. During the winter-spring crop of 1993, Mr Thai's tractor ploughed 150 hectares, earning him over twenty million dong.

The questions that naturally come to mind at this point are: why does land become concentrated and what are the possible consequences of this trend? Such concentration appears to be inevitable from the moment the market system has penetrated the countryside. Only since the market reforms have people been allowed to buy and sell land (though under the guise of ceding user rights). On the one hand, the system itself has created sellers: families who lack the funds or the labor capacity to farm, or are lazy and degenerate (through addiction to drink or gambling); but there are also those who, far from being poor or incompetent, simply want to capitalize their wealth and move into another, preferred, profession. For the latter, the decision to give up one's land to become an agricultural laborer or engage in another profession is simple. (Under the former cooperative system, their only choice was to remain in the cooperative, so that income made by other cooperators could be shared with them). The market has also created buyers for this land: the rich, those with capital, the ability to organize, and the desire to expand production, since expanding production now means increasing one's income.

In addition to the presence of buyers and sellers, the total amount of land also influences distribution. Generally, the greater the area of land per capita, the higher the level of concentration; and trading in land is most frenzied in newly developed areas. Only in these areas is it possible to acquire twenty hectares or more. The vice president of Vinh Hung district is a case in point. Around 1980, the government used the army to clear land on the outskirts of the Plain of Reeds; once the land was cleared, the government resettled urban population in these areas. These settlers found farming exceedingly difficult and, under a pricing system which paid one-twelfth of the free market price for their produce, many became discouraged. Life in the New Economic Zones (NEZs) was far harsher than the life they had been accustomed to in the cities; many therefore sold their land at very low prices and left. The native inhabitants, accustomed as they were to the local conditions, bought this land to plant fruit trees, industrial crops, and timber in order to avoid the liability of forced delivery of rice to the state. At the time, one hectare sold for 0.27 taels of gold (about US$110). The vice president acquired his 100 hectares by buying up portions in this way. At present, the price of land in the same area has climbed to 2.7 taels per hectare (or US$1,100).

The concentration of land is linked not only to a greater differentiation of rich and poor, but also to the emergence of a division of labor within agriculture. This is perhaps the most important process at work in the rural area as a direct cause of the market system. The process is apparent not only in regions where land is abundant, but also, and perhaps to a greater extent, where land is scarce. The rural population need not and can not cling forever to such small plots of land for its livelihood (in some places there is only one-fifth to one-third of a hectare per household). Therefore, some of these peasants have sold their land in order to accumulate some funds and change professions.

Meanwhile, the market economy has begun to open up a number of alternatives in this direction. In fact, it would be more correct to say that it is not poverty, but rather dissatisfaction with their excessively low standard of living that impels peasants both in land-rich and land-poor areas to seek countless alternative sources of livelihood. We not only see poor, incompetent or lazy farmers forced to sell land to richer farmers, but also rich farmers who sell to less rich than they. This process could be called, for lack of a better term, "de-rice-ification" or a move away from rice cultivation by much of the rural population, a trend that will certainly intensify. Simultaneously, rural poverty is clearly in sharp decline. According to a recent survey conducted by An Giang provincial authorities, the number of poor families in the province (incomes of less than 50,000 dong per person per month) has fallen from 16 per cent to 10 per cent. The distribution of incomes in An Giang is as follows (according to the same survey):

- below average (incomes below 85,000 dong per person per month): 43%
- average (85,000 to 330,000 dong per person per month): 49%
- rich (above 330,000 dong per person per month): 8%

Decreased Dependence on Rice Cultivation

In recent years, several factors have created new sources of income for peasants:

- urbanization and the level of consumption of the cities have increased very rapidly (due to higher urban incomes, tourism, etc.);
- the opening of the borders, especially the border with China, has increased the value of a number of goods which previously had practically no market;
- local populations are now allowed to exploit the natural resources of their area (gold, gems, building stone, etc.);

- economic development of the countryside, including plant production, has created a demand for rural services: village shops, services such as hulling rice, transportation, baking lime, making bricks, carpentry, mat weaving, and so on.

These changes have opened up new horizons beyond farming. The land is limited while these other occupations are practically limitless, and as a source of income they provide peasants with an alternative to migrating to the cities (the only option during collectivization). They can remain in their village but still make a good living, without owning a lot of land or even cultivating rice. The next few pages are devoted to presenting some concrete examples of the changes which we observed.

In many portions of the Plain of Reeds which have not yet been cleared, farmers continue to plant floating rice which has a very low yield (during the flood season nothing else can be planted). After the floating rice season (the yield is around 2-2.5 tonnes per hectare or just enough for home consumption) they used to sow mung beans or soybeans straight onto the field, without any fertilizer; and with very low yields they got very little out of it. Since 1992, they have stopped planting beans, and instead planted corn. The peasants discovered the potential of this crop themselves. Using an Indian variety imported from Thailand, they obtain the very high yield of 10 tonnes per hectare, with far less fertilizer than they would need for rice. The seeds are very expensive — 40,000 dong per kilogram in January 1993 — but the final product is also highly priced — 1,200 dong per kilogram, i.e., higher than paddy. One hectare of corn requires 25 kilograms of seed at a cost of one million dong, but the income can reach twelve million dong. Other costs, for ploughing, harvesting, and husking might add up to two million dong. This leaves an income of eight or nine million dong per hectare. The endemically poor areas of floating rice agriculture are now counting on corn to carry them forward.

Why is corn so much more expensive than rice, who buys it, and what do they use it for? Most of the corn produced is consumed domestically, and almost entirely as animal feed. It appears that the biggest consumer of corn is Saigon, a rapidly developing city, where demand for meat is large. This fuels the demand for livestock which in turn stimulates the production of livestock feed. As feed, corn is more highly valued than rice because one kilogram of corn is one kilogram of food, while only 650 grams out of a kilogram of paddy is edible. Intensive urbanization (i.e., not only growth in urban population but also growth in demand and supply of goods) has created a new sector within Vietnamese agriculture: the production of animal feed which previously was insignificant. According to the provincial statistics, the total pig population of An Giang province in 1992 had doubled since 1991, while poultry (chicken and ducks) numbered three million head (an average of two animals per rural inhabitant). This had never happened before.

In addition to livestock farming and the production of animal feed, fresh water aquaculture (using bamboo cages) is also developing rapidly. One cage covering a water surface of 1 per cent of a hectare (100 square meters) can yield an income equivalent to one hectare of rice land, but the investment required is also no less than for one hectare of rice.

All the new opportunities described above have created employment possibilities for peasants. According to An Giang provincial statistics, the non-agricultural sector created employment for 130,000 people in 1992, or 9 per cent of the agricultural population of the province, the equivalent of one-fourth of the increase in population (growth rate of 2.3 per cent in 1992).

On the way back to Hanoi from the Mekong delta, the team stopped in several districts in the center of the country to assess the present situations in these areas whose poverty of arable land is well known. In Quang Tri province, we made a stop in Trieu Phong district, home of the late Secretary General Le Duan. This area carries a reputation a few centuries old for the poverty of its soil and people. By 1980, the average food crop production per inhabitant had reached only 200-250 kilograms of paddy. In 1992 however, many communes achieved levels twice or three times this figure: 610 kilograms in Trieu Thuan, 600 kilograms in Trieu Dong, 430 kilograms in Thanh Cong. Most villages reached at least 400 kilograms per inhabitant.

While the district is no longer plagued by hunger, overall it is still very poor. Even assuming a level 500-600 kilograms of paddy per person, the small amount of arable land per cultivator (Trieu Thuan has 400 hectares for a population of 4,900, Bich La 185 hectares for 2,500 people), means that no amount of increase in yields will allow peasants to enrich themselves if they continue to rely entirely on rice. But these peasants still have no opportunities to move away from rice farming. In contrast to other regions, Trieu Phong is far removed from the large markets of Saigon, Hanoi, and the Chinese border.

Bordering a narrow strip of rice fields are mountains to the west and the ocean to the east. Turning to the mountains as a way of escape requires substantial capital: to clear land, plant trees, and wait out the minimum three to five years before an income can be reaped from the investment. Bich La cooperative has been encouraging peasants to farm mountainous land, but over the past two years has only succeeded in persuading fifteen families (comprising twenty adult laborers) to make the move. Up until now these families have been able to raise only twelve buffalos, in addition to which they farm a few plots of gourds and tea. Their life is very difficult, and nothing ensures that they will remain contentedly settled there. The other alternative is to turn towards the ocean to fishing or prawning. Many have tried this but their income remains very low. In Trieu Lan village, only 1,200 inhabitants grow rice, while 900 work as fishermen; there are 150 fishing boats in the village, which do not venture beyond 5-10 kilometers from the coast because none are motorized. In 1992 the total catch was 400 kilograms of fish and prawns, an average of about half a tonne per fisherman, most of it small fish which were sold locally or dried. To catch more highly priced fish, the fishermen would need motor power in order to go farther out to sea, as well as refrigeration facilities on board. Both improvements require large investment, but where in this impoverished area could they raise the capital? The average fisherman earns only three to four million dong per year. Assuming each laborer must feed on average 1.5 dependants, this works out to an actual income of 100,000 dong per person per month, enough to live on but still very little, although it is quite an improvement over incomes four to five years ago.

Continuing on our way north the team stopped in Ha Tinh province, where we heard the following tale of unexpected good fortune regarding deer farming. In traditional Chinese medicine ginseng and antlers have always been prized drugs. The antler is actually the antler of a male deer. Each pair sells for 2.5 million dong (March 1993 prices). The market for this product is big, and located mainly in Hanoi and Saigon, as demand for the antler rises proportionally to the average wealth and age of the population. Peasants in Ha Tinh farm a total of 5,000 head of deer, and the idea is catching on fast; the number of deer is expected to rise to 7,000-8,000 by 1994. Deer farming does not require any great expenditure of effort or money, the large initial investment aside. The average income from one animal, however, is at least equivalent to that of one hectare of paddy. The vice president of the province said that the herd at this stage could be considered the equivalent of 5,000 additional hectares of land brought under cultivation. For a province like Ha Tinh, arid and poor in arable land, this type of "cultivation" takes on special significance.

The deer farmers' cost accounting is as follows: a male deer costs five million dong (about US$500) and produces one pair of antlers each year, which is removed in April, and is worth 2.5 million dong. In other words the farmer reaps an income of 2.5 million dong per annum for an initial outlay of 5 million dong. The stable and feed cost very little and an elderly person or child easily suffices to care for one or two animals. Thus keeping one male deer is at least as profitable as farming one hectare of paddy. While the female deer does not produce antlers, she produces offspring. A three-month old doe costs 25 million dong; she gives birth to one litter per year. If male, the fawn can be sold for five million dong; if female, it will bring in 25 million dong. The peasants follow this simple calculation: if on average a doe produces a male offspring the first year and a female the next, the income over two years averages 30 million dong. The initial investment of 25 million dong therefore allows a return of fifteen million dong per year.

Breeding deer is far more profitable than raising them for the antlers alone, but the capital required is too large for most people. The peasants have come up with a solution to this problem which serves the interests both of the investors and the person who raises the deer. About one-third of the deer in the province are kept by their owners, while the remaining two-thirds are either jointly owned and raised or "leased" or a combination of the two. The deer is divided into four shares, called "legs"; those with little capital purchase one "leg," others buy two or even three "legs." The profit, on the other hand is divided into five parts, one for each share and a fifth which goes to the person actually caring for the animal — the peasants of Ha Tinh thus say that their deer have "five legs." This illustrates the important role played by the investor among rural population. But in order to make the caretaker more responsible, only the owner of at least one "leg" is allowed to keep the deer; he then keeps two "legs" of the income.

Many officials in Ha Tinh stated optimistically that the peasants would "ride the deer to wealth." It is still unclear how incomes and prices will be regulated by the market in the future, when the number of deer increases. But recently, as we noticed, a couple of thousand families have been able to build new houses thanks to deer farming.

The mountain provinces of the north all seem to be engaged in quarrying building stone and prospecting for gold and gems. In Phu Quang district (Nghe An) a couple of hundred people have made fortunes overnight from rubies, and even those not so lucky still earn far more than they used to. This is not to mention the 20,000 or so people who earn a living from trading and providing services for the mining towns. They are making much more than they could from rice farming. In the provinces of Hoa Binh, Yen Bai, Son La, Lang Son, Bac Thai, and Lao Cai entire districts have flocked to mine and pan gold. Banking experts estimate that in recent years up to 30-40 tonnes of gold nuggets have been excavated by rural prospectors. In fact a large portion of the profit ends up in the hands of gold merchants and contractors, since many peasants simply work as laborers. Even in this case, what they earn as day-laborers when they are not busy farming, brings a considerable improvement in their standard of living. Anyone who visited the districts of Kim Boi (Hoa Binh), Phu Quy (Nghe An), Cam Thuy (Thanh Hoa) or Ngan Son (Bac Can) a few years ago would be surprised to find these isolated, destitute areas now transformed into bustling little towns, crammed with shops and stalls, with new houses going up in every village and hamlet. There is no denying that the lives of peasants here have changed enormously.

A further factor affecting northern and north-central peasants is the opening of trade routes across the border with China, which has created a new source of income through demand for goods which formerly had little or no commercial value. Many food items which previously were consumed by the peasants themselves or sold cheaply in local markets have suddenly increased in value fivefold or even tenfold: eels, frogs, snails, tortoises, turtles, geckos, otter pelts, and scaly ant-eaters. Before resumption of trade across the Chinese border, one kilogram of tortoise cost as much as one kilogram of pork (i.e., between 10,000 and 12,000 dong). Now the going price is 130,000 dong per kilogram, compared to 20,000-30,000 dong per kilogram for pork; snails are 6,000-7,000 dong per kilogram, frogs 70,000-80,000 dong per kilogram, otter skins 600,000-700,000 dong each, and scaly anteater tails 800,000 dong per kilogram. The demand originates from what seems like a whole network that has been set up by merchants all over the country.

We had a closer look at the situation in Tuy Lai, a commune in My Duc district, Ha Tay, about 50 kilometers from Hanoi. Peasants here do not have much land, on average one-tenth of a hectare per family, but the commune includes a lake and a hill. One young man, married with four children, told us his life used to be exceedingly hard as he farmed only three *sao* (1,080 square meters) which did not yield enough to live on. Last year he started catching turtles; the sale of his first four turtles allowed him to buy a sewing machine, three more turtles bought him a bicycle. Five years ago, he said, he could not have dreamed that he would ever own a sewing machine. The commune vice president reported that in 1992 families in Tuy Lai acquired twenty sewing machines and about thirty bicycles thanks to the sale of turtles, frogs, scaly anteaters, snails, and eels.

Of course, the negative side of this economic activity is that the source is drying up; in the past couple of years many of these animals have started to become rare. Vietnam may soon follow the pattern of many developing nations. Only when natural resources have been almost completely exhausted will people think of protecting them and turn to farming as a simple method of obtaining the same products without plundering their environment.

Since the end of 1992, the Chinese market has "eaten" another product — green bananas. All over the Red River delta and northern midlands a trend is emerging to plant banana trees for export to China. Chinese trucks drive right down to villages in the delta and on the spot buy up the fruit by whole truck loads, at a price of 1,300 dong per kilogram. For the peasants, this is twice the normal price they would receive. Today, if you walk along a dike in the Red River delta (banana plantations are usually located on either side of canals), every five to ten minutes you cross a cart carrying bananas to market.

Around the large cities, Hanoi for example, there are probably 20,000 or so peasants who make a living from providing goods and services to the city dwellers. Almost all the peddlers who buy old bottles, scraps of copper or iron, waste paper, etc. come from villages in the periphery of Hanoi some 20 to 30 kilometers distant. Vendors work their way through every street and alley of the city selling brooms, feather dusters, baskets, rice spirits and sticky rice wine, sharpening knives and scissors, and carding cotton quilts. These peddlers usually turn out to be peasants who still work in the fields but because of a surplus of labor have had to find additional work.

In Hanoi, several streets are lined with silk, embroidery, and lace shops which cater mainly to tourists and Vietnamese going abroad. Upon closer inspection, these boutiques turn out to be merely shop-fronts, in the strictest sense, as the goods are mainly produced in the countryside. The embroiderers and lace-makers are peasants living in villages 30 to 40 kilometers from Hanoi. Once a week, the shop owner sends an employee out to the village by motorcycle to bring each family its piecework and bring back the finished work. As a simple test of this fact, just try walking into a shop and asking for some item to be embroidered on the spot and ready in a day or two.

There are many other examples of this kind. But those described above suffice to show that the market economy has opened up many sources of income for peasants other than the traditional and very limited alternative of planting rice.

There are two points that I would like to draw out here. Firstly, that concentration of land does not necessarily go hand in hand with the pauperization of a mass of landless peasants or smallholders. Many contemporary political scientists and economists in Vietnam worry excessively about the political and social consequences of this trend. They are haunted by the history of concentration of land under colonialism, when peasants had almost no decent alternatives to making a living off the land. Their plight is chronicled in a whole series of essays and novels of the period, and has been summed up most recently by Ngo Vinh Long (University of Maine) in the recently republished *Before the Revolution*.[3] Today, however, we are witnessing a very different trend, one which took place long ago in all industrialized countries. To keep 40 million people living off six or seven million hectares of rice land is not a permanent solution, nor is it the best. It would be far better if alternative occupations could be found for a large portion of the daily increasing rural population (the only solution available), leaving only six or seven million people, or even better still, only one or two million people, to farm these six to seven million hectares.

Secondly, the decreased reliance of the rural population on rice cultivation is not synonymous with the urbanization of the population (I refer here to *deriziculturation de la population rurale* and not *deriziculturation de l'economie*).[4] Formerly, when cooperatives existed in the countryside, a subsidized system also existed in the state sector in the cities (industries and state offices). The cooperative system made life unbearable for the peasants, and left them no alternative other than to flee to the city to try by any means possible to obtain a job in a factory or a government office (which provided a salary, ration stamps, lodgings, etc.) As a consequence, the urban population rose quickly under this pressure which the state was incapable of preventing. The population of Hanoi thus went from 300,000 in 1954 to two million in 1990. Of course, this increase did not represent any sort of progress, it was simply the result of the failure of collective agriculture along with the ever increasing parasitism of industry and the state apparatus. In the past three years this pressure has subsided of its own accord. The wave of rural-urban migration seems to have come to an end, although there have been no new measures in this direction from the state. The halting of the rate of urbanization in recent years is only a manifestation of the development and greater health of the industrial and agricultural sector, (as well as a population structure which coincides with the actual circumstances of the economic structure). The market system allowed this miraculous harmonization, a result never achieved by decrees and regulations, though there were a great many of these, or by the city migration police, however powerful.

The Service Sector and the Division of Labor Within Agriculture

Let us return for a minute to the Mekong delta, where in the last couple of years new forms of division of labor have appeared and developed. These innovations are basically peasant initiatives, and even if they are the product of research at a higher echelon, it is still the peasants who really find a purpose and use for them.

I already mentioned ploughing, irrigation, and threshing services. Driving along country roads in the southwest, one hardly ever sees farmers building bamboo drying racks or spreading rice stalks to thresh their rice in the field, as these traditional methods are practically no longer used. Instead, there are entrepreneurs who rent out their services and threshing machines to farmers. This is the product of two new trends: 1) the yields and productivity of farmers have risen to the point where they can afford to hire such services, and to where it is more advantageous to hire out than to do the job oneself; 2) peasants now have the right to sell their services, and they have the capital to invest in the tools of their trade. The result is that ploughing, irrigation, and threshing are consistently contracted out. To cut and carry the paddy to the thresher, farmers hire agricultural laborers. As mentioned earlier, the cost of ploughing one hectare of paddy is 200,000 dong, irrigation for the same area costs another 200,000 dong; threshing costs are computed in two different ways: if it is low quality rice, the fee is 200,000 dong per hectare, if it is good quality rice, the thresher gets 1/25th of the product, i.e., for every 25 baskets of 22 kilograms, he gets to keep the 26th. Harvesters are paid 7,000 dong per day, while carrying bales of paddy is paid at the rate of 12,000 dong (because it involves carrying heavy loads across the fields, and is comparatively harder work).

Needless to say, the owners of ploughs, threshers, and pumps are rich peasants and "proprietors" if not of land then of services, but harvesters and other agricultural laborers also earn incomes around 200,000 dong per month, no less than the income of the average rice producer. In fact many peasants do not want to farm, and prefer to give up their land to work as hired labor because they are freer and the work is easier. This demonstrates one of the points made earlier, i.e., that the concentration of land does not necessarily result in the landless portion of the population being reduced to indigence.

In An Giang, another new service has appeared — pest control. Up until recently, farmers did this themselves (this is still the case in the north and center, as well as much of the south). If the crop was infested, they had to go out and buy pesticides and apply them themselves. Since the fate of the harvest (and their own livelihood) may depend on it, they naturally take a keen interest in this. This is good, but also has its drawbacks. Because of their lack of experience, they cannot fulfil this need satisfactorily; either they spray before it becomes necessary, or they realize only too late that they should have already sprayed. Most households exceed the recommended application, both wasting the pesticide and harming the environment.

In an effort to overcome this absurd situation, the province of An Giang has started to build a system of pesticide application services throughout the province (Integrated Pest Management). The system extends from the provincial to the commune level. At the provincial level, the agriculture development bureau monitors the situation, information, trends, and perspectives of the project for the whole province. The most important unit is the district pest control team, which includes members in every commune of the district (about three people in each). The team contracts with farmers to monitor the pest situation, and takes the necessary measures in time; if the crop becomes infested, causing loss to the producer, then the team must pay compensation. The district employees, delegated by the pest control team to the communes, must therefore monitor the situation in the fields daily, discover pests in time to act, and know when and how much to spray.

The pests naturally do not follow any set schedule, nor do they take into account who is the owner of the field they are destroying. This is why pest control cannot be the responsibility of individual landowners and producers. The centralization of pest control has been in effect for two years with very good results, and the peasants recognize that it is far better than the system followed previously. The province of An Giang had a bumper crop after the terrible infestation of brown hoppers, which caused heavy damage to the 1990-91 winter crop in much of the south, was successfully eradicated. An Giang has also emerged as the country's leading producer and exporter of rice. (Hau Giang, now Can Tho province, had held first place for the previous fifteen years). A further interesting result, is that this form of service makes pest control far cheaper than it used to be. The provincial office estimates that previously peasants could spend up to 400,000 dong per hectare, especially when spraying at the height of an epidemic, whereas integrated pest management has brought this cost down to an average of 100,000 dong per hectare. This is another example of how in the market economy, peasants have finally found the optimal solution to their problems.

Some Remaining Problems

Of course the outlook for agriculture and the rural areas of Vietnam is not entirely rosy. Many problems remain, some which have been in existence for a long time, others which have recently appeared but for which no solutions have yet been found. Perhaps the biggest problem for peasants today is the availability of capital. To increase the division of labor and develop non-agricultural occupations, i.e. to effect a move away from rice cultivation without leaving a portion of the rural population unemployed and impoverished, capital is needed. For those households who have the skills and ability to expand production, increase the yields and quality of their crops, capital is a necessity, in order to buy new seeds and improve farming technology. Improvements in agricultural infrastructure — raising the level of transportation and irrigation services, and strengthening the technological basis — also require capital. Storage and processing facilities also are still very poor, which considerably reduces the value of crops. All these problems can be solved only through investment.

But private investment in agriculture so far has been limited, because by and large the capital held by the rural population is insufficient to solve the problems enumerated above (even supposing all this capital could be mobilized). The national bank clearly does not have the power to fulfil all the agricultural sector's needs for capital. The problem is difficult to solve. In the credit market, the collapse of private credit cooperatives in 1990 had grave consequences, and it is now very difficult to borrow money, because everyone is afraid of lending. The biggest problem with the system of lending on collateral is that poor peasants have nothing to borrow against. In some southern provinces, peasants have invented a new form of credit, which they call "borrowing on reputation," whereby a number of respected members of the community stand as guarantors for the borrower. In some areas peasants can still use their certificates of land usage rights as collateral. Nevertheless, the amount of money borrowed and numbers of people prepared to lend money are still low. Foreign and overseas Vietnamese business people are naturally unwilling, and would find it difficult to invest in an agricultural sector where there is not proper land ownership, and land is still dispersed among too many small producers.

Next in line after capital is processing of agricultural produce. Every year it seems there is at least one commodity which suffers from obstacles at the level of disposing of or processing the crop. Currently the south is flooded with sugar cane and raw sugar. The existing mills can process what the peasants produce, but because these mills are small they cannot extract all the sugar from the cane. Now that the price of sugar has fallen dramatically, the cost of processing has become too high, and the processed sugar must be sold at a loss. Consequently, these mills are no longer buying sugar cane. Even the state-run mills cannot consume the entire production. Farmers contemplate with disgust the heaps of cut cane that no one will buy piling up by the side of the roads. The price of sugar cane has fallen to 700-650 dong per tonne, lower than it has ever been relative to rice. Yet still no one will buy it.

Why does the state not invest in or encourage individuals to invest in developing sugar production in order to consume the cane produced by peasants, since we are at the same time importing sugar? There would appear to be advantages for both sides in this arrangement. The problem is that like every other agricultural produce, sugar cane still suffers from great instability. In many years past, and probably in many years to come, sugar cane production was insufficient to satisfy the sugar mills (because low prices or low profits discouraged producers). Mills had insufficient raw material and had to run on empty; purchasing officers went right to the fields to snatch up the sugar cane for the factories. The price of sugar cane sky-rocketed, the price of finished sugar increased as a result and could no longer compete with imported sugar. Thus, the dilemma which must be resolved is not only investment in processing, but also the state of extreme insecurity in agriculture (insecurity of production and of price).

Vegetable farmers in the Red River delta experienced a similar crisis in January and February of this year. There was a bumper crop of cabbages and tomatoes, but no money to be made from it. In many places, like Thai Binh, Nam Ha, the best quality tomatoes went for only 500 dong per kilogram, i.e., one US dollar would buy twenty kilograms. Still no one would buy them. Cabbages could be cut up and fed to pigs as a supplement to their diet, but farmers had to resign themselves to throwing away the tomatoes. Driving along the highway one could see tonne after tonne of tomatoes dumped in field by the side of the road.

This sorry sight prompted some observers to wonder why no one thought of investing in canning tomatoes? If such an industry existed it would be wonderful, they said, the price of tomatoes would multiply by twenty, and most importantly, it would save tomato farmers from bankruptcy. However, a processing industry requires security, though it may be only relative, in quantity and price of the raw materials. The problem with cabbages, tomatoes, and many other products in Vietnam is that though there may suddenly be an abundance of produce at a very low price, nothing ensures that if a processing plant were completed it would still find enough raw material to operate and avoid failure — this is the present contradiction. No one yet dares to invest in this area of processing, because the level of risk is still too high. Before any investment in processing of agricultural produce goes ahead, there must be investment and a plan (possibly in the form of contracts) to ensure the relative stability of agricultural production. If this were possible, there would be advantages for industry, the export sector, and agriculture, and above all it would contribute to the aim of decreasing reliance on rice.

If the market economy has engendered such contradictions, sooner or later it is bound to find solutions to them as well. The free market in Vietnam has only been developing over the past few years. It would be truly unreasonable to expect it to succeed in solving immediately problems which still occasionally plague even a market economy which has developed over many years. A few years are necessary for the forces of demand and supply to meet. Both forces are still shaky and unstable. If the potential and effectiveness of sugar cane or vegetables production are really proved permanently, and not just temporarily, then there will be investors for the processing industry. This will be tested in the future. For the time being, one need not be too pessimistic about this quandary, although for the producers themselves, who are saddled with a couple of tonnes of unsold sugar cane, or a couple of tonnes of tomatoes that have to be thrown away, there is still cause for absolute pessimism.

A third problem, which in many areas stands out as of first importance, concerns questions of social justice. These are complicated and interrelated; among them are both real problems and false ones, and both material and non-material reasons.

Land use rights is one of these problems. If the concentration of land occurs through transactions such as those described above, then peasants themselves can hardly fail to recognize that it is a reasonable exchange. But in the past twenty-odd years the many changes and reversals in regional boundaries instituted by the state inadvertently caused losses to many areas. This has caused disputes and in places even bloodshed. The role of the state as the only and supreme arbiter in matters of property rights for every type of land throughout the whole country has given local officials the absurd right to give land to this person or that, not least to themselves. This system of administering land rights has created a group of people who have accumulated large landholdings not through land clearing or market transactions but by abusing the power of their position. This of course is unjust and illegal, and causes discontent among peasants. But it is difficult to put things right, when the only alternatives are to use state authority to repair these injustices, or to reject this very authority. In the not so distant future, the government will certainly be forced to introduce regulations which force people who have appropriated land illegally to return it, or to pay to redeem the land they own, as is the case now with the privatization of state-owned housing.

People who have been left unfit for work or disabled as a consequence of the war suffer an historical injustice. By no means are all peasants who sell land to go and hire themselves out as laborers doing well as a result. Quite a high proportion of the rural population, in places up to 10 per cent, cannot keep up with the momentum of the contemporary developments in agriculture, through no fault of their own. If no solutions are found to this social problem, it may not be long before the following situation occurs: the sons and daughters of men who died in the war of liberation, the wounded and disabled, and the veterans who sacrificed their youth and strength in the war, will have to hire themselves out to rich landlords, perhaps the very people who by chance or cunning managed to escape serving their country during the same war. Any society has its injustices, there is no reason why the impartial recognition of the reality of such an evolution should cause us any anguish ... or is there?

Finally, a few comments are in order about the complaints of peasants regarding the level of contributions they pay. Under the product contract system, peasants' obligations were very light: agricultural tax was 8 per cent of the contracted amount only (which represented 70-80 per cent of the total production). In 1991 and 1992, the tax was reduced by half to 4 per cent of the estimated production, in respect of President Ho Chi Minh's wish, expressed in his will, that after the war ended peasants should be given one year of tax exemption. Nevertheless, wherever we went peasants complained about the high level of contributions. The brevity of the study trip and our crowded work schedule did not allow us to investigate all the evidence concerning items of contributions from peasants who submitted their complaints, although in our capacity as government price inspectors we had the authority to do so. In fact we had only one afternoon to interview in detail two farmers in An Giang, who complained that contributions for all items had risen above 40 per cent of production. In the north we spoke to one farmer in Tuy Lai commune, Ha Tay and two farmers in Hai Hung who complained of extortion and oppression at the hands of local administrators. The sample represented here is too small to allow us to generalize.

Nevertheless, we did uncover a few problems. It is clear that the official tax rate of 4 per cent of production is much lower than the real level of contributions, although we have not yet been able to calculate the latter. Local governments in many regions have arbitrarily introduced a number of exaggerated and unlawful levies. For instance, in My Duc district (Ha Tay) the communal authorities imposed a fee to enter the market (Ba Tha market). This market is located next to the Day river which is crossed by a large bridge. The commune on the other shore could not collect fees from the market so they imposed a toll on the bridge. The two communes were at cross-purposes, so finally they removed the planks from the bridge to force people to cross by ferry, and to pay their toll on either side. One commune in Hoai Duc district, Ha Tay, imposed a toll on all motorized vehicles entering the village. It also levied a fee from the young ice cream vendors who enter the village to sell their wares. Hop Thach commune in My Duc district requires people to pay a fee for the right to fish in the communal lake and to trap birds; these taxes have been instigated by local authorities with no legal basis. One village in Hai Hung province made villagers who were constructing new houses to pay a "fine" for the "offence" of building a house. Stories of this kind abound. The only new development is that now peasants can go all the way to Hanoi to sue, and quite often win their cases. But the cost of bringing a group of people to Hanoi to wait for a trial makes legal action expensive. Most peasants just put up with the impositions so long as they do not get excessive.

Conversely, some of these complaints are the result of the peasants' own muddled calculations. Two farmers in An Giang listed irrigation fees, cost of transporting fertilizer, interest on bank loans, etc., among the levies they regarded as excessive. One even included the cost of buying rice seed from the seed station on credit. No wonder then that the level of "contributions" reaches 40 per cent.

It seems that everywhere this year both peasants and local officials complained that the price of many crops was too low. In addition to sugar cane and vegetables, paddy also suffered a fall in price to about 700-750 dong per kilogram on the market. This resulted in a great loss for the producers. But that is the very danger of the market system. Since 1992 the state has sought to protect peasants by instituting minimum purchasing prices (850 dong per kilogram for good quality paddy in the south). In April of this year, the government decided to establish a price stabilization fund, the main purpose of which is to tax commodities which enjoy super profits in order to subsidize prices for farmers. If this fund works properly (and only time and experience will tell), it would be very useful to peasants. It will also be another step forward on the road towards a market economy upon which the Vietnamese state has embarked.

Conclusion

The results of this rapid survey left all the researchers feeling optimistic but not entirely reassured. We feel confident enough to oppose the view that in recent years Vietnamese agriculture has grown too slowly and that the peasants' standard of living has changed very little. We also stand on the side of those who would not blindly believe the statistics published by the General Statistics Office. But the figures of 24 million tonnes of food (in paddy equivalent) produced in 1992, an increase in cultivated land of 3 per cent, and an increase in yield of 7 per cent seem to coincide with the facts which we encountered, heard, and saw in the areas we surveyed. The fact that while export of rice reached two million tonnes in 1992 and an additional 500,000 tonnes in the first quarter of 1993, the price of rice domestically remained stable and at times even dropped, confirms that the country is producing food in abundance.

Growth of 10 per cent per annum in agriculture, if it can be verified, is far from slow. I would emphasize that increases in agriculture are more real than increases in other sectors of the economy. In agriculture there are fewer factors that distort the growth figures, such as favorable interest rates or excessively low depreciation of capital enjoyed by industry. Similarly there is no tax evasion, smuggling or exploitation of workers which contribute to the profit margins of the service sector.

Do I have any personal feelings about the present situation? Certainly. Though the feeling may be futile, I deeply regret that the present evolution of Vietnamese agriculture and the rural sector did not begin as early as the mid to late 1970s, after the end of the war. If this had been the case, agriculture and farmers would already have reached a level that they will only reach by the year 2000. By the mid 1970s peasants had already recognized the advantages of the cooperative system and made use of them. Yet during that period the theories which guided economic policy progressed much more slowly than the economic realities. Therefore the agricultural sector had to wait a couple of decades for the reforms which would allow it to catch up with the rate of change in the private sector. Nevertheless, this slowness, regrettable as it is, at least drives home the lesson that to transform the economic life of a country one must be attentive to the problems and questions that are expressed and act on them in time, and not only take the initiative and lead the way for the new forces born from this lively economic activity, but also help them and protect them along the road.

Notes

1.   Of that two tonnes, 1.4 tonnes were exported by the state.

2.   For the time period covered in this chapter, about 10,500 dong equalled one US dollar [eds].

3.   Ngo Vinh Long. 1991. *Before the Revolution: The Vietnamese Peasants Under the French.* New York: Columbia University Press.

4.   The original is in French.

7

Rice Production, Agricultural Research, and the Environment

Vo-Tong Xuan

Introduction

While other countries have enjoyed peaceful conditions for economic development, it has been difficult for Vietnam to recuperate from the wars that caused immeasurable devastation to people's lives and properties and to the country's natural resources, particularly in the countryside. Social welfare facilities in the villages remain below the standards necessary to support modern living for the rural population. In the Mekong delta, the nation's rice bowl composed of four million hectares, the scars of war are posing many problems for rural development. In the north, where the country was long under a dogmatic socialist system, resources were heavily invested in the struggle for national independence, leaving little available for improving people's living standards. Though for centuries Vietnam has been at the crossroads of Eastern and Western civilizations, it has not been able to capitalize on this during the twentieth century because much precious time and resources have been consumed by war. Once the wars finally ended, food production became the prime concern of the newly unified government. Not surprisingly, until now the government of Vietnam persists in emphasizing rice growing in order to assure a sufficient supply of this basic food for the nation's people.

This chapter first looks at key features of rural development during the mid 1970s-1980s. It then examines some of the important resource and environmental conditions affecting rice agriculture, especially in the Mekong delta, and research and extension work that is being pursued in order to enhance production that is environmentally sustainable.

Rural Development, Mid 1970s to 1980s

Collectivization

During and after nearly 40 years of war, the country has been plagued by a shortage of technical competence to carry out economic development activities. Farmers returned to their lands after 1975 and were pushed by the government into an accelerated rice production program. The new political system favored a top-down approach in agricultural development; farmers were told to follow orders from local government officers and managers of cooperatives. While farmers needed improved technology and agricultural inputs, government officers at all levels, still fresh from military service, did not possess the necessary skills and materials to meet those needs. And yet they were preparing to carry out a comprehensive collectivization of agricultural production in the south similar to what had been done in the north.

The collectivization of agriculture in northern Vietnam involved three phases: the formation of work-exchange teams (1956-1958); the establishment of low ranked cooperatives (1958-1960); and the advancement of cooperatives from low rank to high rank (1960-1980). The work-exchange team arrangement allowed farmers to continue to own land and equipment, but integrated production was encouraged through participation in seasonal or permanent work teams. Members of seasonal teams undertook collective work during peak labor periods, such as planting or harvesting rice. There was no payment for participation in seasonal teams, since this was considered mutual aid. A team could include a whole hamlet or several families. The permanent team was an arrangement by which farming families continued to work their own land but were members of a year-round team, such as the fertilizer team, the pesticide spray team, or the mechanization team. Members of a permanent team were paid according to work days or work points. In a low ranking cooperative, individual ownership of crop land, draft animals, and farm implements were preserved. While all farm operation was done in accordance with a common plan of the cooperative, a member's share of output was proportional to the amount of land, livestock, and farm machinery the member contributed. Each member also received part of the gross yield of the cooperative, a share determined by how much labor each contributed to seasonal and permanent work teams. The high rank cooperative resembled the Soviet collective farm. Members pooled their land and tools to work under a unified management. Land and other factor payments were eliminated and output was shared solely on the basis of the amount of time spent working in production teams. Each worker was assigned points for the quantity and quality of work done each day. Payment at the end of the season was based on the number of points accumulated.

Collectivization in the south was different from the northern provinces because land reform had been completed before 1975 and a private enterprise economy had flourished until 1975. In 1976 the Fourth National Convention of the Communist party adopted Resolution 4, which urged all party leaders in the provinces of southern Vietnam to move gradually toward collectivization, with the goal of completing most rice areas by 1980. The Central coastal provinces and the Western high plateau provinces moved very rapidly toward collectivization: 90 per cent and 52 per cent of the farmers in these regions, respectively, joined the cooperatives (Pingali and Vo-Tong Xuan 1990). Farmers in the Mekong delta provinces, however, resisted collectivization, except in some resettled districts. Even by 1986, less than 6 per cent of the Mekong delta farmers belonged to an agricultural cooperative. Those that did could be classified as low ranking cooperatives or production groups. This does not mean that collectivization efforts did not affect the Mekong delta farmers. Land was further redistributed and farmers were organized into production groups. Households were assigned land as follows: each adult was given 0.10-0.15 hectares of land; each child under 16 years old and adults over 60 were assigned half of that amount. Differences in land allocation per head were based on differences in land quality and irrigation water access. There was no long term security of land tenure on the assigned land; the land could be reallocated at the will of the collective's management. Such reassignments were common and impeded investments which would have helped to sustain the land's productivity.

Unlike in the north, however, agricultural production in the south continued on a family farm basis except in those few areas that were collectivized. Farmers continued to be the primary decision makers for all input and technology decisions on their assigned land, although sharing of labor and production resources became more common. Sharing of labor became especially important for power-intensive operations such as land preparation, irrigation, and threshing, since individual ownership of tractors, roto-tillers, threshers, irrigation pumps, and draft animals was abolished. All such capital assets had to be sold to the province at an assessed value that was substantially lower than the market value of the assets. This equipment was then distributed to the cooperatives or districts for use in equipment pools. The net result was a sharp decline in draft power supply in most of the Mekong delta provinces. Toward the late 1970s, input supplies to the Mekong delta provinces declined because they were being assigned on a priority basis to farmers who were organized into cooperatives. The overall result of these agricultural policies was a situation that wavered between shortages and bare sufficiency in food production.

The Contract 100 and 10 Systems

Faced with rising food deficits and growing farmer unrest, the Central Politburo of the Communist party issued a directive in April 1981 that accepted the contract system (Directive 100/CT, popularly known as Contract 100 system). According to this directive, all farmers would make a contract with the production group or cooperative to produce a certain output on their land. The collective would furnish each farmer with adequate inputs for achieving that output level. While production teams were expected to provide land preparation, irriga-tion, and input distribution services on all farms, each farm household was responsible for crop management on its own land. The contracted output had to be sold to the state at a fixed price. All output beyond the contracted amount could be kept for home consumption or sold to private traders. Conceptually, the introduction of the contract system was equivalent to a switch from a fixed wage to a fixed rent system of production. The introduction of the Contract 100 system had a significant impact on rice production which increased rapidly between 1981 and 1987, and then began to level off. Aggregated rice output grew annually at the rate of 2.8 per cent during 1982-1987 as compared with 1.9 per cent for the 1976-1981 period (National Statistics Bureau 1987). Most of the output growth can be attributed to an increase in yield per hectare per crop rather than an expansion in area cultivated. In the south alone, aggregate rice output grew by over 2.5 million tonnes from 1980 to 1987. The corresponding increase in the northern provinces was around 2 million tonnes for the same period.

The success of the contract system could not be sustained over the long term due to the following reasons: (1) top-down planning on land use and crop choice without consideration of farmer preferences and local market conditions; (2) the government's frequent inability to procure all the contracted production at harvest time; (3) as a consequence, seasonal surpluses at the farm gate led to a crash in the private rice price in several regions, which, while benefiting the urban poor, had severe negative effects on farmers; (4) the persistence of centralized input supplies resulted in inadequate and untimely provision of inputs to farmers; and (5) lack of security of land tenure resulting in inadequate farm-level investments for maintaining long term land productivity.

The party and the government have now realized that to ignore the social values of a backward economy can result in deteriorating conditions. This "new change" is reflected in new policies prescribed in the Sixth Party Congress Resolution and a series of other resolutions of the party's Central Executive Committee. These "new change" (*doi moi*) policies are much more realistic because they are appropriate to Vietnamese society and take into consideration the social values of the people. The drawbacks of Contract 100 system were eliminated almost entirely by the Central Committee of the Communist Party Resolution 10 passed in mid 1988 (commonly known as the Contract 10 system). The Contract 10 system was legalized by a number of government ordinances to free up the prices of rice and inputs, privatize the distribution of inputs, provide longer term land user rights, and reduce land tax and provide more freedom of choice of crops. After 1989, farmers were no longer required to sell a contracted amount of rice to the state. Ordinance 170, issued by the Council of Ministers on 14 November 1988, stated that the individual family would have the right to own all products it generated after subtracting taxes and other commissions owed to the local collective (where one still existed). Private traders now had equal rights to the state in the purchase of food grains from farmers. Subsidized sale of food grain to government employees and to the army, which was the primary reason for government food grain purchase, was also discontinued. In 1993, the National Assembly passed two important laws concerning farmers: the new land law and the Agricultural Land Use Tax law.[1] These assure farmers land use rights and reduce their taxes.

General Conditions of Resource Base[2]

Vietnam's rich biodiversity will continue to be eroded if a national strategy for environment protection and sustainable development of natural resources is not quickly implemented. Environmental management has thus become a serious concern of the central government and the scientific community. Natural calamities such as typhoons, severe drought, flash floods, various pests, and other abnormal natural phenomena continue to afflict rural Vietnam. Rapid socio-economic development, particularly with a high rate of population increase, has brought pollution and degradation wherever economic intensification is occurring, leading to adverse effects on the quality of life of present as well as future generations. The magnitude of environmental damage can be judged through the following overall assessment.

The government's previous policy on *in situ* food self-sufficiency legalized many environmentally deleterious activities, such as clearing forested land and empoldering of problem soil areas for rice fields, and applying high doses of chemical fertilizers and pesticides in intensive crop production areas. In less than a decade (1978-1985), the amount of cultivated land increased more than 50 per cent, including the reclamation of lands damaged during the war (Reddy et al. 1988:28). The policy of land settlement and food self-sufficiency has resulted in various types of environmental degradation that are difficult to correct. These include: the disappearance of forests; heavy infestation of rice pests due to the chemical suppression of their natural enemies; chemical pollution of soils and water; acidification of empoldered areas; and salinization of downstream arable land due to upstream over-extraction of river water for new irrigation systems.

The national forest resources have been reduced to the least tolerable area. In 1943, total forest cover was 19 million hectares; in 1992, only 7 to 9 million hectares remained, representing 20-28 per cent of the national forest cover. This implies that the forest cover is being depleted at an annual average rate of about 160,000 to 200,000 hectares. In addition to losing substantial flora, logging and wanton hunting also result in loss of a large quantity of fauna.

Soil resources are being used wastefully in several places. Deforestation has left the denuded upland watersheds completely exposed to very high intensity rainfall. Serious erosion is occurring on approximately 70 per cent of 33 million hectares of Vietnamese territory (Sharma 1992:462). The rapid population increase has also put great pressure on the land. Per capita land holding has declined and in the Red River delta, it is now only 462 square meters per person. Soil fertility is being degraded by erosion and heavy exploitation. In deltaic areas, about three million hectares of land are affected by salinity intrusion or acidity. In other regions, the soils are becoming unusable due to shortages of water and are polluted by industrial wastes or overuse of agricultural chemicals. In the uplands, shifting cultivation will continue to ruin the forest and contribute to soil erosion as long as the food problem cannot be solved by other means.

Marine resources are beginning to experience pollution, especially near the oil drilling platforms and along the passages of ocean-going ships. Fresh water sources are being depleted in watershed areas, polluted at estuary areas, in intensive agricultural production areas and swamps as well as around industrial areas, affecting water quality and the breeding grounds of inland fish species. Fresh water fish are becoming scarce in many regions due to exploitation by the rural poor. Minerals development activities are also resulting in pollution of waterways, and are responsible for disrupting the natural beauty of the scenery.

Urban environments are seriously polluted by industrial as well as household solid wastes and sewage. In Hanoi and in Ho Chi Minh City, more than 50 kinds of toxic gases have been recorded at toxic levels more than ten times higher than internationally permissible levels. Excessive noise in the cities and around factories is becoming a major concern.

The post-war effects of chemical defoliants can be observed on tens of thousands of hectares of ruined forested and arable lands together with the disappearance of numerous species of fauna which inhabited those areas. Certain residues of dioxin may be left in the soils and water, endangering human health.

Rapid population growth in Vietnam, at 2.2 per cent per annum, is placing great pressure on the environment, both within cities and in intensive production areas.

Among most ordinary Vietnamese an environmental consciousness is poorly developed. What an environmentalist refrains from doing is often normal practice for average people. It is often incomprehensible to local people when someone asks them to quit these "habits" for the sake of environmental friendliness. Children in rural areas learn the practices of their immediate relatives and neighbors: dumping trash on road sides or in the waterways, felling trees, shooting birds, killing young animals, catching fingerlings, urinating on the road side or in the backyard, etc. As adults, they are unaware that something may be wrong with these daily habits.

Agricultural Research Directions and Needs in the Mekong Delta

The resolution of the Sixth National Congress (1986) of the Vietnamese Communist party marked a milestone in Vietnamese economic history. It signalled a deviation from the Soviet style in managing the country's economic activities. For more than three decades in the north and a decade in the Mekong delta, rural development was not able to move as fast as it potentially could have.

The 1986 resolution determined that due to its relatively favorable climate, soil, and water resources, the Mekong delta would become the nation's largest region for food and merchandise production. Thereafter, scientific and technological activities in the Mekong delta began to be geared to achieve that role. The mandate of the science and technology sector in support of the country's three major economic programs, namely production of food, consumer goods, and exportable commodities, is to do the following research and development work:[3]

- determine and apply technologies which are both suitable to the environment and the managerial skills and approaches of the population;
- design appropriate economic policies which foster people's participation in making best use of resources to achieve the economic targets set forth by the Sixth Congress; and
- determine social factors that cause under-utilization of scientific manpower, infrastructure, and back-up services.

Events during the last few years show clearly that macroeconomic policy plays a key role in agricultural development and that such policy should also include science and technology components. The Seventh National Congress in 1991 recognized the past mistakes when paths for future economic development were prescribed. Significantly, the "self-sufficient, self-empowered" mentality has been replaced by policy which emphasizes the exploitation of the country's resources according to the comparative advantages of each region. Because the country's resources are very diversified, an integrated approach in agricultural research and technology transfer (ART) needs to be organized with the following objectives in mind:

1. to mobilize internal and external capabilities and explore agricultural systems management for various agro-ecosystems in order to assure optimum food production, especially rice, while supplying more plant, animal, and aquaculture products, and maintaining the sustainability of household farming systems;
2. to improve production efficiency for all major agricultural, forestry, and aquacultural products;
3. to increase the value of all agricultural products by appropriate processing techniques;
4. to increase farm income by developing an appropriate agricultural extension system coupled with credit facilities and internal and export markets for projected farm products.

Proposals for the integrated ART approach can be illustrated with reference to the Mekong delta (Vo-Tong Xuan 1992). Proposed is a regional institute, supported by the central government and foreign assistance, to coordinate ART activities. Research programs will be defined according to a delta-wide development plan and assigned to accredited organizations together with appropriate budgets. Each organization will combine research with extension while servicing an area consistent with its capacity and capability. Specific ART programs for the Mekong delta will evolve from detailed studies of the natural and human resources, socio-economic conditions, and market opportunities. Based on what is known now, the broad outlines of those conditions suggest the following emphases for research and extension in the delta.

First, for the next decade or two, rice will remain an essential commodity. In Vietnam, ART for rice production will aim at developing varieties of higher grain quality and yield with built-in resistance to brown plant hopper, sheath blight, blast, and red-stripe diseases. Promising varieties emerging thus far from collaborative work between Vietnamese scientists and the International Rice Research Institute (IRRI) include MTL89, MTL105, MTL119, and MTL125. Techniques for minimizing chemical fertilizers and pesticides, while stabilizing grain yield, are needed to reduce farmers' production costs and environmental pollution. Presently, integrated pest management procedures are being introduced in many parts of Vietnam with the help of IRRI and the Food and Agriculture Organization (FAO). Soil management techniques on saline and acidic areas (such as zero tillage seeding in the spring-summer rice crop followed by dry seeding in the summer-autumn rice crop, and shallow drainage practice) need to be introduced widely. Zero tillage rice cultivation is now widespread in acidic areas such as Long An, Dong Thap, and Tien Giang provinces. This unique method saves farmers considerable expense and prevents the soil from becoming acidified during the dry season. More efficient water management methods need to be developed in order to improve energy usage and reduce costs. Rice-based farming systems are being studied to find additional ways to increase farming households' income and maintain environmental sustainability. Systems that combine rice and shrimp, rice and fish, rice along with duck raising and orchards, rice and upland crops are among the appropriate ones being encouraged now.

Second, increased attention in research will be given to suitable hybrids of pig, poultry, water buffalo, beef, and milking cows; and suitable land areas will need to be determined and reserved for production of feed and forage. Thus far little research has been done on this front due to lack of funding and trained personnel.

Third, fish and shrimp production techniques, either in intensive semi-industrial or fully industrial systems, or in integrated systems with rice and animal production, will be carefully studied both at research stations and on farms. Promising initial results include successfully hatching tiger prawns for farmers' use and supplying fish fries and new fish farming technology to some villagers.

Fourth, fruit trees and annual industrial crops will be developed to enable a quick response to market conditions and promote diversification. This is a very new area of agricultural research in Vietnam.

Fifth, agro-forestry techniques needed for the very acidic soils, and mangroves management procedures for protected coastal regions, will be tested in long term projects. Early success in coastal management involves mangrove-cum-shrimp farming.[4]

Sustainable Development and
Research Issues for Rice Farming

The research and extension work emphasized above includes attention to "sustainability." Since being put forward in the international development community in the early 1980s, the concept's definition has become clearer as more aspects of the agro-ecosystem have been taken into consideration. Research for integrated rural development in Vietnam follows the guidelines of the following established sources: the Asian Development Bank's (1991) policy on sustainable management of all agricultural projects, the criteria of the Technical Advisory Committee (1988) of the FAO for the evaluation of sustainability, and the FAO's (1989) own definition for sustainability. For Vietnam, particularly in the zones where rice production prevails, the main elements of sustainability must include (1) conservation of land and water and of plant and animal genetic resources; (2) minimal adverse technological impact and environmental degradation; (3) economic viability; and (4) social acceptability.

High on the agenda of agricultural research in Vietnam is helping farmers to develop sustainable agricultural methods, especially for rice since that crop is vitally important for the country. Some of the problems and possible answers can be illustrated by looking at different rice growing environments, especially in the Mekong delta region.

Irrigated Rice

Irrigated rice receives the most attention from scientific circles because it is done intensively in densely populated rural areas. Since land holdings are small, farmers tend to over-work the land and reduce fallow periods. Soils become exhausted and lose their natural balance with the result that rice yields decline or stagnate, agricultural inputs are increasingly used to replace natural nutrients, and in general, farming incomes begin to decline.

In mono-culture rice farming systems, the declining or stagnant yields is thought to be caused by the following factors:

Rice Varieties. Varietal performance *per se* does not change significantly the yield potential if the same variety is used only a couple of times on the same piece of land. However, after the third continuous crop with the same variety, yield reductions start to occur. Advanced farmers never plant the same variety of rice consecutively more than three times, indicating an awareness of the problem, but until now there has been little scientific understanding of this phenomenon.

Empirical observations and farmers' own accounts in Vietnam suggest that each rice root system exploits the rhizosphere in a specific way. When the same root system is fed with a constant quantity and type of fertilizer during consecutive crops, certain changes begin to occur in the soil solution and in the rice micro-atmosphere. Thus the dynamics of soil nutrients in the rhizosphere vary from one variety to another. This phenomenon has been demonstrated clearly in experimental plots and in farmers' fields where unbalanced fertilization practices are known to occur. In addition, other biotic factors occur, such as certain insects and disease organisms tend to adapt to the new environment and resurge. The result is lower yields.

Soil Conditions. While scientific understanding is not fully developed, farmers apply their practical experiences to avoid declining yields mainly by refreshing soil physical conditions. In most cases, they rotate their rice varieties. This practice results in new rhizospheres every time the crop is planted. Thus the continuous development of new rice varieties is essential. Farmers also alter the physical conditions of the soil. During the early period of the "green revolution," some scientists recommended strongly that keeping rice soil in a reduced condition year after year would conserve soil nitrogen, a big saving for farm families. This recommendation is contradictory to Vietnamese farmers' practice. The famous Vietnamese saying "A clod of well dried soil is worth more than a basket of fertilizers" is still valid. So, it is crucial that the rice field should be ploughed and dried thoroughly before being flooded again for the following rice crop.

The agricultural economy facing farmers in the Mekong delta today is quite volatile. In many cases farming incomes are declining as a result of imbalances in farming costs and returns. Farmers are typically applying more inputs in order to maintain yields, but production costs are increasing correspondingly. As more rice is being produced, the quantities presented to the market are increasing and, with resultant price decreases, farm incomes are in many cases declining. Many farmers are wondering: what should they produce instead of rice? Who will buy their new produce? What rotation might they follow? Can there be a subsidy? How might they make full use of farm household agro-ecosystems? Through research and experience some possible answers are being explored.

During the last few years, the animal component of rice-based farming systems has shown encouraging results (Preston 1992). Rice farmers who also grow some sugar cane, for instance, have taken to raising pigs in a manner that uses a locally made feed mixed with sugar cane juice. Besides having pigs to sell or eat, these farmers also end up with sugar cane bagasse and pig manure, which they use to produce methane gas for cooking. The residues from this gas-making process become an organic fertilizer that is free of CO_2. Vietnamese farmers especially favor multipurpose livestock. Using these animals farmers can recycle crop residues and by-products, produce cash income, obtain organic fertilizer (manure), gain additional food and income, and provide employment for women and children, who often are the ones tending the livestock. Other farmers are introducing perennial crops with high biomass-producing capabilities that can be transformed into food, feed, and fuel, which help to restore soil fertility and act as sinks for the greenhouse gases, carbon dioxide and methane. Other farmers and researchers are investigating technologies for on-farm fuel production using low-cost biodigestors and gasifiers.

Rain-fed Lowland Rice Farming

For the sake of stabilizing the natural environment across land units, irrigation systems have to stop where additional extraction of fresh water from rivers or the ground endanger downstream areas. Hence, rain-fed lowland rice farming continues to predominate from the hillsides to the plains in Vietnam. Water is collected early in the cropping season to facilitate land preparation before transplanting. Such wet land preparation — puddling — has been practiced by farmers for centuries. But because no one can predict rainfall patterns precisely, despite elaborate studies on rainfall characteristics of each region in Vietnam, puddling is not the optimal way to establish rice stands in the rain-fed areas. Drought damage to transplanted seedlings is a common problem. Studies show that dry land cultivation followed by direct dry seeding (DDS) minimizes the risk of drought damage, and by using this technique with very short duration rice, an extra rice crop under total rain-fed conditions is possible. However, to switch to a more successful DDS-based rain-fed lowland farming system, agricultural research and experimentation must perfect the following techniques.

- Early ploughing in preparation for the dry fallow period: This operation is a "must," particularly with heavy clay soils, although ploughing can be delayed on soils high in organic matter. To many farming communities, early ploughing is considered abnormal, but once farmers realize its value, they adopt this practice. The method is now widespread in Long An, Tien Giang, Tra Vinh, Soc Trang, and Minh Hai provinces, which as a result also have an extra rice crop using a variety with a short period (90-105 days).
- Regenerating the soil's granulated structure before DDS: Appropriate machinery is required for heavy clay soils, although less sophisticated equipment is required for soils high in organic matters.
- Preventing early flooding of DDS fields: Early rain water is good for flushing away toxic substances accumulated on the soil surface during the dry fallow, but impounding water in the field may submerge the young seedlings.
- Caring for the sown seeds: Appropriate means need to be developed to cover the dry seeds and help protect them from bird and rat damage.
- Controlling weeds: This is one of the major constraints to the quick adoption of DDS.
- Fertilizers: This remains an important research issue for rain-fed agriculture in general; it is especially important for DDS. Minimizing the losses of nutrients and optimizing yields will depend on the timing of fertilizer application and the kind of fertilizer materials.
- Alternate, complementary crops: Crops other than rice that can be planted by DDS during the early part of the rainy season need to be found. Also needed is research on possible crops for planting after harvesting the main rice crop, provided some way of on-farm ponding to conserve rain water can be applied.

Upland Rice Farming

The uplands remain a great national concern both in terms of socio-economic equity, given that the least privileged and usually most remote portions of the nation's population live in upland areas, and in terms of environmental management. Rice farming is but a small component of upland farming. Researchers must give more emphasis to other food crops and to methods for improving land conservation and food production stability. One issue with respect to sustainable upland farming is determining appropriate technology for use on sloping land and measures to reduce erosion. Other issues concern crop rotation and crop mixes, as well as methods for integrating animals into the farming system.

Deepwater and Tidal Rice Farming

In regions where water depth is greater than 100 centimeters, floating rice used to dominate the agricultural landscape. But now, virtually all floating rice areas in Vietnam have been transformed into double cropping with short duration rice, with a flood fallow in between. Another large part of the rain-fed areas has less than 50 centimeters of water during the peak of the rainy season. Rice growing is still the main occupation of the farmers in these areas. Single and double transplanting of long duration rice varieties used to be the predominant practice. The ingenuity of some farmers, however, has resulted in important changes in these practices. For instance, they have shown that direct dry seeding (DDS) with very early rice can also be applied in these areas during the early rainy season and can be followed by transplanting traditional two-month-old rice seedlings. Some farmers have found that growing rice in a shallow drainage system can increase rice yield by three to four times over the traditional methods. The integration of an upland crop during the early rainy season or of fish, shrimp, or other water life into the rice system can be an environmentally sound and economically advantageous method. The rice-shrimp system was accidentally discovered by one farmer and then spread widely. Similarly, combining molting (soft-shelled) crab production in the dry season's brackish water with rice growing during the rainy season is an ingenious discovery by one farmer in Long An province.

But the sustainability of such farming systems is questionable at this time. Higher-yielding rice varieties (greater than five tonnes per hectare) with a tall stature are not yet available. Further knowledge is required about integrated pest management in deep water areas. Also, shrimp production is constrained by the availability of shrimp fries and the suitability and supply of local feed for shrimps. Coastal lands are flooded daily to a depth ranging from 30 centimeters to four meters, according to tidal movements. In these areas, wetland rice can be transplanted only during the rainy season as this provides the only source of fresh water. Research issues for the promotion of this ecosystem include the production of saline tolerant, short duration, tall stature rice varieties and experimentation with direct wet seeding to reduce labor costs.

Looking Ahead

During the past two decades, food grain supply-driven farming models, typified by green revolution agriculture, have increasingly been recognized as unsustainable because of their excessive dependence on inputs derived from fossil fuels and their negative effects on the environment. Declining rice yield is a common phenomenon in many countries. And as rice supplies increase, rice prices decrease, resulting in an economically unsustainable enterprise, as has been observed in Vietnam since early 1992. If this situation is not corrected, it will eventually lead to a decrease in rice acreage wherever a market for other commodities exists. If present and future rice-based farming systems are to be sustainable, they must produce benefits for the farm family, for the environment, including its flora and fauna, and for the society at large. Ecosystem-based rice research has been addressing constraints faced by farmers in both favorable and unfavorable regions in terms of different aspects of sustainability, but overall, the research seems to be centered on a single component rather than on the entire agro-ecosystem of the farming household. Unless this trend in research is corrected, it is unlikely research will assist farmers to improve farm and resource management.

Although Vietnam today has become one of the world's leading rice exporters, the income of most Vietnamese farmers is still low compared to that of their neighbors. A resolution of the Central Committee's Fifth Plenary Session (August 1993) emphasized integrated rural development and family farming. During the transition from collectivized agriculture, farmers have received assistance from government research and extension services, but it is still far from adequate. Agricultural researchers and technicians have a crucial role to play during this transition, but it is essential that a participatory, integrated farming systems approach be adopted and this must be institutionalized at every level. More natural and social scientists are needed to work with poorer farmers, especially in remote areas of Vietnam. When combining participatory research and farming systems research methods, technicians will better understand the situation of the rural poor and with them develop new proposals for policy to be adopted by the government. This, I believe, will create a better milieu in which the Vietnamese populace may prosper.

Notes

1. For more about the land law, see Kerkvliet's chapter, this book.
2. For an elaboration, see Vo-Tong Xuan 1993.
3. State Commission on Science and Technology 1987.
4. Keeping in mind these five emphases and using the land resources inventory of the Mekong delta and growth requirements of various economic crops, I have estimated elsewhere the acreage of land capability for each of the various production systems found in this region (Vo-Tong Xuan 1987).

References

Asian Development Bank. 1991. "Sustainable Agricultural Development Concepts, Issues and Strategies." Agricultural Department Staff Paper No. 1. Manila.

Food and Agriculture Organization. 1989. "Sustainable Agriculture Production: Implications for International Agricultural Research." FAO Research and Technology Paper No. 4. Rome.

Pingali, Prabhu L. and Vo-Tong Xuan. 1990. "Vietnam: De-collectivization and Rice Productivity Growth." IRRI Social Science Division Papers No. 84-16, October 1990, IRRI, Los Banos.

Preston, T.R. 1992. Private communication.

Reddy, Y., G. Reddy and K. Prasad. 1988. "Vietnam's Policy of Farming Land Expansion: An Environmental Disaster." *Asian Environment* 10(4):26-35.

Sharma, P. 1992. "Status and Future Needs for Forest Watershed Management in Vietnam". *Applied Engineering in Agriculture* 8(4):461-469.

State Commission on Science and Technology. 1987. "Report to the Mekong Delta Science and Technology Planning Conference," Ho Chi Minh City, 5-7 October.

Technical Advisory Committee (TAC). 1988. "Sustainable Agricultural Production: Implications for International Agricultural Research." Report of the TAC, Consultative-Group on International Agricultural Research (CGIAR), Washington, D.C.

Vo-Tong Xuan. 1987. "Land Suitability for Various Crops and Cropping Systems in the Mekong Delta," in *Report of the Program 60B, Integrated Inventory of the Mekong Delta.* July.

_____. 1992. "Report to the Mekong Delta Master Plan Project."

_____. 1993. "An Assessment of Environmental Policies and Policy Implementation in Vietnam." Report at the Problem Assessment Workshop, Initiative for Development of Environmental Alliances through Leadership Project. IRRI, Los Baños, 26-27 July.

8

Changing Rural Institutions and Social Relations

Tran Thi Van Anh and Nguyen Manh Huan

Introduction

Rural social and economic institutions and relations have changed profoundly since 1981 when renovation effectively began in rural areas. Emerging social and economic relations are combining elements of past traditions and modern techniques and aspirations. Vietnamese farmers, and women in particular, are the main people who have created these significant changes. This chapter reviews several changes in institutions and social relations resulting from the renovation policy.

Before 1958, the household was the basic economic unit in all aspects of the rural economy from production through distribution and consumption. Between 1958 and 1980 Vietnam's countryside, however, was collectivized. The autonomous role of the household economy was replaced by a new form of organization, the agricultural cooperative. Organizing production in this way brought about several adverse consequences in the countryside. Land was left fallow not only in cooperatives in northern Vietnam but also in the production groups created in the south after 1976. Agricultural labor was underemployed. Collectivization fostered a concentration on food production in the cooperative, a decline in other means of livelihood, and the domination of rice monoculture in the countryside. The capital and assets of cooperatives were used ineffectively. Average investment in labor and land rose dramatically between 1960 and 1980 as did the value of assets, but the effective use of this capital declined to only 33 per cent of the 1960 level.[1] Food productivity and output per capita gradually decreased. In 1959 rice productivity was 2.15 tonnes per hectare, in 1980 it was 2.08 tonnes per hectare. In 1959 average rice per capita was 322 kilograms, in 1980 it had declined to 268.2 kilograms. Rice productivity decreased rapidly while the size of cooperatives increased.

Contract 100 and Contract 10

From 1981 to 1987 Vietnam's countryside applied a contractual system, in line with Resolution 100 of the Communist Party's Central Committee (here referred to as Contract 100). Since 1988 further changes have occurred in accordance with Resolution 10 of the Political Bureau of the Communist Party of Vietnam Central Committee (Contract 10, in short). Each of these two contract systems are similar in that the state returned a degree of autonomy to farming households which did not exist during collectivization. Under Contract 100 the state did not specify that farming households had long term use rights to specific parcels of land. These rights came only with Contract 10. Contract 100 still had a cooperative-style work-point system; and farming work teams were still responsible for tilling the land, irrigating it, and spraying it with insecticides. Products continued to be distributed to households according to the number of days they worked for the cooperative. The work-point system was removed under Contract 10. Households are now obligated only to provide the cooperative with an amount specified by contract.

Economic renovation of the countryside proceeded more rapidly than in other sectors of the economy. In 1981, while subsidization increased in other sectors, the contractual quota system replaced collectivization in the agricultural sector. The return to household-based production is the most important reversal, and is the origin of other diverse changes in politics, economy, culture, society, public health, and education in rural Vietnam.

Changes in the Cooperatives

During the renovation process, cooperatives changed in different ways in different localities.[2] The agricultural cooperative still exists mainly in only three regions: the Red River delta, the former fourth zone's delta and the lowland areas of central Vietnam. In the Mekong River delta, eastern south and northern mountain areas and central highlands, cooperatives have disintegrated.

Where cooperatives still exist, they have had to adjust in accordance with the production system based on farming households. In the Red River delta, for example, some cooperatives have successfully changed to providing advice and other services, especially with regard to types of seed, fertilizer, and crop care. Consequently, such cooperatives have helped many households to better manage their resources, particularly those households short of labor and households headed by single women. Other cooperatives, in the Red River delta, however, suffer bad management and their relationships with households are still overbearing and monopolistic.

In numerous surviving cooperatives on the central coast of north and central Vietnam, many households have yet to become separate production units. They remain passive and depend on cooperatives for most phases of production. Peasant participation in cooperative management remains limited. The services which cooperatives provide are often of lesser quality and more expensive than available from private services. In fact, cooperatives often constrain peasants' independence and activeness.

Significantly, new voluntary cooperative organizations have appeared throughout the country even in the three regions where state cooperatives still exist. These are based on the principle that households must benefit mutually. Other economic organizations also exist in the countryside such as gardeners' associations (known as VACVINA) and private centers for agricultural materials. As of December 1993, there were 35,000 voluntary cooperative organizations in Vietnam.

In the Mekong River delta, the farmers cooperate with each other in various forms of road and water groups, credit arrangements, service groups, and farming promotion groups. In Can Tho province, farmers have created self-managed credit systems. In the southeast, voluntary action creates roads, electricity systems, and other infrastructures that are beyond the capacity of individual households. Cooperative action also includes production, gardening, and livestock raising. In the Red River delta and central coast of the north, voluntary cooperation includes a range of farming tasks and exploiting marine resources. These collective organizations, which have arisen alongside the previous cooperatives, have been very beneficial for farmers.

In the northern mountains area village chiefs and heads of clans play important roles in forming associations to make a living from the forests and in safeguarding their production, especially in times of shortage and illness. In the coastal areas, many fishing cooperatives have sold their boats and other gear and the proceeds have been distributed to members. Now fishing households establish boat groups or contribute capital to build fishing vessels. They also help each other regarding technology, supplies, and marketing their catches. In the state-owned agro-forestry enterprises, families have been allocated land and contracts to grow tea, coffee, and rubber. Now households are working together to improve production and renew processing technology.

The diverse forms of agricultural production organizations indicate the rapid transformation of old-style cooperatives. Wherever farmers dare to withdraw from old-style cooperatives, the state resigns itself to losing control over the management of farmer production. But wherever people are docile and the old-style cooperatives survive, the state does not allow farmers to abandon that form of cooperative. The knell of the old-style cooperatives has been tolled, new and varied forms of rural associations are appearing and progressing. The basic difference between the old and the new cooperative organization is that the new respect private ownership rights, and consequently are more acceptable to rural households.

Household Differentiation

Contract 10 recognizes the household as an independent economic unit. Consequently, economic differentiation is occurring amongst households. Some households are faring well from these changes, others however are adversely affected.

In Thanh Hoc on the outskirts of Ho Chi Minh City, the Nguyen Van Ot family averages 100 million dong in income annually.[3] Yet in 1975, Mr Ot was a bicycle repairman who barely earned enough to feed his family. With borrowed money in 1978, the family profited from pig raising, and, in 1980 it bought a milking cow. Since then, the family has been raising both pigs and milking cows, having now 50 pigs and 20 cows and selling 300 piglets per year and 100 liters of milk per day. In Thanh Tri district, Hanoi, the Hung family changed how it used 3,680 square meters of land. Instead of planting two rice crops annually, the family grew one rice crop and raised fish the rest of the year. Since then, their annual income has doubled each year.

Many households have benefited from "VAC" practices — the Vietnamese acronym for combining gardening, fishing, and animal husbandry. In Ha Nam Ninh province, for example, 10 per cent of the total surveyed households earn from a square meter of garden the equivalent of eight to ten square meters of rice land; 30 per cent earn from one square meter of garden the equivalent of three to five square meters of rice fields, and the remaining 60 per cent earn from one square meter of garden the equivalent of two square meters of rice. For example, Nguyen Trong Khanh's family in Kim Bang district, Nam Ha province planted mandarins and persimmons on 720 square meters. Earnings equalled what the family would get from 7,200 square meters of rice land.

In coastal areas many households raise shrimp and crabs. Illustrative is the Mai Xuan Han family, who successfully bid for a contract beginning in 1989 to use the 50 hectares of land adjacent to the sea in Thai Binh province. That first year the family invested 100 million dong to improve the land. By 1990, the Han family earned 50 million dong after deducting expenses; after two years of producing shrimp, the family had re-couped their capital investment.

In mountainous areas, numerous households developed agro-forestry to earn income. For example, a family at Ham Yen district, Tuyen Quang province, has planted four hectares of styrax and one hectare of fruit trees and tea. After eight years, the family earns 80 million dong from the four hectares of styrax and ten million dong from fruit trees and tea each year.

In the central highlands, land is available and the climate favorable for the development of industrial crops, plant and cattle breeding. Some households make full use of such potential to become rather well to do. For example, the Amalot family in Krong Pac district, Dac Lac province, received 3.5 hectares of land under the contract system. The family plants coffee and raises ten cows. The Amalots also have a Kubota tractor and a pump which they use to service other households for additional income. The household's average net income is now 75 million dong per year, making this once average family quite rich.

While there are signs of expanding prosperity in the countryside, there is also evidence of poverty. At present, needy people account for about 30 per cent of the rural population. The percentage increases to about 50-60 per cent in some remote and mountain areas (Ministry of Labor, War Invalids, and Social Affairs).[4] More than 30 per cent of needy households are headed by women. Many are also ethnic minority households. If the average income of a household family of the Kinh ethnic majority is 100, the average income of ethnic minorities is 83 for Tay; 43.7 for Dao; 58 for Muong; 55.8 for Thai; 40 for H'Mong, 72.2 for Ede; and 29 for Xedang (State Planning Committee 1993). A socio-economic survey conducted in the rural areas in the central province of Quang Tri has shown that 61.2 per cent of household families run short of food from three to seven months a year, and 18.5 per cent run short of food all year round (they are the "desperately poor"). Of the needy households, 21.5 per cent have children dropping out of school and 45.7 per cent have insufficient surplus income to buy medicines (Reports from KX-08 1993).

The causes of poverty include insufficient land, capital, and experience to engage in production or business, or too many children. Results of a survey in Quang Tri province indicate that 25.7 per cent of the needy households are poor because they have many children but too few members are old enough to work; 15.7 per cent have insufficient land; 28.5 per cent are short of capital; 14.3 per cent lack experience in production and business. About 7 per cent of households are poor because of illness (Reports from KX-08 1993).

Not often mentioned, however, is that poverty is also provoked by macro-policies of the central government and practices of local authorities. From 20 to 40 per cent of household families in most communes in northern and central provinces have been forced to return a part (as much as 30-40 per cent) or all their land because they could not pay their debts or could not fulfil their contractual obligations to the cooperatives. This can be linked to the 1981-1988 quota system (under Contract 100) during which households did not have the right to manage their own economic activities and had to contribute from 70-80 per cent of their products to the cooperatives. Those who did not contribute enough were in debt in the next year. The debt became a reason for the cooperatives to take away a part or all of their land. Household families who were deprived of land (almost all were headed by women) encountered further difficulties due to the shortage of land. Such families are becoming poorer, gradually losing any possibility of being able to eliminate hunger and poverty (Tran Duc 1993).

Local policies have also contributed to poverty. Under the slogan "the state and the people work together," cooperatives and local authorities, in addition to collecting agricultural tax and land taxes stipulated by law, made peasants contribute to ten to twenty other payments. According to a September 1993 survey conducted in the Red River delta province of Thai Binh, the peasants had to make fifteen payments totalling 100 kilograms of rice per capita annually (Nguyen Manh Huan 1993). In a five-member household a family would contribute 500 kilograms or 500,000 dong annually. This is an important reason why poor households become poorer.

Since late 1992, and particularly in the first six months of 1993, the state has launched a campaign for the abolition of famine and reduction of poverty. Thus far the effects have been minor. The most important component of the campaign is to grant low interest loans to the poor. By June 1993, about 3,000 billion dong from the national budget were granted to farmers as loans. Average loans per household were 167,000 dong. But poor households constituted only 30 per cent of the loan recipients. The majority of households were not poor; some were households of cadres that pretended to be poor.

Unemployment

Unemployment in Vietnam is rising at an alarming rate. An estimated eight million people throughout the country are jobless. Each year, about 1.2 million more people reach working age; most (840,000) of them are in the countryside. Meanwhile the average cultivated acreage per capita is low (0.51 hectare per household) and declining due to urbanization. Employment in the state sector declined by 200,000, and nearly 120,000 of these returned to the countryside each year in 1991 and 1992. About six-to-seven million unemployed laborers now are in the countryside. At the same time more and more people go from the countryside to the cities looking for employment. Labor markets are now common. In Hanoi alone, there are dozens of places where people from the countryside gather to sell their labor. In this situation women have to accept more arduous jobs and are paid less than men both in the cities and the countryside (Reports on Survey Results 1993).

There exist many obstacles to the generation of rural employment. Small rural industries are underdeveloped due to poorly developed markets and infrastructure. Farmers have been reluctant to invest in the development of production and the state has not encouraged the development of private enterprises. Insufficient capital has been mobilized to generate jobs. Although the state has played a role, about two million dong are needed for the generation of a job; the state budget is far too small to create jobs for six-to-seven million people. Job generation policy does not encourage those with capital to invest in job creating activities. Surveys by the national rural development program indicate that, on average, a rich household in the countryside could hire 100 days worth of regular labor and 186 days of seasonal labor (Reports from KX-08 1993). With 15 per cent of rural households being rich, they could absorb millions of laborers. Furthermore, the countryside now lacks people who have the ability to organize businesses, operate in markets, and be competitive, as a consequence of 30 years of state subsidies.

Inequality between men and women is increasing. The role of the husband as the master of the household is being reinforced in the new economic environment. Surveys conducted in Bac Thai, Nghe An, Ha Tinh, and Song Be provinces show that 80 per cent of decisions regarding the selection of trees to be planted and animals to be raised are made by the husband. The demands of the market-oriented economy and the ambition to be wealthy have increased farmers' desire to have sons instead of daughters. Rural women, particularly women of poor families, have to work even harder now. Meanwhile, the responsibility for reducing population growth also falls mainly on women.

The proportion of children able to go to school is very low, particularly among ethnic minorities. Educational levels generally are declining. At present, 9 per cent of adult laborers in the countryside are illiterate, 40 per cent have not yet completed a basic level of education. Educational opportunities for women and girls are much more restricted compared to those for men and boys. The disintegration of kindergartens and creches adds to the difficulties of mothers and of daughters who have to look after younger siblings. In many families girls now have an educational level much lower than their mothers.

Problems Regarding Land

In the context of land reforms and renewal of a market economy, certain problems have emerged regarding land. One is land disputes, of which there are now several varieties (Reports on Survey Results 1993).

In several parts of Mekong delta provinces, some families whose lands were previously taken from them as part of earlier land reforms are trying to regain those lands. When they succeed others are then left with no land again. Another form of land dispute evident in mountainous regions involves indigenous people reclaiming land that recent arrivals have occupied. In the Red River delta, some people who during collectivization were organized into teams of carpenters, blacksmiths, and other tradesmen now are awarded no land to farm. To get land they believe they deserve, they come into conflict with those who were organized into farming teams under the old system and want to continue to farm. Other disputes occur between husband and wife. The new policy that issues land licences to heads of household families has disadvantaged women. Another category of disputes is those between individual households and organizations — such as army units or religious entities — over parcels of land that each claims. Finally, numerous conflicts set one village or commune or district against another because they disagree about where the boundary should be.

Many factors explain these disputes. We want to highlight two. The first is tension between the idea that rural households are autonomous units of production, on the one hand, and the law that considers all property to be public, not private. Collectivization deprived peasants of the right to central production so that they became indifferent to land. Since Contract 10, peasants have become independent and renewed their interest in having land.

Another contributing factor is that officials have sometimes abused their authority, by taking for their own use, property that is supposed to be used for all or be assigned to others. In some cases, such officials have illicitly sold land use rights, making considerable money for themselves. Such actions have provoked people to object (see Kerkvliet's chapter, this volume).

Freedom of movement has gradually replaced the policy to move people to "New Economic Zones." The period of collectivization (1958-1980) involved moving families from the Red River delta to build New Economic Zones" in the mountain and coastal regions. During these years, 1,675,000 people moved to New Economic Zones (Reports from KX-08 1993; Reports on Survey Results 1993). Resettlement was intended to reduce population densities in the Red River delta and increase arable land per capita. But the annual population growth rate of 2 to 3 per cent resulted in no net gain in land availability. Meanwhile, those who did leave were not free to choose where they would go; they had to follow plans worked out by provincial and district authorities. Many were dissatisfied and only 60 per cent of the household families who were moved to New Economic Zones stayed there. The rest returned to their homeland or moved to cities or industrial centers.

Since 1981, and especially since 1988, people have been free to move as they wish. Between 1981 and 1990, 2.145 million people resettled, or 1.28 times the number of resettlers during the previous twenty years. From 1991 through 1993, another 1.5 million people were relocated. Unlike before, these people moved voluntarily. Usually the families planned their relocation carefully, sending one or two healthy people ahead to survey possible resettlement areas and prepare the chosen area. Afterwards remaining family members sold their houses, land, and property and then moved the entire family to the new place. After three to five years, living conditions stabilize for about 90 per cent of these settlers. Only one-tenth of resettled people appear to encounter great difficulties and a small percentage return to their native land.

Changes in Village and Commune Management

Before French colonialists invaded Vietnam in 1858, villages managed their internal affairs by themselves while meeting such obligations to the central feudal regime as paying taxes, giving military service, and providing free labor. Under this self-management system, leadership was entrusted to a few people in each village, called mandarins, who were selected in one of two ways: by their diplomas or other educational achievements, or by seniority. Under this regime the provincial administration only reached the "gate" of the village; it did not directly intervene in a village's internal affairs. There was substance to the adage, "the king's rule takes second place to village customs". While this system had advantages when local mandarins governed well, it had disadvantages when the village mandarins were tyrants. In that system, it was not easy for villagers to get their complaints about injustice to higher authorities.

The French tried to take advantage of the village self-management system in order to wipe out peasant resistance. From the 1920s, under the banner of "Rural Reform," the French step-by-step interfered in community management. They took hold of the village headmen responsible for collecting taxes and implementing the laws, regulations, and decisions made by higher levels. Now the headmen were required to report to higher levels on all aspects of village affairs. This policy made the commune headmen tools of the colonial power.

After the August Revolution in 1945, the rural socio-political structure remained much the same until 1954 in the north and 1975 in the south. Thereafter commune-level Party Committee instructions were direct orders to all units within the commune, village, and hamlet administrations. The People's Council and the Fatherland Front of the commune remained formalistic. The cooperative took over as supplier of materials, managing money, and marketing produce. The role of the peasant in these matters was abolished. Community self-management was replaced by mass organizations such as the women's union and the youth union. All these organizations were under the party's management and supervision.

Since 1988, the cooperative's functions have gradually been replaced by household producers and the market economy. The diminished supply of subsidized materials, money and commodities for the People's Committee, People's Council, Party Committee, and Fatherland Front of the commune meant that these organizations also had to change.

One consequence of these changes is that the commune's People's Committee has assumed the cooperative's former functions of land management, tax collection, setting social policies, and much of the role of the Party Committee. Meanwhile the role of villages and hamlets has also heightened. Local people are again becoming active in civic projects like road construction and erecting electricity lines. Provinces most noteworthy in this regard are Thai Binh in the north, Nghe An in central Vietnam, and An Giang in the south.

Another consequence is that local people's self governance, which in the past was obstructed, now may develop. Many villages have rehabilitated their rules which can be regarded as their own "law." Thanks to these rules, conditions in villages are more orderly and cultural life has improved.

Many rural political institutions have not yet changed. There are tensions between the re-vitalized village and hamlet institutions and the political apparatus carried over from the pre-1988 system.

Renovation of State Services to Farmers

The advent of economic renovation has also meant the renovation of the system for agricultural services to farmers. The yards for drying rice and other crops, storage facilities, animal stations, industrial machinery, and other facilities that were created for collectivized farming are not suited to the household production system. Since 1988, when many of these previously collectivized services were privatized, many people thought the quality was being down-graded. Often, however, the outdated facilities were improved in a manner consistent with the needs of the new household-based agricultural economy.

Now many peasants have, on their own initiative, purchased vehicles and agricultural equipment as they pursue higher outputs and more efficient production methods. Compared to the period of collectivization, the number of oxen and buffaloes, assorted engine machines, threshers, and insecticide sprayers, has increased 1.3 to 2.5 times. Although the machinery is small, its quality is high (Reports on Survey Results 1993).

Agricultural Extension

According to some official sources, the transfer of agricultural, scientific, and technological knowledge is two or three times faster now than in 1981. The main reason seems to be that research institutions and producers cooperate better due to mutually-beneficial economic agreements.

Because of changes that peasants initiated, the state has come to recognize the need to renovate agricultural extension. In the third quarter of 1993, the state announced that agricultural extension would have two levels: a provincial Agricultural Extension Department and a commune Agricultural Extension Station. Agricultural extension services mainly supply information and give guidance to farmers, most of whom throughout the country now make their own decisions about what to plant, what animals to raise, and what methods to apply. Provinces where agricultural extension work is apparently being done well include Bac Thai in the north and An Giang and Can Tho in the south. Cadres doing agricultural extension work generally respect village producers' sovereignty. Agricultural extension work includes training courses and seminars, distribution of literature, and demonstration through film and other media (Report on Survey Results 1993).

Regrettably, in some provinces, particularly in central Vietnam, agricultural encouragement has not been well conducted. Throughout the countryside women typically are excluded from extension meetings and training courses. Also, on account of their heavy workloads, women have less opportunity than men to hear extension messages on the radio and television and to read leaflets. Official communication channels have yet to use small meetings and informal communication methods that are more effective for reaching women.

Credit Services

In the collectivization period, the state granted loans only to state-run units and cooperatives. But now peasants can borrow directly from agricultural banks under certain conditions. This is a fundamental reform in the state's policy to support farming households. To date about 20 per cent of households nationwide have been granted loans by the agricultural banks (Reports on Survey Results 1993). This achievement, however, does not yet satisfy the demand from rural households. Bank branches in some localities have been hesitant to expand their loans to households. Credit rules, with their complicated procedures and collateral arrangements, effectively exclude many households from getting bank loans.

The lack of district and commune branches, poor transport, and inadequate information have meant that poor households, especially those headed by women, are unable to borrow despite the soft interest rates now available in many state agricultural banks. Other obstacles, particularly affecting women, are encountered in the private credit markets. Helping to overcome some of these difficulties are women's thrift groups recently encouraged by the Vietnam Women's Union. These groups can make loans without requiring that borrowers provide collateral.

Health and Education Services

During the collectivization period, cooperatives underwrote many of the expenses for health and education with subsidies for basic salaries and some other programs coming from the provincial and central government. Now, such subsidies are disappearing, meaning that more of the costs are being shouldered by individual households. These changes have also contributed to other problems in health care and school facilities.

Many community health stations have degenerated, and the number of people using them have gradually decreased.[5] Those who can afford it go more often to the medical stations in the provincial cities and to private medical services. Commune budgets have declined, and consequently their contributions to medical stations have decreased. Professional health knowledge and skills are deteriorating. Meanwhile, the network of kindergartens and creches has also deteriorated, and the education system has failed to meet new requirements. For many years funding to improve and construct school buildings has been extremely limited. Teachers have few opportunities for attending refresher courses. Students' learning motives have dropped markedly because there are too few employment opportunities.

Experience in various parts of Vietnam shows that the switch in public health and educational services from state subsidization to liberalization has had mixed consequences. On the one hand, they better meet what is needed by people who can afford to pay. On the other hand, their accessibility, particularly to poor women and children has decreased.

Conclusion

The renovation process has allowed farming households to become more autonomous and independent, but the consequences have been diverse and there are losers and winners amongst households and regions. Throughout the countryside households can be found exploiting agricultural and marine resources in new and innovative ways, sometimes within the organization of cooperatives that have not changed greatly as a result of renovation. In most cases, however, the collectivized forms of organization have ceased to exist other than in name, and in many regions there are few signs remaining of the rural organizations created since 1954 in the north and since 1975 in the south. The bureaucracy of state management has been disintegrating as a result of economic liberalization. Meanwhile, traditional forms of self-management have been revived, though often they sit uneasily under political arrangements designed for the past era. There are contests amongst these various kinds of organizations for control and influence over rural production and distribution. Land disputes are common since they involve one basic aspect of rural production.

During rural transformation, men seem to have obtained more advantages than women. Women have been adversely affected by the decline of commune-financed services, like child care, and typically they have less access to agricultural services, credit, or the basic means of production like land and agricultural machinery.

In general, Vietnam's countryside remains poor and farmers' living conditions are difficult. The results of five years of renovation cannot compensate for the failure of 23 years of collectivization. This requires the Vietnamese state to do more to improve conditions, but the wealth being accumulated by rich rural households needs also to be productively invested in ways that have wider benefit. In these ways, rural Vietnam may have a chance to advance rather than continue to lag behind other countries in tropical Southeast Asia.

Notes

1.   From statistical data 1962-1981. Figures are standardized at the 1962 exchange rate of 1 US dollar equals 2.40 Vietnamese dong.

2.   The rest of this section is based on Reports from KX-08 (1993).

3.   This and the following examples come from Reports from KX-08 (1993) and Reports on Survey Results (1993).

4.   According to the definition of the Asian Development Bank, a needy household family has insufficient income to cover its essential requirements in food, clothing, medical treatment, and housing with minimum hygienic conditions. The Job Center under the Ministry of Labor, War Invalids and Social Affairs worked out a concrete definition: a poor household has less than 40,000 dong per person per month an average family has from 40,000-60,000 dong per person per month, a middle family has 60,000-80,000 dong per person per month, and a rich household has more than 80,000 dong per person per month.

5.   This paragraph is based on Nguyen Manh Huan 1993.

References

Ministry of Labor, War Invalids and Social Affairs. Unpublished data.

Nguyen Manh Huan. 1993. Eight evaluation reports on development projects in Vietnam for international organizations.

Reports from KX-08. 1993. Reports on results of research during the first six months of ten projects under Program KX-08 concerning rural development, land, household economy, and political-social systems in the countryside. Unpublished.

Reports on Survey Results. 1993. Results of surveys in the provinces of Ha Tay, Bac Thai, Nam Ha, Quang Tri, An Giang, Dong Nai, and Thua Thien-Hue. Unpublished.

State Planning Committee. 1993. Information Center. *Tap Chi Kinh Te Ke Hoach* [Economic Planning Review], nos. 3, 4, 5, 6, and 7.

Tran Duc. 1993. *Nen Van Minh Song Hong, Xua va Nay* [Civilization of the Red River, Now and Before]. Hanoi: Social Science Publishing House.

9

Economic Liberalization, Marginality, and the Local State

Doug J. Porter

Introduction

It is evident from earlier contributions to this volume that, with some relatively minor provisos, the social and economic results of economic liberalization are regarded as positive. On a national basis, average incomes have improved, agricultural production has increased remarkably over the past five years and we have read reports, from throughout the countryside, of innovation, experimentation, and a new sense of optimism about the future.

Whilst disparities existed before liberalization, the social and spatial inequalities are significantly greater now. Income statistics are a poor and sometimes misleading surrogate for what is occurring in the lives of everyday people. But it is already clear that some social groups and some regions are being favored by a liberalized economy, just as other areas are being bypassed, or in some respects, may actually be disadvantaged by the play of market forces. Until recently, it is fair to say that the pace of differentiation in the countryside was not fully appreciated. In some degree this was fostered by a blind spot in international thinking about economic liberalization. As others have observed, this fostered "a vision of the countryside as homogeneous, diametrically opposed to the city and the 'state', and waiting only for price hikes and free markets to turn into small, efficient entrepreneurs" (Uvin 1994:264). Now, in the mid 1990s this vision is accepted as being dangerously simplistic, indeed, deceptive if allowed to form the main basis for national policy. Earlier chapters in this volume should contribute to a more fine-grained appreciation of the consequences of economic liberalization for people and places in different parts of Vietnam.

Two reasons are being advanced within Vietnam to explain the different social and spatial impacts of economic liberalization. Neither reason is unique to Vietnam, although few observers have yet analyzed the details, nor how they inter-relate in the Vietnamese countryside. First is the obvious point that some areas and people are favored by a conjunction of factors, such as their relative infrastructural endowment, their geographic location, and various agro-ecological features, which accelerate the penetration of market forces and people's ability to access the opportunities afforded by this penetration. Contrarily, a different mix of the same factors can pose significant constraints for other regions and people. Whilst liberalization has removed some of the more obvious fetters on economic development on the national scale, in doing so, it has set the scene for highly differentiated developments at the local level.

A second explanation, sometimes offered in tandem, sometimes building on the first, focuses more closely on the role of the state with respect to both alleviating the constraints faced by some areas and social groups, and actively promoting a more even-handed spread of the benefits of economic liberalization. As noted in the comparison with other Asian nations in Chapter 1, Barrington-Moore's "social co-ordination" questions involve state actions which foster the geographic spread of market forces (such as provision of infrastructure), those which promote diversification in the rural economy and thereby the inclusion of wider sections of the population (such as micro-economic policies, access to credit, etc) and finally, those actions which are deliberately designed to provide safety nets for people unable by their own means to accumulate sufficient surpluses to participate in the renovated markets or to sustain a toe-hold in new patterns of production and consumption.

This chapter refers to experiences in parts of two provinces, one in the south and one in the central region, which show how policies implemented by national government for economic liberalization result in diverse local consequences, in part as a result of particular geographic, social or historical factors, in part resulting from what are called "knock-on" effects of national policy. Knock-ons are the unintended effects of policies introduced in one area of national government which have consequences elsewhere. The central government has for instance, instituted a range of procedures designed to improve control over the national budget deficit. These procedures, whilst technically necessary in this arena, have contributed to important shifts in the way that public expenditure decisions are made; in turn this alters the kind of facilities and services to which public resources are allocated at the local level.

The first example, from a district in Ba Ria-Vung Tau province in the south, illustrates the way in which policies associated with economic liberalization (such as the privatization of health care) can block poor households' ability to accumulate surpluses necessary for participation in the renovated markets. More pointedly, experience from this locality suggests that rapid privatization of social services, in the absence of improved access to employment or income earning opportunities, can result in a deterioration of living conditions, often with little prospect of improvement in the long term. A second example, from Quang Nam Da Nang province in central Vietnam, is more concerned to illustrate the changing patterns of control over public resources, in particular, capital resources for public facilities, which are appearing as a result of national policies associated with economic liberalization. In some respects, the central government appears to have maintained a practice of redistributing public revenue from richer to poorer provinces, a step that is essential to the stability of local government. However, relations between provincial, district, and commune government are changing rapidly and this has major consequences for patterns of public investment and, ultimately, for accelerating or arresting the marginalization of people and areas within the country.

Linking National Policy with Local Circumstances

Xuyen Moc District, a coastal area some three hours drive north from Ho Chi Minh City, is part of the recently formed Ba Ria-Vung Tau province. Prior to 1975 the district was settled by less than 5,000 people, then living in a heavily forested zone of intense military activity. Large tracts of the district were affected by aerial bombardment and chemical defoliants. In 1976, Xuyen Moc was declared a New Economic Zone and an additional 30,000 people were settled in eleven communes throughout its 64,000 hectares. By 1990 population had reached over 100,000 drawn from over ten provinces and very diverse backgrounds.

Environmental conditions vary considerably. Although climatic conditions vary little over the district, the central and northern parts of the district are less productive for agriculture than are the better soils in the long settled communes adjacent to the main coastal road. Present agricultural practices in the central northern part of the district do not yield sufficiently well throughout the year. Chronic food deficits occur throughout these predominantly sandy-grey soil areas (about 40 per cent of the district) where settlement densities have increased greatly over the past decade.

Government land use, settlement, and recent economic policy has resulted in rapid intensification in all forms of agricultural production. Although small enclaves of two and three crop paddy have persisted since the early 1960s and were extended in the late 1970s (600 hectares), the area of land available for food production has declined (to just over 10 per cent of total land) and relative to population density. More than 20 per cent of land is now devoted to industrial crops (rubber, sugar, oil plants), and forest plantations (36,400 hectares) and forest reserves (15,000 hectares eucalyptus planned) continue to encroach on agricultural land. The area for food production including corn, cassava, and rain-fed rice now comprises less than 7,000 hectares. The combination of poor soils, high settlement densities on poor land, and the general poverty characteristic of new settlers, all indicate that malnutrition and chronic food insecurity is widespread. Table 9.1 provides a general overview of the demographic and economic characteristics of the population in each commune.

When compared with the summary of the income situation found throughout the countryside, as presented in Chapter 5 by Dao The Tuan, the poor socio-economic conditions faced by people in Xuyen Moc are quite evident. While around 20 per cent of the farming population enjoys incomes in excess of 200,000 dong per person per month, equal to or better than the national average, the 40 per cent classified as "poor" and "marginal" households cope with less than 80,000 dong per person per month, and most subsist well below what is regarded locally as the "poverty line." The proportions of poor and marginal households are most marked in the inland localities settled mainly since the mid 1980s under the national resettlement program. In Phuoc Tan and Hoa Binh communes, 60 per cent and more than 80 per cent respectively of households are in the poor and marginal categories. The proportion of households classified as "marginal" varies considerably, ranging up to 20 per cent of the rural population, although most often it is between 10 and 15 per cent.

The income figures presented in Table 9.1 are estimates which include both cash incomes and food equivalents, according to a statistical measure which is applied throughout Vietnam. However, the figures record only one aspect of poverty, what is more correctly termed "income-poverty" (Chambers 1994:6-7), and say little about the quality of life nor circumstances which these figures reflect. Among many of the people classified as "marginal" for instance, low income is seldom regarded as an adequate defining characteristic. Men and women from marginal households consistently refer to two aspects of

TABLE 9.1: Xuyen Moc District: Socio-Economic Features (1993)

	Total	Bau Lam	Hoa Hung	Hoa Binh	Phuoc Tan	Phuoc Buu	Xuyen Moc	Hoa Hoi	Hoa Hiep	Bong Trang	Bung Rieng	Binh Lam
Population	102,86	11,429	4,767	11,480	13,441	46,294	10,276	7,561	8,205	3,539	3,854	12,022
Total rural households		1,199	518	1,034	2,151	2,551	1,848	781	1,218	635	739	1,966
Farming households		1,094	518	855	1,510	1,662	1,743	781	1,218	490	689	595
Total farming population		5,447	2,735	4,874	10,308	8,791	9,256	3,708	6,168	2,420	3,463	3,150
Income Groups: Rural Households												
Middle-rich	3,973	515	28	195	215	1,490	370	230	245	125	45	515
Middle	5,657	412	117	254	480	741	924	136	348	235	257	467
Poor	4,766	262	438	585	1,154	330	554	136	348	235	257	467
Marginal	1,192	55	50	285	124	42	195	73	98	83	18	169

Notes: Middle-rich households have income (cash and rice equivalent) greater than 500,000 dong per month per adult labor; middle income between 200,000 and 500,000 dong per month per adult labor; poor includes less than 200,000 dong per month per adult labor. Marginal households, a sub-category of the poor, include those with income/food equivalent incomes of less than 20,000 dong per person per month. Data recorded under 'Income Groups' does not always tally with 'Total rural households' due to different sources and collection dates.

Source: Field surveys 1992-93.

their marginality, one which refers to their "endowments" and a second, increasingly important, which refers to their "risks to livelihood." The various aspects of "endowment" marginality show the multi-sided difficulties they face. Typically, many of the following six aspects are noted:

- a high incidence of morbidity and mortality with respect to "diseases of poverty," notably malaria, dengue, diarrhea, obstetric problems, and respiratory tract infections;
- an inability to accumulate savings (for food security or health care) or capital in terms of farm assets (tools, basic consumer goods) and agricultural investments (inputs to enhance productivity);
- settlement on land of poorer quality (ie., sandy-grey soils) with less reliable rainfall than "non-marginal" people;
- living in areas remote from commune markets, health, and educational facilities or linked by poor quality tracks well beyond transport services;
- tendency to grow crops of poorer nutritional value, lower market values, and with lower yields and from poorer seed stock, and often tend to sell more nutritious, higher value crops to raise income, and;
- tendency to have a higher proportion of female single heads of households, less than 1.5 adult labor units per family, high dependency ratios (many children and aged dependents) and a greater proportion of children under five years old in the family.

Amongst the greatest immediate concerns for marginal households are the ways in which these endowments limit their opportunities or "room to move" in the face of the many risks they are exposed to in the normal course of rural life. All poor rural households must cope with a variety of situations which increase their exposure to risk. Risks of climatic perturbations which affect their ability to sustain their livelihoods have always been problematic. Those with land are perennially concerned about whether the rains will come too late, too heavily, too lightly, or not at all. Those without land are similarly affected since climatic conditions quickly translate into the vagaries of daily and seasonal rural employment markets.

A striking feature of peoples' accounts of recent experience is the way they highlight and rank what they regard as "risks to livelihood." Climatic perturbations remain, but more commonly the risks associated with illness are ranked higher. In some respects this is surprising, since the "supply" of health care in Xuyen Moc district has improved markedly since 1990, although it is still below average national conditions. Nationally, the number of hospital beds per 1,000 population is 2.5, whereas in Xuyen Moc the figure is approximately 0.77 per 1,000. The average number of university trained doctors and assistant doctors per 10,000 population is 7.13 in the south. Although Xuyen Moc still compares poorly, with less than 1.9/10,000, this is still a considerable advance on four years ago — prior to the equipping of health stations in all communes, which attracted more qualified health workers to the area. Poor households' more recent concern is directly attributable to health sector policies associated with economic liberalization. Nationally, as has been observed in earlier chapters, expenditure on health care has increased and now about 3.1 per cent of the national budget is allocated to health (up from 2.1 per cent five years ago). However, in districts like Xuyen Moc there has been a decline in health sector funding in real terms and in proportion to the growing population since 1989. A second consequence of national economic policy has been the decision, in May 1989, to introduce fees for medical services and, shortly thereafter in Ba Ria-Vung Tau province, to authorize a rapidly emerging private health sector.[1] In effect, this further reduced the already meagre attention given to primary or preventive health care in rural areas and fostered a rapid expansion in private, curative care. By 1992, just two years after private care was authorized in the district, the value of private health services exceeded six billion dong annually. The total annual turnover of the Xuyen Moc district public health services was in the order of 220 million dong for the same period.

How did these nationally endorsed policies become "risk factors" for marginal households? For most marginal households[2] the impact of national policy needs to be considered in terms of their "endowments" noted earlier. More than half have assets (housing, utensils, farm implements, transport) worth less than US$50, and have debts persisting longer than two harvest seasons that often amounts to three times the value of their assets. Most maintain a complex portfolio of debt obligations. Sometimes the debt is garnered from friends at low interest rates (5-10 per cent per month), but because they are recent settlers, the safety nets provided by friends and relatives are weak (a situation that contrasts markedly with the national one, cf. Ronnas 1992:107ff, 144). None of the marginal households, of course, enjoy access to bank loans. Consequently, a high proportion, greater than 80 per cent, of chronic debt, is typically owed to multiple sources in the private, informal network of usurers that has flourished since 1991. In this market the interest rates range between 15 and 30 per cent per month. For a few of these households, chronic indebtedness has been a constant companion since well before economic liberalization in the mid 1980s, but for a much larger proportion it is recent and directly attributable to two aspects of economic liberalization. First has been the now complete withdrawal of communes from responsibility for financing commune health services and from providing preferential, subsidized access for the so-called "SOS cases." Second, of more widespread significance, is the cost of medical care. For a large majority of marginal households, and an increasing proportion of the relatively better-off "poor," more than two-thirds of chronic indebtedness has been accumulated to cover costs associated with episodes of ill-health.

The costs of illness arise in two main ways. One includes the direct payments to health workers for curative services. These services are often over-prescribed and involve unnecessary surgical treatment for ailments diagnosed in accordance more with the pecuniary appetites of privatized health workers in mind than the illness requires. Episodes of ill-health costing between 800,000 to one million dong and more are common. The funds must be borrowed, and it is not uncommon to find "middle-poor" households with total cash incomes of 400,000 dong per month supporting debt-service obligations, accumulated through ill-health, in the range of 200-300,000 dong per month. The debt-service obligations of marginal households are frequently found to exceed their monthly cash incomes.

A second cause of health-related debt has to do with the local labor market which has become more pervasive since 1989. Such a supply of labor is another aspect of the uneven penetration of the market economy into rural areas. While the figures available do not support confident generalizations, it is clear that since most poor and marginal households are food deficit from between four and eight months each year, they would not survive without access to off-farm employment. Most households in Xuyen Moc report an improvement in demand for labor, and daily wage rates (in the order of 12,000 dong for women and 15-20,000 for men) are regarded as sufficient to cover food costs for an average family of five. However, two points emerge from accounts given by local families. First is that labor markets are extremely erratic and unreliable and second, following from this, employment opportunities are almost always tied to on-farm work. There are few indications of a diversified non-farm rural enterprise economy emerging and where such is occurring it is well away from the localities where poor and marginal households typically reside. This feature of the local economy quite clearly increases the exposure of such households to increased indebtedness. Poor households generally do not have surpluses or accumulated savings. When afflicted with frequent bouts of ill health, they are not able to turn to loans at reasonable rates of interest nor to alternative sources of employment to generate cash.

To what degree can it be argued that national privatization of health and other services is similarly affecting the "not-so-poor" in rural districts like Xuyen Moc? In other words, is it possible that the ranks of poor and marginal households, whose lives may in some respects be deteriorating under economic liberalization, are being swelled by new entrants from previously more secure households? Research so far seems not to have documented this issue systematically, but anecdotes from families who regard themselves as "the-recently-poor" provide some insights. On the positive side, in resettlement areas like Xuyen Moc, it appears that households who have been able to weather the impact of privatized social services and increase their incomes, assets, and consumption of services include those who have been better off since before liberalization took root. These are typically extended households with much adult labor, with good land holdings close to roads and markets, and very frequently, with access to investment capital from outside the locality, either from relatives overseas or in nearby urban areas. Accounts from "the-recently-poor" point to the beginnings of a new twist to the age-old cycle of poverty witnessed by heavily indebted marginal households. People in marginal circum-stances live with the anxiety of debt and new bouts of illness, but they also are aware that when repayments cannot be met, "you can't take nothing from nothing." In a small community, word gets around, and unpaid debts make it doubly difficult to borrow again. But few have capital assets which would be targets for repossession in the event of loan defaulting.

The situation of households with land, however, is different. The advent of the officially sanctioned "land use market" in Xuyen Moc, combined with the slowly diversifying non-farm rural economy, has created a further twist to the "spiral of poverty" being experienced in rural areas. Whereas concern in the past has been voiced about what is often termed "the cycle of poverty," for "not-so-poor" households, the risk is now that they will enter a "cycle of decapitalization." Decapi-talization is a more recent side effect of government policy on land titles and the emergence of a market for land. Household debt is now being tied to land title, and failure to repay is resulting in more severe consequences. Few households are able to recover once land has been lost to the money lender. The "not-so-poor" households, which include families in the middle income category of Table 9.1, believe that in slightly different circumstances they would be resilient to the shocks of weather, ill health or other events that prove calamitous for poor and marginal households. Amongst the "endowments" that distinguish middle income families is a lower dependency ratio, in particular, a higher proportion of adult labor in the family. Labor is one essential resource they can mobilize in times of adversity. However, in the absence of a diversified non-farm employment market, this resource goes underutilized and cannot therefore be mobilized as a block to eventual decapitalization. According to national research, rural under-employment and poorer than expected rates of diversification are not a reflection of lack of opportunities. Indeed, the farm sector in districts like Xuyen Moc is diversifying; individual landowners are for instance investing in a wider range of crops. Rather, the poor performance of agro-processing and servicing enterprises is directly attributable to the shortage of enterprise capital. "It is notable that shortage of capital is considered by the enterprises themselves to be by far the most important constraint to the development of the enterprise" (Ronnas 1992, 110).

Liberalization and Provincial-Local Government

Various studies and position documents highlight two ameliorative actions necessary on the part of central government to extend the liberalized market and to provide access for areas and people who are presently marginalized from beneficially participating in the liberalized economy. One is facilitating the provision of credit, the second is market-relevant infrastructures. Credit provision is much highlighted, as noted in the chapter by Fforde and Sénèque, and the recent International Labor Organization study quoted earlier concluded that "the extremely limited access ... to external sources of capital is a major constraint to enhanced employment and income generation" (Ronnas 1992:110; cf. World Bank 1993:150). The government has argued that credit should receive a high priority in Vietnam "because the level of education and institutional development provides unusually favorable conditions for efficient, disciplined growth of agricultural credit" (SPC and FAO 1993:62).

These two ameliorative actions, credit and infrastructure, are closely related. Rural enterprises, essential for diversification, are constrained by shortage of credit and, because they require a much wider geographic network of suppliers and buyers than urban enterprises, are greatly affected by the condition of rural infrastructure. This is particularly apparent in Vietnam, where about two-thirds of rural enterprise inputs are reported as being of urban origin, and where about two-thirds of sales are, perforce of the parlous state of transport infrastructure, highly localized (Ronnas 1992:147). Rural enterprises note inadequate power supply, market facilities, and transport networks high on their lists of "constraints." Markets tend to be highly localized and fragmented and, as the government has noted, "market towns cannot develop if the bulk of their hinterland is not joined to them through all-weather road grids" (SPC and FAO 1993:45). This contributes to inefficiency, hampers competition, and encourages localized monopolies. Transport and irrigation infrastructures are known to increase off-farm rural employment opportunities and, by reducing costs, increase both consumer demand and prices enjoyed by the farmer. In the same way the Green Revolution demonstrated, although not consistently, the positive link between wages for unskilled rural labor and intensification in agriculture through infrastructural investment (e.g., Lanjouw and Stern 1993).

Given the previous remarks about credit, as well as references to the topic throughout this volume, the focus here will be on infrastructures. Following convention, a distinction will be made between social infrastructures — schools, clinics, and other social facilities — and economic infrastructures designed to directly improve productive activities. The distinction is to a degree artificial, given contemporary awareness of the high economic returns that accrue to investments in educational facilities and services, particularly for females. Economic infrastructures include public utilities — such as power, piped water supply, sewerage, and public works — commune and district markets, farm-to-market roads, irrigation, and drainage. The precise links between infrastructure and development are still debated, but there are close, lineal relations between incremental investments in infrastructure and increases in GDP (e.g., World Bank 1994:2ff, 14). The links between infrastructure and poverty are subject to more debate, although the kind of infrastructure has a great impact on whether growth reduces poverty. An important factor in the early growth in farm productivity and non-farm rural employment in China was the package of transport and power created at the village level, along with incentives to local government from fiscal reforms, which fostered rural enterprises (Oi 1993). This is a marked contrast with the Vietnam situation.

The point is not to assert that increasing government investments in infrastructure are failing to alleviate this constraint on economic growth. Infrastructural investment, such as the US$250 million per year over ten years proposed by the SPC and FAO (1993:57-58) for rural roads, does have great potential to access remoter regions. However, this investment may exacerbate the problems of marginalization referred to in the earlier section. There is a wide variation in total per capita public expenditure across the country, but central government appears to have maintained the longstanding principle of reallocating funds to revenue-poor provinces. It is reported that the same redistributive principles once applied in relations between provincial governments and the districts and communes. Since the reform measures introduced in 1991, district and commune officials often complain, this redistributive process may be being eroded. To explore the possibility, it is necessary to examine aspects of the political and administrative processes which control the allocation and implementation of public infrastructure investments. Public sector reforms undertaken to achieve national objectives associated with economic liberalization may be reinforcing a bias for investment in localities within provinces that are already greatly benefiting from economic intensification, thereby contributing to the differentiation among areas and peoples noted throughout this volume. The point made at the end of this analysis is that coping with infrastructural constraints involves far more than making appreciative remarks about the role of infrastructure in development and then simply creating inventories of requirements against existing infrastructure stocks and computing financing requirements. The systems developed for planning and allocating publicly financed infrastructure, as well as the tenurial rights of different levels of government to identify and own these infrastructures, are also crucially important.

National Revenue and Expenditure

Vietnam has undertaken a number of important reforms in public financing since 1989 as part of the broader program of economic

TABLE 9.2: Government Revenue Sources 1988-1991 (per cent of total revenue)

Source	1988	1989	1990	1991
1. State enterprises	63.8	47.0	40.0	36.2
2. Non state sector	18.4	18.9	15.7	21.3
Agricultural tax	7.8	7.9	4.8	7.1
Non-agricultural tax	10.6	11.0	10.8	12.8
3. External trade	7.5	9.3	11.9	13.4
4. Other revenue	10.3	24.8	32.4	29.1
Fines/lotteries/fees	–	–	8.8	6.3
Crude oil	–	–	19.9	22.0
Foreign remissions	–	–	4.8	0.7

Source: Based on World Bank 1992. Table 3.2 p. 57.

liberalization. Alongside the dismantling of central-state planning, the elimination of subsidies, reforms to banking, investment and property laws, and the adoption of austere monetary and fiscal policies, have come actions to reduce the budget deficit, the structure and distribution of taxation, and changes, still underway, in fiscal relations between central and local government.

Since 1991, these reforms have seen a doubling, in constant prices, in government spending, and revenue has increased by 80 per cent (Table 9.3). In large part these revenue and expenditure trends reflect the macroeconomic situation. GDP growth rates have been above 5 per cent since 1988 and exceeded 8 and 7 per cent in 1992 and 1993, respectively. (See the analysis by Fforde and Sénèque, Chapter 4). The national fiscal situation has improved as a result of reversals from the situation in the late 1980s when the government sector experienced negative savings, a large overall deficit, and strong reliance on borrowings. By 1992 however, the fiscal deficit was down to around 3.8 per cent of GDP (from 8 per cent in 1989).

Revenue collection is reported to be quite low in Vietnam, ranging between 11 and 13 per cent of GNP since 1988. Important shifts have however occurred in the sources of revenue as a consequence of the government's structural reform in the economy. Table 9.2 indicates the percentage of total revenue according to sources over the 1988 to 1991 period. State enterprises accounted for about 75 per cent of government revenue prior to 1988, and other sources, such as agricultural tax were minor. From 1987 however, there was a steady decline in revenue collection from state enterprises, declining from 9.5 per cent of GDP in 1986 to 5.3 per cent in 1990. By 1993 just over one-third of tax revenue was raised from state enterprises. Revenue from the countryside primarily occurs through agricultural taxation. This source of revenue has always been low, although the low figures for 1990 and 1991 reflect the government's decision to implement a "tax holiday" provided for in Ho Chi Minh's will.

Recurrent expenditures (as indicated in Table 9.3) have continued to rise, to an estimated 20.4 per cent of GDP in 1994, largely as a result of the growth in state salaries (doubling at the province level in 1992). Interestingly, the social service component of current expenditure has increased from 3.2 per cent of GDP in 1986 to 6.4 per cent in 1992. But these figures are deceptive; the bulk of increases have been expended on pensions and social relief programs, as a result of restructuring and layoffs in the state enterprise sector. It is important to note therefore, the different rates of increase in current and capital expenditure; the reduction in the fiscal deficit has largely been achieved through a reduced rate of increase in capital expenditure on both social

TABLE 9.3: Revenue and Expenditure 1990-1994 (billions of current dong)

	1990	1991	1992	1993	1994P
Domestic government revenue	6,153	10,353	18,970	28,660	37,700
Current expenditure	6,156	8,728	15,005	23,860	30,600
Capital expenditure	2,124	2,135	5,710	11,120	12,800
Primary deficit	2,127	510	1,745	6,320	5,700
As a Percentage of GDP					
Domestic government revenue	16.1	14.8	18.6	22.9	25.1
Current expenditure	16.1	12.5	14.7	19.1	20.4
Capital expenditure	5.6	3.1	5.6	8.9	8.5
Primary deficit	5.6	0.7	1.7	5.1	3.8

Sources: Based on Ministry of Finance, *Statistical Yearbook* (various years), Ministry of Finance figures.

infrastructure (health, education, etc.) and economic infrastructure, as can be seen in the comparative proportions of GDP allocated to capital and current expenditure in Table 9.3.

Although a steady increase in government capital expenditure can be noted (apart from 1991), for many reasons this does not accurately reflect trends in investment over the country. A large, but varying, proportion of capital expenditure by provinces goes unrecorded (and is not reflected in Table 9.3). Provinces also regularly "adjust" the use of capital and current finances once they have been approved first by the State Planning Committee (for capital expenditure) and then by the Ministry of Finance. For instance, a recent analysis of seven provinces concluded that 18 per cent of designated education funds (including both capital and recurrent funds) coming from the center are lost from the provincial education budget — suggesting these funds are being allocated to other budget categories by the province (Unicef 1994). Finally, even though an increase in capital expenditure is noted in national figures (Table 9.3), almost all of the increase in 1992 and 1993 was due to spending on the national power transmission project linking the north with the south. Across the country, the current level of public investment is barely adequate to maintain the national infrastructure. Little funding is available to improve or rehabilitate infrastructure and services even though, since 1989, direct government capital investment has been targeted solely toward infrastructure and social services. State enterprises, previously the recipient of a large proportion of public investment, are now required to access capital only through the formal banking system. Maintenance of the existing capital stock is becoming particularly difficult. Government sources indicate, for instance, that in the school year 1992-93 a total of 68,248 classrooms were either destroyed or became unusable due to poor construction and materials and lack of maintenance (Porter 1994).

The prognosis is for an expanding revenue base in the medium term as a result of sustained economic growth. But serious problems remain. Government domestic revenue is expected to reach 25 per cent of GDP in 1994, having risen twice as fast as economic growth. Direct government investment is now as high or is higher than any other government in East or Southeast Asia. Some macro-economic observers believe it will be difficult to sustain this level of public investment, or that a ceiling has been reached.

Province Revenue and Expenditure

Central government is responsible for around two-thirds of total public spending and one-third of national revenue collection, which does not differ markedly from comparable countries (World Bank 1992:40ff). The government plays a significant role in moderating regional inequalities. The tax and expenditure system redistributes income from higher to lower income provinces, and poorer provinces are at times permitted to retain larger shares of tax revenues and receive higher provincial subsidies. The rules for revenue sharing between the central and provincial governments include negotiated retention ratios, and as a basis for negotiation, proforma rates of per capita allocation are used to derive first estimate budgets for social services and administration.

The wide variation in per capita public revenues is depicted in Map 9.1. The fundamentals of the revenue redistribution system are conveyed in Figure 9.1 which is based on national figures for provincial resources and central government transfers in 1993.

Revenue collection by provinces has traditionally been quite closely correlated with per capita GDP. An Giang, a relatively wealthy Mekong delta province, collected 136,054 dong per capita revenue in 1993 but expended only 70,729 dong per capita. Ha Tinh, a poor province along the north central coast, collected only 30,363 dong per capita, but after a central government subsidy was able to expend 93,425 dong. Important changes are however occurring in provincial revenue and expenditure. In 1989, half of the 44 provinces were net contributors and half were net recipients of revenue transfers. By 1993 however, 35 provinces of 53

230

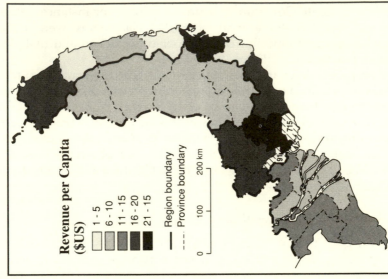

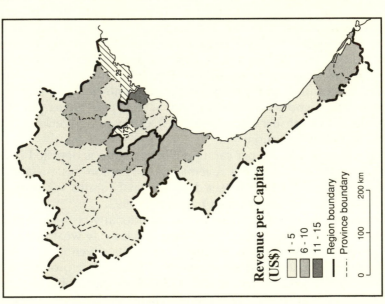

MAP 9.1: Public Revenue per Capita by Province

(or 66 per cent) received central government resources and only 19 (or 36 per cent) of the 53 raised more in revenue than was expended in the province. This indicates greater provincial dependence on the central government, which is a consequence of moves toward centralizing budget and expenditure control. Of course, it is important to note reservations about data of this kind. The size of the tax base of particular provinces is a surrogate, but not necessarily a good measure of relative provincial wealth. On the expenditure side, there is a range of other, unreported, revenues raised by government at all levels. Households pay fees and levies in kind, or through cash donations for maintenance of local facilities. One cannot assume these various practices (of under-reporting the tax base, or the scale of unrecorded taxation) occur evenly across the country — indeed, practices can be quite different in two neighboring districts (as will be discussed later). Nationally, it is understood that the reported level of GDP is understated by 20 per cent or more on average, but more importantly, it is acknowledged that provincial GDP estimates vary so markedly from the real indications of relative wealth or deprivation as to be of little use in comparisons across the country.

With these provisos in mind, however, Figure 9.1 demonstrates the enormous range of public resource allocations across the country.[3] Against a national average public sector expenditure of US$10.88 per capita, many provinces (e.g., Hai Hung, Nghe An, Nam Ha) expend slightly more than half this amount, whereas others particularly in the northern mountains and central highlands, where preferential policy applies to areas with a predominance of ethnic minorities, the rate of public sector expenditure ranges between 50 and 100 per cent higher than the national average. In 1989, per capita revenue raised ranged from 15,900 dong in the north central coast region to 128,000 dong around Ho Chi Minh City, a factor of 8 to 1 (World Bank 1992:41). By 1993, the per capita amounts collected had increased, but the difference between these two regions, one rich, the other comparatively poor, appears to have declined, from around 61,000 dong in the north central coast to close to 400,000 dong on average in the Ho Chi Minh City environs, a factor of 6 to 1. This is an interesting trend in light of the enormous differentials between these two regions in terms of benefits from economic liberalization. On the per capita expenditure side, however, there remains a strong sense of redistributive equity and less variation is evident. In 1989 the per capita expenditure contrast between these two regions was a ratio of just 2 to 1, with a low of 21,500 dong and a high of 44,200 dong. By 1993, however, the ratio had declined to less than 2 to 1, with a low of 97,539 dong and a high of 157,160 dong.

FIGURE 9.1: Provincial Public Sector Revenue and Expenditure (1993)

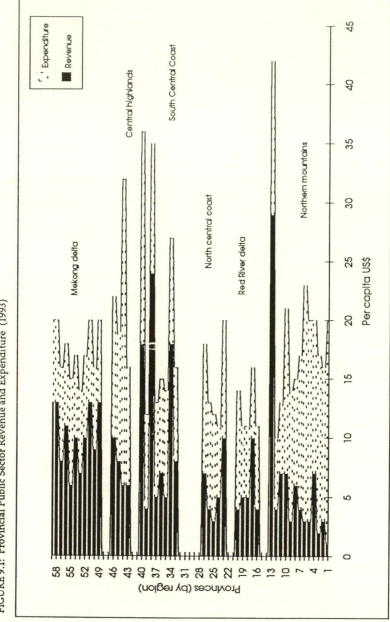

Source: Ministry of Finance 1994.

Across the country, there is little indication in 1993 figures that there is a close relation between relative needs and corresponding attention via public sector expenditure. Table 9.4 illustrates aspects of this point with respect to infant mortality rates and per capita expenditure in selected provinces.

On the basis of existing data, it is difficult to discern patterns of public investment in infrastructure. Trends in national data are extremely deceptive; since 1989 an increasing share of public investment (in public enterprises) has been shifted from the national budget towards the banking system. Regional state investment figures (reproduced in Fforde and Sénèque's Tables 4.10 and 4.11 for instance) indicate a constant increase in investment in transport and communications between 1989 and 1991, but that investment in poorer regions (such as the north central coast) was particularly volatile where sharp falls in investment were recorded. However, aspects of the decentralization process have increased the responsibility of provinces to finance a greater proportion of capital investment from their own revenues. Unfortunately, at the provincial level it is even more difficult, due to the paucity of data, to determine the results of allocation decisions. Interviews with Quang Nam Da Nang province officials, and selected districts and communes within this province, do however, provide indications of recent developments.

Provincial Resources and Capital Investment

Quang Nam Da Nang is one of only two provinces in the south central coast region where revenues exceed expenditure (largely as a result of state enterprises and trade taxes). However, in many respects it is typical of provinces in the region. As evident in Maps 9.2 and 9.3, the bulk of the province's 1.9 million population are concentrated in the lowland and nearby undulating hilly areas adjacent to the main north-south arterial routes and in the urban center of Da Nang. However, excluding the urban area of Da Nang, 40 per cent of the population are resident outside these areas, either in the mountainous areas or the extensive sandy coastal zone. There exist great differences in the standards of living and infrastructural endowments enjoyed by this population compared with people resident in communes adjacent to urban centers. Illustrating this difference is an infrastructure index which reflects a composite of endowments in education, health, market facilities, agriculture, electricity, and roads[4] (Map 9.4). More than 60 per cent of communes in the mountainous region record index scores of less than ten, and many are close to half this score, which indicates that infrastructures either do not exist or are in a parlous state. Fewer than

TABLE 9.4: Selected Provincial Expenditure and Health Indicators 1993

Region/Province	Population	Expenditure per Capita (US dollars)	Infant Mortality Rate (1994 est)
Hai Phong	1,568,786	11	21.6
Northern mountains			
Bac Thai	1,157,541	9	33
Vinh Phu	2,214,183	6	31.2
Ha Bac	2,266,123	6	35.2
Red River delta			
Ha Tay	2,218,151	7	36.6
Hai Hung	2,652,732	6	38.4
Nam Ha	2,578,025	6	31.2
North central coast			
Thanh Hoa	3,311,322	10	30.4
Ha Tinh	1,284,448	9	40.2
Quang Tri	512,768	11	32.4
South central coast			
Quang Nam Da Nang	1,925,083	9	34.2
Quang Nai	1,160,053	9	39.6
Binh Dinh	1,375,395	8	37.2
Central highlands			
Gia Lai	746,007	10	50.5
Kon Tum	252,123	26	50.5
Lam Dong	732,604	12	33
Ho Chi Minh City & Environs			
Song Be	1,101,600	12	31.8
Tay Ninh	898,989	10	38.4
Dong Nai	1,833,421	8	27.2
Mekong delta			
Long An	1,281,052	7	37.6
Can Tho	1,831,840	7	32.4
An Giang	1,675,748	7	35.4
National average		10.88	34.5

Sources: Based on figures from Ministry of Finance and UNICEF Vietnam.

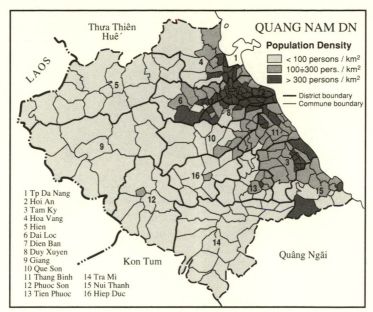

MAP 9.2: Population Density

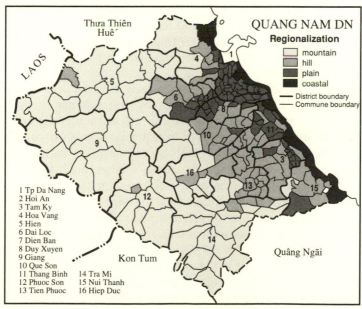

MAP 9.3: Regionalization

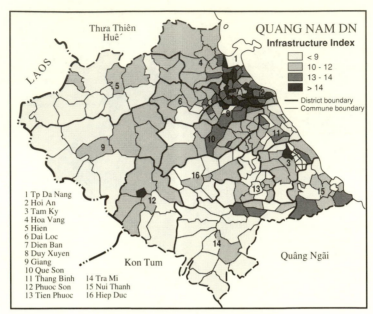

MAP 9.4: Infrastructure Index

10 per cent of communes on the plain region however record such scores. More revealing is the fact that fewer than 8 per cent, or 17 of 216 communes in the province, have an index score greater than fourteen and all (excluding one anomaly) are nestled on the coastal plain area close to the urban center of Da Nang.

In one respect, the wide variation merely underscores the priority accorded to infrastructural investment by the national government. However, the spatial distribution of the infrastructure scores attests more firmly to the skewed pattern of investment in this province. There are no figures available for actual investment by district and by commune since 1989 and, as will be noted further, such figures would provide no reliable indications of actual investments made over time. However, the infrastructure index is a measure both of the physical existence (or absence) of the infrastructural facilities and the quality of those facilities. Communes with relatively high scores, above thirteen for instance, are those where the facilities both exist in good measure and are of recent origin. It is these communes, as will be argued, that have enjoyed the benefits of capital investment decisions made under provincial allocation procedures that have been in place since 1991.

What are the main features of the provincial capital allocation process and what changes have been underway since 1991? In brief, capital allocation occurs in the context of overall provincial budgeting. Within the province, there are three levels of fiscal authority: the provincial, the district, and the communal level. The provincial planning process is based on five yearly and annual plans. The five year plans result from an interaction between priorities determined at the district level (by various offices of provincial departments and the District People's Committee) and at the provincial level. However, both levels are obliged to operate within the context of targets and priorities communicated from the central government, both by ministries, for recurrent expenditure, and the State Planning Committee, for capital expenditure. Every June, the Ministry of Finance instructs all provinces to prepare for the next fiscal year (coinciding with the calendar year). Three months are provided for submission of proposals, during which time districts make submissions, for recurrent and capital allocations, to the province and repeated rounds of negotiation and adjustment occur prior to October when the province makes its first submission to the central government. The actual revenue sharing that eventuates between the provinces and the central level is not determined by law but is fixed by the central committee of the party. The process, as evident in the wide-ranging provincial expenditures per capita recorded in Figure 9.1, is highly political and whilst a degree of redistributive justice prevails, the increasing dependence of provinces on the central government for revenue transfers is reported to have increased the "arbitrariness" of the outcomes. Moreover, prior to 1990, (later in some cases) districts and communes tended to set budgets against expected revenue and then pass the unallocated surplus up to the next level of government administration.

The negotiation and bargaining between districts and the province has always been highly political. But this budget process has tended to be less variable across communes and districts with regard to recurrent budgets which correspond, in their initial calculations by districts, to guidelines issued by the central government. Guidelines stipulate the amount to be spent per pupil in education, per kilometer of road, per district and provincial administration employee, and so on. Capital budgeting and allocations involve a great deal more discretion and complication. Before fiscal reforms were introduced, districts and communes were able to allocate funds to capital investment projects and, although there was never complete certainty, there was greater confidence than now prevails that a high proportion of their proposals would be honored in the final allocation approved and incorporated into the overall provincial budget. Currently however, only two budgeting levels operate; province and commune. Districts are in practice merely spending units of the provincial government and this practice is likely to be ratified in the State Budget Law considered by the National Assembly in 1994 for enactment in 1995. After the ratification of this law, districts will effectively operate only as revenue collection and spending units of the provincial government. The commune, on the other hand, appears set for revitalization. This is said to be underway through support for reviving traditions of village self-government and, through multilateral assistance, the government is investigating a range of progressive communal conventions, rules, and regulations to give this effect.

The public sector reform process initiated by the national government has resulted in important changes in the capital budget allocation process. Responsibility for infrastructure provision and maintenance is increasingly decentralized to the provincial level, with the expectation that districts and communes will take a correspondingly greater role. However, running against decentralization has been a rapid centralization of control over revenue and capital expenditure. This centralization is attributed to efforts to increase the central government's capacity for effective macroeconomic management, in particular, to reduce the budget deficit, which stood at 6 per cent of GDP in 1993. The implications for provinces in relation to central government are mixed. On the one hand, all capital expenditure allocations are required, on an annual basis, to be authorized by the State Planning Committee. And, as noted earlier, fiscal austerity measures instituted by the central government appear to be curtailing the capital budgets available to provinces. This is indicated in Table 9.5 which summarizes, by proportions, the revenue and expenditure pattern for Quang Nam Da Nang for the three years since 1990. No figures are available for actual budget amounts, but if Quang Nam Da Nang follows the national budget trend, it is reasonable to assume the province enjoyed a doubling of expenditure levels in constant prices since 1991. The declining percentage of expenditure allocated to "investment in capital construction," from 18.5 per cent to 13 per cent of total expenditure, would indicate a tightening of resources available for infrastructure. However, due to other factors, it is more reliable to conclude that provincial capital resources have increased quite dramatically and, importantly, the degree of administrative oversight exercised by central government may have actually declined. The budget category "administrative expenditure," traditionally considered an item of recurrent expenditure, is now officially available for capital expenditure.[5] The total level of funds available to the province for these categories are authorized by central government. However, the individual activities to which these categories are devoted are at the discretion of the Provincial People's Committee. Notably, these funds

TABLE 9.5: Revenue and Expenditure Allocation (per cent of totals)

	1990	*1991*	*1992*
1.0 Total Government Revenue	100.00	100.00	100.00
1.1 Central state enterprises	33.8	24.4	28.47
1.2 Local state enterprises	15.8	20.6	21.86
1.3 Tax on non-state enterprises	10.9	10.4	10.42
1.4 Agricultural tax	2.4	4.6	3.79
1.5 Export-Import tax	16.3	22.8	9.96
1.6 Others	20.8	17.2	25.48
2.0 Local Revenue	52.3	60.2	64.48
3.0 Local Expenditure	100.00	100.00	100.00
3.1 Investment for capital construction	18.5	18.4	13.03
3.2 Allocative working capital	0.2	3.4	5.10
3.3 Subsidy	0.3	0.6	0.75
3.4 Administrative expenditure	62.1	55.1	63.77
Including: Economic activities	17.6	14.7	19.16
Social-cultural activities	61.4	60.9	56.96
Administration	21.0	24.4	23.8
3.5 Others	18.8	22.4	17.35

Source: From Annual Statistics of Quang Nam Da Nang 1992, Table 19.

comprise the province's own revenue sources, not central government transfers, and as a consequence of recent central government decisions, provinces are drawing an increasing proportion of capital expenditure resources from these items. This suggests the percentages referred to as "capital construction" in Table 9.3 are misleading.

How do these developments relate to the skewed pattern of capital infrastructure evident in the provincial maps presented earlier? First it is important to reiterate the increasing political significance of provincial government viz. the two levels it now administers. Districts and communes retain no rights to independent budgets, the former is now simply an appendage of the province, and neither is entitled to capital budgets. Measures introduced by central government in the past three years to improve fiscal discipline and reduce wastage and corruption have been seized by provinces, along with the above administrative changes, to almost entirely concentrate control over the recurrent and capital allocation process at the provincial level. In effect, allocations for all kinds of infrastructure, including social and economic investments, are centered on the provincial government. Two conclusions are suggested by these developments, neither of which can be demonstrated statistically, but both regularly are decried by district and commune levels of government; one concerns capital allocations, whereas the second relates to the stability of district and commune budgets overall.

First is the major change in capital allocations already indicated. Previously the bulk of infrastructure investment proposals came via annual commune and district budgets prepared at the respective levels. In many cases, depending on the wealth of the administrative unit, small scale infrastructures like schools, clinics, farm-to-market roads and commune markets, could be financed from own-sourced revenues.

Larger infrastructures, or those beyond the fiscal capacity of the district, would be subject to bargaining and compromise with the province and subsequently, if successful, funds would be allocated through the provincial level department responsible for the construction and oversight of such investments. Under recent arrangements, however, the overwhelming majority of infrastructure investments derive from proposals made initially by provincial technical departments controlled by the Provincial People's Committee. The scope for projects nominated by district and commune authorities is greatly curtailed and focuses, in the main, on renovations to administrative structures and the construction or rehabilitation of public monuments and such like. The consequences of these changes are clear, at least to district and commune officials on the margins of economically favored localities. An increasing proportion of capital expenditure for individual projects draws on what were previously administrative, recurrent budgets operated on a near "discretionary" basis, without State Planning Committee oversight. Capital construction is now completely controlled by "Provincial Construction Management Boards." These tend to be a small coterie of provincial technical department officials whose main administrative benefits and salaries are derived from the various service charges, fees, and levies on the design, execution, and oversight of public construction contracts. The "fee content" of capital construction is tied proportionately to the size of the individual project, and since most of the senior departmental officials reside in or near the urban centers, it is a relatively short step to appreciate why capital allocations favor larger infrastructural projects in localities in or adjacent to the main centers of economic privilege. More densely populated areas logically require more infrastructural investment. However, the infrastructure development index scores referred to earlier take most of this factor into account. Long-serving district and commune officials in the poorer regions of Quang Nam Da Nang argue that the fiscal centralization which has accompanied public sector reforms has allowed the political influence of provincial officials and technicians residing in districts close to the urban centers to prevail in public resource allocation to a much greater extent than prior to 1989.

The fiscal centralization instituted in support of economic liberalization appears to have undermined district and commune governance in other ways as well. In relations between the central and provincial governments, as indicated in earlier sections, there are wide variations in per capita expenditures across the country. However, there is a degree of stability, as was evident in comparative remarks on revenue and expenditure ratios between 1989 and 1993. The extent to which provinces are able to institute routine procedures for forward planning of all government functions is greatly dependent on the reasonable expectation that expenditure allocations will have some incremental relationship from one year to the next. The increasing dependence of districts and communes on provincial government, a dependence that is about to become legislatively enshrined, does not appear to have brought with it a similar degree of stability in district and commune fiscal capacity. Once again, broad statistical measures are not available to adequately explore this development, but data from three districts in Quang Nam Da Nang points to a highly volatile situation which is contributing to the weakening of local governance implied in the earlier discussion (Porter 1994).

Tables 9.6 and 9.7 illustrate the volatility in revenue budgets for three districts in Quang Nam Da Nang. Hien is a mountain district adjacent to the border with Laos which depends greatly on allocations from the provincial government and special transfers for mountainous areas from the central government. Neither Nui Thanh nor Que Son districts, both in the hilly/plain regions, can be regarded as well-endowed; they have infrastructure index scores below ten, but include households with a wide variation in wealth and standard of living.

Table 9.6 shows the increase or decrease in revenues by source and in total over the 1991-93 period against a 1991 base year set at 100. Taxes and levies are raised in the district, whereas grants indicate the proportion of budget derived from provincial government transfers. Clearly the pattern for every source and in total is completely irregular and the increase in total revenues varies greatly amongst the districts. The 1993 budget for Que Son district increased by a factor of 3.3 over 1991, whereas that for neighboring Nui Thanh increased by 2.1, and for mountainous Hien district increased just by a factor of 1.6 over 1991. As evident in Table 9.7 the same irregularity can be observed in the proportions of total revenue derived from different sources. The

TABLE 9.6: Revenue Flows, Selected Districts, 1991-1993

	Revenue Source	Taxes	Levies	Grants	Total	Annual Increase %
	1991	100	100	100	100	–
Nui Thanh District	1992	125	347	184	208	108
	1993	146	166	348	210	1
	1991	100	100	100	100	–
Hien District	1992	356	79	105	135	35
	1993	211	46	208	156	16
	1991	100	100	100	100	–
Que Son District	1992	145	169	326	326	87
	1993	226	151	524	524	75

Source: Interviews, district officials, June 1994.

TABLE 9.7: Variation in Revenues, Selected Districts, 1991-1993

	Revenue Source	Taxes	Levies	Grants	Total
	1991	41	30	29	100
Nui Thanh District	1992	25	49	26	100
	1993	29	23	48	100
	H/L	1.6	2.1	1.8	
	1991	16	32	52	100
Hien District	1992	41	19	40	100
	1993	21	9	70	100
	H/L	2.6	3.6	1.8	
	1991	42	40	18	100
Que Son District	1992	32	37	31	100
	1993	38	24	38	100
	H/L	1.3	1.7	2.1	

Notes: H/L indicates the ratio between the highest and lowest proportion of the budget derived from the specific resource.

Source: Interviews, district officials, June 1994.

TABLE 9.8: Revenue Distribution, Selected Districts, 1993

Revenue Source		Share of Tax	Levies	Grants	Total	Grants Actual	Revised Budget
Nui Thanh District	Million dong	740	606	1,250	2,596	824	1,727
	Per cent	29	23	48	100	32	68
	Per capita dong (1,000)	5.9	4.8	9.9	20.6	6.5	14.1
Hien District	Million dong	412	187	1,379	1,979	480	1,499
	Per cent	21	9	70	100	24	76
	Per capita dong (1,000)	14.8	6.7	49.2	0.7	17.1	53.6
Que Son District	Million dong	1,596	1,037	1,594	4,227	1,629	2,598
	Per cent	38	24	38	100	39	61
	Per capita dong (1,000)	13.5	8.8	13.5	35.8	13.8	22.0

Source: Interviews, district officials, June 1994.

High/Low ratio indicates the degree of instability and unpredictability in revenues available for district governments.

In the actual resources available to district governments in these three cases (Table 9.8), a similar erratic situation can be observed. The heavy dependence on the province for grants is evident in the range from 39 per cent to 70 per cent. The per capita budgets vary greatly (from 14,100 dong to 53,600 dong), just as there is considerable instability in the relation between approved and actual grants received on an annual basis from the provincial government.

Conclusion

"The truth is...," writes Jose Guilherme Merquior of his native Brazil, "that we have simultaneously too much state and too little state" (Merquior 1993:1,265). The epigram can be used to sum up the debate in Vietnam about the future role of the state in economic liberalization. It is recognized now that the overwhelmingly negative views of the state that often attended earlier debates about economic liberalization on the international stage need to give way to a more refined awareness that effective economic and social development requires capable states. Previously the role of the state was defined in terms of what it must not do, that is, negatively, whereas now it is replaced by what Miles Kahler terms the "orthodox paradox," the need for a relatively effective state to implement the reforms necessary for economic liberalization (Kahler 1990:55). The state's role is not to be the earlier "developmentalist state" which too often acted alone without regard for private activity or the demands of civil society. Rather, the "capable state" view underscores its role in creating both an "enabling environment" for development, and the obligation to intervene to protect the environment, regulate market forces, and promote social policies that alleviate poverty and the long term marginalization of some localities and peoples.

Most contributors to this volume have drawn attention to aspects of differentiation occurring in the Vietnam countryside. There is no overall agreement at this stage regarding the degree of differentiation that is occurring, whether it reflects an inevitable, temporary, or regrettably irreversible trend, nor indeed, whether it is possible, through the normal means available to the state, to make any appreciable difference to these trends. All chapters have acknowledged the complexity of the situation, just as each contribution has been modest in the confidence with which trends and conclusions may be drawn at this stage. This is quite appropriate for observers drawn, largely, from the academic sphere.

For many rural people, however, there is no such reticence in their observations. They remark on the profound transformation underway. Most vocal are those who applaud the transformation that has occurred in the past decade and call for "more" and "sooner, rather than later." But once clear of the centers of power and privilege, other voices can be heard as well, less audibly, but no less stridently. For these people, change, and what I have termed here "marginalization," is occurring at a breath-taking pace. Here too there is applause, but it does not amount to the peels of thunder that in large measure have greeted economic liberalization. The views and advice from marginal areas and people have, by and large, yet to be heard. Rural people, particularly the poor and politically unconnected, are less visible and less apt to be organized. Politically rational leaders hear and favor those who reside alongside them in the towns and cities, where the benefits of economic intensification are most pronounced.

It is too early to remark on the character of government services and institutions that will develop as a consequence of public sector reforms implemented alongside specific policies on economic liberalization, and this discussion provides no more than a speculative glimpse of what appears to be developing in parts of two provinces.

Further, in light of the broad support for decentralization and more responsive governance at the local level emanating from national fora, it can hardly be asserted that these developments, amounting as they do to an undermining of capacity at the lower levels and a corresponding concentration of power at the provincial level, are outcomes desired by national policy makers. It is inevitable that policies and procedures introduced at one level, for a specific purpose, have knock-on effects elsewhere. The critical judgment for government is whether these knock-ons, to the extent they may be observable elsewhere, should be regarded as unfortunate effects of policies which should, in the interim at least, have precedence. And this judgment will involve assessments of the degree to which the concentration of political control over public resource allocation processes are resulting in the privileging of some localities and the marginalization of others, and whether this will yield significant long term consequences for social stability and the consolidation of market reforms.

Notes

1.   There is a large grey area between purely public and private health care which makes an analysis of the importance of each difficult. Most health services are provided in public facilities under private remuneration arrangements.

2.   These remarks are based on longitudinal surveys of 98 households since early 1992 in Xuyen Moc district.

3.   Not shown in these figures are high revenue provinces/cities which provide major subsidies to other parts of the country. Ha Noi for instance raises per capita revenues of US$173, whereas its total expenditures amount to US$31 per capita. Similarly, Ba Ria-Vung Tau, via oil and gas revenues, raises a total of US$715 per capita, but expends only US$10 per capita.

4.   The infrastructure index derived for each of 216 communes, includes six elements, each of which includes a scale of three categories: 1. Number of school aged children per classroom, ranging from >600 persons per classroom to <400 per classroom; 2. Status of the commune health clinic (with qualitative judgments on conditions); 3. Status of the market facility and category of market (commune or inter-commune); 4. Percentages of households with electric light; 5. Road density, ranging from <3m per km^2 to >10m per km^2; and 6. Percentage of paddy land which is irrigated, ranging from <10 per cent through to >50 per cent. Scores for each indicator were combined to create a total infrastructure development index. The index was developed by the

Center for Rural Planning and Development (CERPAD) and applied in Quang Nam Da Nang province with the author during 1993.

5. Authorized in Inter-Ministry Circular "Guiding the planning and management of economic-affairs funds and other-affairs funds, invested for construction works that are newly built, or rehabilitated, or significantly repaired," State Planning Committee and Ministry of Finance, 28 March 1994.

References

Chambers, R. 1994. Poverty and Livelihoods: Whose Reality Counts? Overview Paper 11, UNDP Stockholm Round Table on "Change: Social Conflict or Harmony?" 22-24 July. Mimeo.

Kahler, M. 1990: "Orthodoxy and its Alternatives: Explaining Approaches to Stabilization and Adjustment," in J. Nelson, ed., *Economic Crisis and Policy Choice*. Princeton: Princeton University Press.

Lanjouw, P. and N. Stern. 1993. "Agricultural Change and Inequality in Palanpur, 1957-84," in K. Hoff and J. Stiglitz eds., *The Economics of Rural Organization*. Oxford: Oxford University Press.

Merquior, J. 1993. "A Panoramic View of the Rebirth of Liberalisms," *World Development* 21(8):1,263-1,270.

Oi, J. 1993. "Fiscal Reform and the Economic Foundations of Local State Corporatism in China," *World Politics* 45(July):99-126.

Porter, D. 1994. "The Planning, Budgeting and Project Management Process in Vietnam." Discussion Papers, 2, New York: United Nations Capital Development Fund.

Ronnas, P. 1992. *Employment Generation through Private Entrepreneurship in Vietnam*. Geneva: International Labor Organization.

SPC and FAO (State Planning Committee and Food and Agriculture Organization) 1993. *An Agriculture-led Strategy for the Economic Transformation of Vietnam: Policy and Project Priorities*. Contribution to the Preparation for the Round Table Meeting of Donors, September.

UNICEF 1994. *Towards Universalised Primary Education in Vietnam: A Study of the Cost and Cost Effectiveness of the Pimary Education System*. Hanoi: UNICEF, March

Uvin, Peter. 1994. *The International Organization of Hunger*. London: Kegan Paul International.

World Bank 1992. *Viet Nam: Restructuring Public Finance and Public Enterprises: An Economic Report*. Washington: Country Operations Division, Country Department I, East Asia and Pacific Region.

_____. 1994. *Infrastructure for Development: World Development Report 1994*. Washington: World Bank, New York: Oxford University Press.

About the Book

Since the mid-1980s, Vietnam has experienced remarkable economic, political, and social change. This is the first study in English to focus on rural Vietnam — where nearly 80 per cent of its people live, much of its economic production occurs, and political upheavals earlier this century changed the course of history.

Analyzing the impact of economic liberalization on the countryside, the contributors note that despite significant improvements in real income for most rural Vietnamese, poverty is still pronounced and socio-economic inequality appears to be growing. The poorest now appear to have less access to educational and health services. Environmental conditions also pose significant problems. Highlighting the dynamic political scene in Vietnam, the contributors also consider the interplay between national policymaking and local pressures and activity.

Index